To D.O.T. and P.Y.E.

What This Book Is About

This book brings together the most up-to-date information about:

1. Measurement of *advertising messages* (Part One)
2. Measurement of *advertising media* (Part Two)

In other words, this is a book about creative research and media in the advertising industry of today and with emphasis on practical details.

Part One explains both the planning of advertising measurement and the techniques of measuring advertising messages. There are separate chapters on recognition tests, recall and association tests, opinion and attitude ratings, projective methods, laboratory testing and analyses of content, and inquiries and sales measures. Since no single technique of advertising research could possibly begin to answer all research questions, various combinations of research techniques should be considered in dealing with a specific research question. Accordingly, both the advantages and the disadvantages of each research method are analyzed and appraised separately.

Part Two explains the basic media concepts. There are separate chapters on printed-media audiences, television and radio audiences, exposure of advertisements, audiences of advertisements, kinds of people in media audiences, and attitudes of media audiences; the book ends with a discussion of audience accumulations and combinations and the implications of mathematical programing. So far as we know, this is the only comprehensive study of media research and evaluation; and a great deal of the material analyzed is not available in most libraries.

Measuring Advertising Effectiveness represents the combined efforts of two psychologists, who between us have spent over fifty years in advertising work. To produce this volume, we have drawn upon our psychological knowledge, our experience as teachers, our own research studies, and our work as advertising consultants.

Our previous book, *Advertising Psychology and Research* (McGraw-Hill Book Company, Inc., 1950), provided a great deal of background material, but the present book is in no sense a revision of that work. The earlier book is still useful in its discussion of advertising appeals, location and size of advertisements, mechanical factors affecting advertising, and so on—and the present book is a logical extension of the research and media phases of that book. We are presenting here the latest information and a critical evaluation of all the principal methods for measurement of advertising messages and advertising media.

We believe, therefore, that *Measuring Advertising Effectiveness* will be useful to students in the classroom and useful also to those people in business who are concerned with the evaluation and improvement in methods of measuring advertising effectiveness. In other words, it is our sincere hope that this book will be a "must" for teachers and students of advertising . . . and a "must" for practitioners of advertising.

Special thanks are due to the following, each of whom has read the entire manuscript in detail, but no one of whom is to be credited with any debits:

Seymour Banks, Vice-president and Manager of Media Planning and Research, Leo Burnett Company, Inc., Chicago

Harper W. Boyd, Jr., Chairman of Department of Marketing, Northwestern University

Edward C. Bursk, Professor of Business Administration, Harvard Graduate School of Business Administration, and Editor of *Harvard Business Review*

John S. Coulson, Vice-president in Charge of Research, Leo Burnett Company, Inc., Chicago

Albert W. Frey, Professor of Marketing, University of Pittsburgh

Vernon Fryburger, Chairman of Department of Advertising, Northwestern University

John C. Maloney, Manager of Research Development, Leo Burnett Company, Inc., Chicago

Charles K. Ramond, Technical Director, Advertising Research Foundation, Inc., New York

Charles H. Sandage, Head of Department of Advertising, University of Illinois

F. Robert Shoaf, Associate Professor of Marketing, New York University

Eugene J. Webb, Assistant Professor of Advertising, Northwestern University

Clark L. Wilson, Vice-president in Charge of Research, Batten, Barton, Durstine, and Osborn, Inc., New York

To many people in many different departments of our respective universities and in the Leo Burnett Company, Inc., and Batten, Barton, Durstine, and Osborn, Inc., our appreciation is also expressed for continued cerebral stimulation.

Darrell Blaine Lucas

Steuart Henderson Britt

Contents

are more likely than others to produce *predispositions to buy* the advertised product or service. After all, a great deal of advertising is not designed to make sales, but rather to predispose people to buy.

Although it is a shock to many a business executive to face the bitter truth—there is *no* method of advertising research which can *guarantee* that his cash registers will ring if certain advertising is run—nevertheless, almost every business executive wants more and more information as to what his company's dollars spent in advertising produce for his company. And he usually wants this information in advance of running the advertising.

But to come by such information is not easy. In fact, it is a slow, laborious process, and it is going to take years and years of research to establish general principles which may not even be applicable to *all kinds* of advertising.

One of the main problems is that so much advertising research has to be particularistic rather than generalistic. As Norman Heller of MarPlan says:

> This is due, of course, to the predominant requirement in advertising that each research project must pay off, that research be conducted to answer a specific problem for a specific client. Rarely is an attempt made . . . to extend the data beyond the immediate problem, to interrelate it with other studies, to theory-build, or to understand beyond the immediate boundaries of the study. Our copy tests tell us which of two or three specific ads looks most promising; our motivation studies tell us which themes to develop for brand X—but when the next research request comes through, the only benefit derived from these previous studies is perhaps an improvement or refinement in some research technique. To put it another way, our studies, for the most part, provide us with islands of isolated data, which live short lives.[2]

And too many advertisers inflate their own egos by having the kinds of "research" done for them which will produce nice, pleasant score cards—like the report cards that they hope their offspring will bring home from school.

True, most advertisers give lip service and even hearty "amens!" to the statement that more money should be invested in advertising research. But most stop short with the "amens." They have been agreeing with each other, especially in public addresses, for the past thirty years or more that advertising research is desirable, but very few really carry out advertising

[2] Norman Heller, "The Next Development in Copy Research," speech before the Copy Research Council, New York, March 19, 1958.

research on any significant scale. Too many prefer to rely entirely on their own personal judgment as to advertising effectiveness, while at the same time they may pay many thousands of dollars a year for rating services which are circulation figures rather than measures of advertising impact.

Yet advertisements are business investments; truly effective advertisements may be two, three, or four times better than weak ones.

What needs to be determined with respect to any advertising that is to be tested is: *What was its real objective?* Was the purpose to close an immediate sale? Did it aim at some specific step leading to a sale? Was the objective to impart information? Was the purpose one of building good will? Was the building of imagery the main idea; if so, what imagery? Was the advertising designed to build a long-range consumer franchise?

These are the sorts of questions that need to be asked (and there are many more) and to which answers need to be given *before* research is undertaken as to the effectiveness of an advertising message.

> Advertising attempts to move consumers from *unawareness* of a product or service . . . to *awareness* . . . to *comprehension* . . . to *conviction* . . . to *action*.[3]

> A variation is that advertising should move people from *awareness* . . . to *knowledge* . . . to *liking* . . . to *preference* . . . to *conviction* . . . to *purchase*.[4]

So we must start with the fact that every successful advertisement must make contacts with enough people, must hold contacts long enough to make an impression, and must make useful, lasting impressions.

NEED FOR ADVERTISING RESEARCH

The purpose of an advertisement is to produce for the advertiser a profit in terms of money, reputation, good will, or understanding—or all of these. However, the problem has become increasingly complicated.

As advertising becomes national, as the time lapse between advertising and sales increases, as products become more alike, as the variety of advertised

[3] Russell H. Colley (editor), *Defining Advertising Goals for Measured Advertising Results* (New York: Association of National Advertisers, Inc., 1961), especially p. 55.

[4] Robert J. Lavidge and Gary A. Steiner, "A Model for Predictive Measurements of Advertising Effectiveness," *Journal of Marketing,* Vol. 25 (October, 1961), pp. 59–62.

VALUE OF RESEARCH

Chapters Two to Eight deal with methods of researching advertising messages and material. These methods cover tests made both before and after circulation. Some of the test methods should be applied before circulation, since the information they produce can just as well be obtained before major advertising expenditures are made. Other tests may require at least a limited amount of circulation in order to be applied properly and therefore apply only after circulation has occurred.

The value of testing should not be too limited by cost considerations. When advertising money is well spent, it may influence sales and profits far beyond the advertising cost. If research helps to guide or improve advertisements, the gain may relate much more to company profits than to either advertising cost or to research cost. It was a wise advertising director who said that he tested his advertisements not because they cost money, but because the advertisements made money.

Possible Omissions or Misunderstandings

Here is a specific example, in the words of Perham C. Nahl, of how research can uncover significant omissions or misunderstandings.

> We were developing plans for advertising a new Johnson's Wax product. . . .
>
> We wanted to find out whether women understood the headline WASH YOUR KITCHEN WITH WAX.
>
> We showed the layout to a number of women. Through open-end questioning, we found out whether such a product might interest them. We asked what they might use the product for. The ad states that kitchen wax is especially for kitchens: "It's an easier way to clean your refrigerator, range, cabinets, woodwork, and walls."
>
> An unexpected windfall in this simple copy research project was the discovery that most women got the wrong impression of the product. They thought it was to be used on floors, as well as on other surfaces. . . .
>
> A serious omission was corrected. The revised ads stated that Kitchen Wax could be used on everything except the floors. We avoided some very real misunderstandings by a very inexpensive test.[8]

Another example has to do with a proposed headline for the detergent All: "Wouldn't I be dumb to use thick suds when the instructions prescribe

[8] Perham C. Nahl, "Speedy, Inexpensive Pretests of Ads: Capsule Case Histories," *Proceedings of the Fourth Annual Conference, Advertising Research Foundation, Inc.* (New York, October 2, 1958), pp. 51–52.

All!" Copy research demonstrated that lots of women bristled at the head-line because of the word "dumb"—for them, it was the wrong word psy-chologically. So an advertising campaign was continued that emphasized that All leaves no suds scum on clothes.

Aid to Creativeness

While evaluation of advertising may be desirable at several different stages, research can only assist—rather than control—the creative process. Research never wrote an ad. Unfortunately, though, there have been many misunderstandings among some creative advertising men and among some research men. As Richard D. Crisp has well said:

> These roadblocks are largely mental. . . . Roadblock No. 1 is the creative adman, who is afraid of research. He sees research as something that is some-how a threat either to his job or to his creative freedom. He sees research as something that is going to "fence him in." Roadblock No. 2 is the research man who is inclined to try to overuse or misuse research, or who understands imperfectly the role of research in the field of advertising, and/or the rela-tionship between creative research and creative advertising.[9]

Luckily, a good deal of the former antagonisms between the people who "make the ads" and the people who "make the research" have been ironed out in recent years. Members of each group realize more and more that they will be better off if they form mutual-admiration societies.

Both groups recognize that research is useful chiefly in challenging tradi-tional practices and in calling attention to possible oversights. Research may aid the choice among alternative advertising designs and give assurance at various stages of the creative process.

In other words, research is not a substitute for creativeness but does pro-vide facts upon which creativeness can go to work.

Importance of Scientific Methods

While advertisement building is an art, advertising measurement tends to be a science. Methods of evaluating copy which are not scientific are likely to lead to misinformation. Measuring methods which conform to the principles of science may not always get conclusive answers, but can be depended upon as far as they go. Copy research is necessarily a tenuous kind

[9] Richard D. Crisp, "How Research Can Help Increase Creative Effectiveness," speech at *Advertising Age* Summer Workshop on Creativity in Advertising (Chicago, July 24, 1958).

commonly, the buying act provides a number of cues and becomes more a process of *aided recall*. The consumer wants to recall what brand or product will best satisfy a particular want. *Recognition* requires even less mental effort, since it is only necessary to pick out and identify the product or idea.

THE USE OF JUDGMENT

Sometimes research has been looked upon as a substitute for judgment in advertising procedure. Research itself, of course, requires a good deal of judgment. It requires judgment to decide when to test, where to test, what to test, how to test, and how to use the results.

All these decisions must be made if the research practitioner is to aid the advertising practitioner in making still more important decisions. At times these important decisions can be little more than guesses, and the real challenge for the researcher is to provide facts which will reduce guesswork to a minimum.

Take the case of an advertiser who has long used a reverse plate for his logotype, but is considering a change to dark type on a light background for print advertising. The typographer and layout artist have shown him that he can drop the background plate entirely and, by enlarging the lettering slightly, achieve a good appearance. The advertiser tries to judge what he is sacrificing in order to increase legibility and keep up with contemporary styling. Obviously, he will be losing continuity, contrast, and possibly identification and recall, and there may even be some effect on the amount of copy read.

A research executive, coming onto the scene at this point, may or may not recommend some kind of test. A check on the reading patterns for other advertisers may give assurance that the proposed logotype change will not reduce reading. Available data may also show that identification at the time of advertisement reading is unlikely to suffer. The problem may come down to the simple question of whether the trademark or logotype is vivid enough to be highly memorable. If there is an immediate loss in ease of recall as the result of making a change, is the loss likely to be only temporary?

The research executive may recommend a recall test with matched sample or samples for each design under consideration. He may select other prominent and competitive designs for the purposes of establishing a uniform environment and basis for comparison.

After the research and the choice of a new design, suppose it performs almost as well as the previous logotype and both are among the best of the entire group tested. What has been gained by the research? Does it provide a definite basis for decision, or is this new evidence merely a vague indicator?

The point is that most tests of advertising do not dictate decisions. If test results are not evaluated carefully, the hazards may be greater than any likely gains. Not only must tests themselves be evaluated, but also the results of the tests as they relate to the advertising problem.

> Good consumer research is alive and dynamic, revealing new ideas and changes of buying habits as they occur. It can bring fresh ideas to the copy writer before they have been spoiled by competitive use. It provides a part of the working substance from which he creates. But a seasoned advertising man frequently finds a solution entirely apart from day-to-day research.[13]

Accuracy, Timing, and Cost

Finally, consider the problem: Under what circumstances should tests of advertising messages be used? There are three basic considerations: (1) accuracy, (2) timing, and (3) cost.

We should always decide in advance what degree of *accuracy* is required because this affects the size of sample and the methodology of the tests.

We should also determine how much *time* is available in order to have meaningful tests. One way of stating this might be to ask the question: After what date will the test results do us *no good?*

Finally, we should make a decision, based on probable *costs* of the tests, as to whether the expenses are justified for what we might learn from making them.

IMPLICATIONS

Advertising represents a business investment which, when properly conceived and executed, can bring highly gratifying returns. It is also a business in which judgment plays a prominent role. Among its record of successes are both big and little successes; there are also records of mistakes. The purpose of advertising measurement is simply to try to extend the percentage of big successes and to try to reduce or eliminate the mistakes.

Measurement is concerned largely with evaluating the effectiveness of advertising messages and campaigns and with appraisal of the media which

[13] Darrell Blaine Lucas and Steuart Henderson Britt, *Advertising Psychology and Research* (New York: McGraw-Hill Book Company, Inc., 1950), p. 150.

spring, it was concluded that people were judging acceleration of their cars by ease of gas-pedal operation!

The problem of finding and reporting meaningful answers when people cannot or will not report their buying motives accurately is not as discouraging as might at first appear. Politz has likened the problem to that of the adversary system in courts, where a witness might be assumed to be biased and even defensive. While consumer respondents need not be put in a defensive role, the questions and their sequence must be planned in such a way that dependable conclusions may be derived by studying the response patterns collected.

Learning to make the necessary records during an interview without causing confusion or embarrassing pauses is an art. Memorizing questions usually enables the interviewer to get the respondent started answering the next question, even while he records the answers just given.

The best that an interviewer can do is to execute skillfully and conscientiously the patterns laid out for him by the designer of the survey. He cannot correct for faults in the questioning any more than he can improve a poor sample design; in fact, if he tries to remedy what he believes to be some weakness in questioning or sampling, he cannot avoid introducing bias.

A good interviewer is one who accepts instructions which completely govern his field activities and then conforms to those instructions in minute detail.

It seems doubtful that interviewing procedures can be developed which will entirely erase the differences between superior and inferior interviewers. But an ingenious device has been developed for increasing interview reliability.[8] Called a *Recorditron,* it has several features which help to control the administration and recording of the interview. The questionnaire operates on a continuous roll, like a camera film. Each roll contains a full field assignment printed in continuous pattern. Forward motion is produced by turning the knob, but the roll cannot be reversed; this prevents editing by the interviewer. As an additional control, the Recorditron contains a clock mechanism which can be used on specified occasions to indicate the length of time of the questioning. The supervisor is enabled to observe the speed of the interview and to detect any

[8] Bertram Gold, *A Device for Increasing Interview Reliability,* paper presented at the Seventh Annual Conference of the Advertising Research Foundation, Inc., New York, October 3, 1961.

short-cut methods that might tend to invalidate the interviewing work. Small tape recorders are another of the means used to ensure adequate fieldwork, and their use probably will increase.[9]

SELECTION OF RESPONDENTS

The technical and financial problems associated with high response from a representative sample are of great importance in consumer surveys. Yet frequently the demands on time or the limitations of budgets encourage shortcuts on both time and money. The essential question is how good a sample needs to be for a particular problem solution. When is a local, convenient selection of willing respondents adequate? When is it necessary or desirable to secure a high rate of response from a large sample selected on a truly random basis from the population under study?

Basically, the answer is simple. Sampling economies and shortcuts are justified to the extent that one can afford not to know the extent of his risks of sampling error. Stated positively, a random or known-probability sample of a particular size is essential when it is important to know the extent of risk of error in the sample.

Sampling

The essential feature of a known-probability sample is that everyone in the intended universe has a known chance of being drawn into the sample. Since populations keep changing, the sample design may not determine the exact chance ratio until it is executed. Unlike population, land changes very little and a known-probability selection of land areas is a common basis for samples. Area-sample designs may begin with a random selection of large cities and nonmetropolitan counties.

These *primary sampling units* are then divided into smaller land areas called *clusters*. These are small, recognizable areas, such as groups of city blocks or rural land areas with designated boundaries. Clusters are intended to contain approximately equal numbers of dwelling units. Clusters are further divided into *segments* containing a convenient number of dwelling units for field assignments. The households or dwelling units may all be included or selected on a random pattern within the segment. *Individuals* within the households may then be selected on a random basis

[9] James F. Engel, "Tape Recorders in Consumer Research," *Journal of Marketing*, Vol. 26 (April, 1962), pp. 73–74.

speak of "inevitability of bias," which means that none of the measures of advertising effectiveness can or should be interpreted in *absolute* terms.

In a sense, the advertising researcher must of necessity inject a certain kind of bias into his work—such as that which comes from the artificial exposure of the advertisement to the respondent or from the artificial responses in that the respondent's memory is "massaged" in order to produce the responses.

As an example, the statement that "28 per cent noted the advertisement" is really a *relative* statement, rather than an absolute statement (although most people think the latter). The point is that the 28 per cent would have been 14 per cent or 56 per cent or X per cent *if* the sample had been constructed differently, *if* the questions concerning the noting of the advertisement had been asked differently, and so on. Just as psychological measures of intelligence have only *relative* meaning, the same is true of measures of advertising effectiveness. The researcher must realize that he should try to be as objective as possible but that he cannot avoid bias completely and that his job is to try to keep the small amount of bias *constant* as to any variable that is being compared with any other variable.

Sensitivity

The problem of sensitivity is a difficult one to state explicitly. It is even more difficult to solve.

So many of the measures of advertising are both reliable and valid—at least, in terms of "face validity"—but *without being sensitive enough to be meaningful*. As an example, the evidences concerning reliability and validity of most measures of advertising research are derived from analyses of results from quite different kinds of advertisements—advertisements for automobiles as compared with advertisements for cake mixes, for example. However, these measures have value only when they are applied to much finer kinds of discriminations, that is, discriminations between (or among) advertisements for the same brand of the same product under essentially the same conditions, including the amounts of money involved for the advertising.

As a case in point, the Starch scores of recognition of advertisements (see Chapter Three) have high reliability and give the appearance of validity, but for the most part they are useless for spotting better or poorer advertisements within a given campaign. Instead, their value is almost entirely limited to gross comparisons of average results from one campaign to another. Although this point has been made repeatedly by research people who have made statistical analyses of Starch data, most other people in advertising continue to "evaluate" *separate advertisements* on the basis of Starch scores!

Prediction

A third problem has to do with prediction. A research executive cannot always tell in advance whether the test he has devised will produce the kind of information he is seeking. Another way of stating this is: Testing methods sometimes will give fairly clear-cut answers—as between (or among) advertisements—as to which is most effective with respect to a particular objective, but under certain circumstances they will not.

It is just too much to expect a test to differentiate too accurately between (or among) advertisements which are all extremely good. In other words, the principal use of a testing method is to show up differences between two (or three or more) advertisements, *if* there really are great differences.

Here is the dilemma. If only a single element is different, in two advertisements that are to be tested, the measurement of results may become extremely difficult. The reason is that changing only one element may make the difference unmeasurable. On the other hand, if there are a great many major differences in two advertisements to be tested, then the differences may be easily measurable. What we can then say is that one combination of elements is better than another, although we may not necessarily learn too much about whether this is due to differences in art, headline, body copy, or other elements of the advertisement.

IMPLICATIONS

Much of the interpretation of the findings of advertising research is dictated by the preliminary planning. If the purpose is to test a hypothesis uncovered in exploratory stages and if techniques have been adapted and coded for proper tabulation and reporting, the results and their meaning should be almost self-evident.

Techniques of measurement are the working tools of the advertising research executive. Some techniques are well fitted to certain problems, and other techniques may be indicated to solve other problems.

Basically, there are only a few different techniques for evaluating advertising messages—certainly fewer techniques than the myriad of problems or advertising objectives to which they must be fitted.

three

Recognition Tests

ADVERTISING AND REMEMBERING

THE REGULAR RECOGNITION METHOD

WHAT DOES RECOGNITION MEASURE?

A CONTROLLED-RECOGNITION METHOD

EXTENSIVENESS OF RECOGNITION METHODS

IMPLICATIONS

Advertisers and advertising agencies spend a considerable share of their print research dollars on tests *after* advertisements are circulated. By far the most popular of the posttesting methods is the measurement of noting and reading of copy, based on *recognition* of the advertisements.

Certainly the simplest memory performance which can be checked with a respondent is to present him with an advertisement or advertisements and ask him to identify the advertisement or advertisements as seen or noticed, or not seen or noticed previously. There are many refinements and variations of this method and also a number of problems as to the significance of the method. But because recognition tests have been used so long and so widely in connection with publication advertisements, this first of six chapters dealing with specific methods is devoted to a discussion of *recognition* methods.

The very next chapter is devoted to a discussion of *recall* and *association* methods. As a simple example of a test of aided recall, a respondent may be told the name of an advertiser in a magazine issue he has seen or read previously and then asked to describe the advertisement and what it said.

By contrast, in a test of pure recall (approaching as nearly as possible *un-aided* recall), fewer or almost no cues are given to the respondent, and the questioning procedure is less likely to be directed to specific advertisements.

Although both recognition tests and recall tests are used to measure memory, this should not be their exclusive purpose or function. After all, any method of copy research that involves a response some time after advertising exposure must depend—in part, at least—on memory. An advertiser who finds that 90 per cent of his potential audience can recognize or recall his advertising message may be much less concerned with the evidences of memory than with the fact that his message got attention in the first place. This is an example of how important it is for the research executive to have a clear understanding of the advertising objective.

ADVERTISING AND REMEMBERING

A continuing problem for all advertisers is that people may not remember the advertising to which they have been exposed. But it must be realized that *learning* and *remembering* occur on the same time continuum; that is, remembering is in certain respects a temporal continuation of the learning process.[1] Thus

Learning   Remembering
——————————————
Time→

"Learning and remembering can be separated only for purposes of logical analysis. There is such an interrelation and integration of the activities of learning and remembering that it is accurate to speak of the learning-remembering process. . . . Our diagram should really look like this."[2]

Learning   Remembering (opposite aspect, Forgetting)—
measured in terms of Recognition-Recall-Relearning
——————————————
Time→

In any case, numerous experiments over the years by psychologists have demonstrated that most of us rapidly forget (do not remember); that the speed of forgetting (not remembering) rapidly accelerates; and that differ-

[1] Steuart Henderson Britt, "The Learning-remembering Process," *Psychological Review*, Vol. 44 (November, 1937), pp. 462–469, at pp. 466–467.
[2] Citation in footnote 1.

ent measurement scores are obtained, depending on whether we measure by the recognition method or by the recall method. In an important study of meaningful material conducted by some Yale University psychologists, the amount *recognized* after twenty minutes was 97 per cent, but two days later was only 75 per cent; but the amount *recalled* after twenty minutes was only 68 per cent and after two days was just under 10 per cent.[3]

Advertising men have long been concerned over the problem of how to keep people recognizing and recalling their advertising and the products and services advertised. In fact, advertising practitioners make use of many psychological principles or "rules" of learning.[4]

A practical problem in the psychology of advertising is—how should advertising be scheduled? Should an advertising schedule be concentrated in an intensive "burst" (thirteen weeks) or should it be spread out over a longer period (fifty-two weeks)? For the same expenditure, a relatively small number of consumers can be exposed to advertising many times, or a larger number can be exposed a smaller number of times.

It seems obvious that advertising will be quickly forgotten if consumers are not exposed to it over a period of time. It also seems obvious that as the number of exposures to advertising increases, the rate at which it is forgotten is likely to decrease. But neither of these statements really answers the questions asked in the previous paragraph, although they have been answered tentatively at least by some experimental work which suggests the following hypotheses:

> If the objective of the advertising schedule is to make a maximum average weekly number of people at least temporarily remember the advertising, then: (1) Spreading thirteen exposures over the year would be preferable to an intensive burst of thirteen weekly exposures. (2) Thirteen exposures per consumer, among a relatively small group of consumers, would be preferable to fewer exposures per consumer among a larger group. (3) The dollar efficiency of advertising increases as additional exposures to the advertising are purchased, at least up to thirteen exposures.[5]

This discussion obviously gets over into the complex problem of setting up proper media schedules, to be discussed in Part Two of the present

[3] Carl I. Hovland, Irving L. Janis, and Harold L. Kelly, *Communication and Persuasion* (New Haven: Yale University Press, 1953), especially p. 249.

[4] Steuart Henderson Britt, "How Advertising Can Use Psychology's Rules of Learning," *Printers' Ink*, Vol. 252 (September 23, 1955), pp. 74, 77, 80.

[5] Hubert A. Zielske, "The Remembering and Forgetting of Advertising," *Journal of Marketing*, Vol. 23 (January, 1959), pp. 239–243, at p. 243.

book. But the matter is also brought out here because the appropriate methods of measurement of what is remembered are so important. Every advertiser is interested in what he may call "advertising penetration"—he wants to know how many people remember and how many do not remember his current advertising.[6] For further discussion of this matter of *penetration*, see Chapter Nine.

Following are brief statements of certain basic principles relating to advertising tests based on memory:

1. *All memory tests of advertising effectiveness are necessarily based on two separate reactions to the advertising:* (*a*) whether or not the respondents *noted* the advertising (or how much attention they gave to the advertising) in the first place; and (*b*) whether or not the respondents *remembered* the advertising (or how well they remembered it) in the second place. And the problem is that one can never be sure of the extent to which a memory test reflects *noting* as compared with *recall*.

2. *Both noting and recall of advertising are importantly mediated by many factors other than the advertisements which are being studied.* These include the respondents' interest in, need for, or usage of the product or service being advertised, the respondents' responsibility for buying the advertised product or service, the frequency of the respondents' exposure to previous advertisements for the product or service, and the similarity of the advertisements studied to advertisements to which respondents had previously been exposed.

3. *To the extent that the advertisement itself dictates noting or recall of a single advertisement, the major factors in noting and recall are the size, color, and amount of illustration.* These factors are often held constant among advertisements being compared by memory measures for any one product or service. Thus, the advertising researcher needs to be sure that the measures of memory that he employs are *sensitive enough* for making the kinds of discriminations called for by the research problem.

4. *All recall is "aided" to some degree.* It cannot be elicited by a blank stare from an interviewer and nothing more. Whatever question is used to elicit recall determines the degree of aid given to respondents in stimulating them to remember. Thus, all recall and recognition measures are *relative measures*—comparable only when recall or recognition is elicited in exactly the same way.

[6] Compare Rosser Reeves, *Reality in Advertising* (New York: Alfred A. Knopf, Inc., 1961), p. 10.

The methods used to obtain Starch Advertisement Readership ratings were carefully reproduced, with two objectives in mind. One was to see how well the results would correlate. The other was to see whether additions to sample and design would reveal facts not hitherto known about the method or the commercial applications of it.

The Advertising Research Foundation selected a single issue of *Life* containing 125 one-half page and larger advertisements, for a tryout of the recognition method. A relatively large probability population sample was designed, sufficient to permit over 600 interviews with admitted readers of the *Life* issue. A summary analysis, including a comparison between the ARF recognition scores and those produced by Daniel Starch & Staff on the same issue of *Life*, is enlightening. Only the scores on noting of advertisements will be discussed, and conclusions rest solely on one issue. Interpretations beyond the reported facts are those of the present authors.

The regular recognition method, as used commercially, is definitely reproducible. Correlation of women's scores, based on 96 full-page and larger advertisements measured by both ARF and Starch, is +.92. The scores for men correlate +.86. Actually, the average ARF score for both sexes is 21.7 per cent, which is significantly below the average Starch score of 26.4 per cent. This difference is secondary in significance in comparison with the pattern of correlation.

According to this single-issue test, sampling, one of the most controversial points surrounding commercial recognition ratings, had little effect. The Starch sample was of the judgment quota type. ARF tried to throw further light on the sampling influence by tabulating separately those persons more difficult of access for physical or personality reasons; it is assumed that these people are less likely to be included in a judgment sample. The "more difficult" group had only slightly lower scores for noting advertisements, however, and there was no evidence to support the additional expense of probability sampling.

The passage of time—up to two weeks after magazine issuance or last reading of it—had no significant effect on average noting scores for all 125 advertisements, as shown according to the following interviewing dates:

Interview date	Per cent
May 13–15	19.5
May 16–19	18.8
May 20–22	18.6
May 23–28	20.7

This steady pattern is reassuring from the standpoint of interview scheduling, but it is a serious challenge to the term "recognition," since all memory functions are expected to decline with the passage of time. The question as to whether the method is really a memory technique will be discussed shortly.

One interviewing factor logically related to actual advertising exposure is the particular method used to identify readers of the issue. The commercial method accepts as readers those who identify by means of the cover or a quick inspection of the issue. Audience research (see Chapter Ten) has demonstrated that there is a 25 to 50 per cent overclaiming of the reading of popular magazine issues on the basis of covers and inspection. People who have not seen inside the issue must surely depress recognition scores— or so one would think. But they do not! Apparently those who make erroneous claims of issue reading also make erroneous claims of advertisement noting.

ARF added a small sample in which claimed readers were required to recall (see Chapter Four) an article or picture story in the issue to *qualify* for the recognition interview on advertisements. This more rigid reading test produced no significant improvement in recognition scores for women. Men's scores actually dropped, when based on the more selected group of issue readers. The evidence indicates that accurate recognition is *not* the full basis for response to advertisements.

ARF had the supervisor rate each interviewer for competence in order to estimate the influence of interviewer skill. No significant difference was found in the recognition scores for the better and poorer field workers. The method apparently is not very sensitive to interviewer skill.

The large ARF sample made it possible to compare noting scores according to age, education, and socioeconomic level of readers. There was no significant variation for these groups. On the other hand, women showed consistently higher noting scores than men, with average scores of 20.7 and 17.6 per cent, respectively, on the 125 advertisements one-half page and larger. This same tendency has long been noted for advertisements intended to appeal equally to women and to men.

Recognition ratings are definitely sensitive to the size of advertisement, the class of product, and whether the respondent is a "real" prospect or has no use for the product. The size factor and product influence have long been identified as rating determinants, and the large ARF sample made possible a comparison between scores for those subjectively judged to belong to the

Reasons for Inaccurate Recognition

There are a considerable number of factors which may account for the demonstrated tendency to claim recognition of advertisements not actually seen or heard previously. Some of the more commonly accepted causes of inflation would include the following:

Genuine confusion with other advertising

Guessing when uncertain

Deliberate exaggeration

Deduction that advertisement was seen, based on recognition of surrounding material

Deduction of likely noting, based on memory or knowledge of one's own reading habits

Eagerness to please the interviewer

Hesitation to appear ignorant

Misunderstanding of instruction given by the interviewer

Guessing, on the basis of general familiarity with or interest in the advertised product or service, and its advertising in general

Tendency to rate or not rate advertisements on the basis of whether they look like advertisements that the respondents *think* they would have noticed

Relative ratings in different publications or issues may go up or down, depending on the following:

Thickness of issue

Average reliability of the people who make up the reading audience

Position of the advertisement in the issue or the interview

Variations in the interviewing staff and in the emphasis on care in recognition

Proper design of controls can either eliminate or equalize the effects of all of the above factors, assuming that the respondent has at least a fairly good idea of what is expected of him.

Design of Recognition Controls

Controlled-recognition measurement requires that magazine advertisements be removed from context. This may appear to put some extra burden on memory, but it has the advantage of eliminating the chance of false identification based on context or sequence of reading the issue.

Since the advertisements have to be put into a portfolio or mounted in a scrapbook for interviewing, it is possible to rotate positions so as to equalize any possible effects of interview position. The use of a portfolio with equal numbers of items in all tests makes it possible to rule out the variable influence of thickness of magazine issue on the length of interview.

It seems desirable to provide some balance of familiar and unfamiliar advertisements in the kits for both preexamination and postexamination. Since the test advertisements are unpublished in the preexamination, there should be approximately as many familiar, published advertisements mixed in at random as a background. Later, in the postexamination, the test copy may have become familiar through circulation, so that the additional filler advertisements should be still newer, unpublished copy.

Identifying Issue Readers

The fact that the measured magazine issue is not shown in its complete form permits still one further precautionary step. The regular recognition method has been criticized for accepting claims of issue reading, based on cover identification alone. Some nonreaders are allowed to go through the issue and make spurious claims of recognizing advertisements in it. Since the main editorial features are not used in the advertising part of the interview, they can be shown *first* for determining who is *qualified* as a reader (as in magazine-audience studies—see Chapter Ten).

Eight or ten main editorial features can be bound inside of the issue jacket for the purpose of identifying genuine issue readers. In the postexamination, the contents of the measured issue will be used; the preexamination will use the cover and contents of an issue the same age in relation to interview dates. When the magazine part of the interview is reached, the respondent is asked if he has read any copy of the particular publication in the past six months. Those who have done so are then shown the cover of the issue and asked to look at each editorial feature and state whether or not they think it is interesting. This, in brief, is the widely used method of measuring magazine audiences, and it provides a definable base of respondents to test for advertisement recognition.

Taking the respondent through the editorial features and asking about his interests has two advantages. First, this procedure gets the main issue features before him, so that it is then safe to ask whether he happened to read the issue before. People are usually able to discriminate accurately by that time, and since they have talked only about their interests, they do not have the embarrassment of reversing earlier claims of having read the issue. Second, having scanned the editorial features, the genuine readers have had a chance to revive the associations which may help them better to identify the advertising content.

3. This noting set, or tendency to note ads, is related to multimagazine readership. Multimagazine readers are more likely to note ads falsely than non-
multimagazine readers.[9]

Appel and Blum were able to demonstrate that high consumer interest
in the product and high share of a market, relative to other brands, gen-
erated increased false claims of noting. Multimagazine readers and readers
of magazines with small audiences were found to make more false claims
of ad noting. These points accentuate the problem of developing a precise
measure of actual ad noting. Appel and Blum concluded that such an
attempt is futile, but did develop a regression procedure for estimating
relative audience sizes. Indeed, by use of regression, it is possible to make
meaningful forecasts based on false claims measured in advance of publication!

Blum has also introduced a new type of "ad-evaluation" technique.[10]
The advertisement ratings, reported as percentiles, are based upon recognition claims of people exposed to the magazine issue and nonexposure recognition claims obtained from people in the sample who have not yet seen the
issue. The nonexposure scores are used in place of prepublication scores, as
indicated above, to predict recognition scores for exposed people on the
basis of regression. The difference between the predicted exposed score and
the actual exposed score is used to compute the ad-evaluation score. The latter is expressed as a percentile and relates directly only to other advertisements in the issue.

This percentile procedure is conservative in that it does not designate an
absolute performance on each advertisement. It avoids some of the controversy surrounding the controlled-recognition formula, which requires
acceptance of the absolute premise that respondents who are confused or
unreliable on a particular advertisement will later see or note the advertisement in the same ratio as the more reliable individuals. The use of a nonexposed group, which may not easily be equated with the exposed group for
sampling purposes, offers a great advantage in economy over pretesting with
preexposed people. Only one survey is required to establish the final percentile scores. Early results also suggest that the percentile ad-evaluation
scores may have a rank order closely corresponding to controlled-recognition
scores. At least, Blum's ad-evaluation method dramatizes the fallacy in
following absolute recognition scores obtained after exposure, and it makes

---

[9] Valentine Appel and Milton L. Blum, "Ad Recognition and Respondent Set,"
Journal of Advertising Research, Vol. 1 (June, 1961), pp. 13–21, at p. 14.
[10] Based on discussions with Milton L. Blum.

considerable headway in establishing a relative evaluation of advertisements in noting or perception performance. Blum also emphasizes the implications in large nonexposed scores of the cumulative effects of previous advertising.

Final resolution of the problem of precisely correcting for false recognition of advertisements appears as far back as 1951, when William T. Moran (now with Young & Rubicam advertising agency) made one of the more exhaustive analyses of the underlying factors.[11] Moran was not satisfied to assume that all false responses are in the affirmative, as is implied by the controlled-recognition-correction formula. He proposed a procedure calling for a choice between two advertisements, rather than merely identifying one advertisement at a time. Norman Heller challenged Moran's assumptions,[12] and the latter defended his position on theoretical grounds.[13] While Moran did not solve the problem of how to select suitable copy for pairing with each test advertisement, he raised questions of theory which continue to be unsettled.

Such explorations and others highlight three shortcomings of the controlled-recognition method which have been acknowledged from the beginning. These are as follows:

1. People forget ads which they actually have seen.

2. For prestige reasons, people may deny having seen some ads and may falsely claim to have seen others.

3. There is a fallacy in assuming that unreliable respondents later actually see ads in exactly the same pattern as do the more discriminating respondents.

The first two questions are met by the assertion that the chief fault of uncontrolled recognition is assumed to be inflation, not deflation. The controlled method does not correct for deflation.

The third and most serious point cannot be fully resolved. The formula usually adds only a minority to the audience established by simple subtraction of the prepublication score from the postpublication score. It may be that when prepublication scores approach or exceed 50 per cent, there is some loss in validity, as there certainly is in statistical reliability, of the formula score. But when prepublication scores are of such a magnitude, it

[11] William T. Moran, "Measuring Exposure to Advertisements," *Journal of Applied Psychology,* Vol. 35 (February, 1951), pp. 72–77.

[12] Norman Heller, "Moran's 'Measuring Exposure to Advertisements,'" *Journal of Applied Psychology,* Vol. 35 (February, 1951), pp. 77–78.

[13] William T. Moran, "A Reply to Heller's Note," *Journal of Applied Psychology,* Vol. 35 (February, 1951), pp. 78–79.

is even more ridiculous to treat uncontrolled-recognition scores seriously as measures of audiences of individual advertisements.

EXTENSIVENESS OF RECOGNITION METHODS

The regular recognition method is used so widely that Starch Advertisement Readership ratings can be obtained on almost any half-page or larger popular magazine advertisement within approximately one month after publication of the issue. Recognition ratings of specified issues of a considerable number of newspapers are produced by the Starch service, as well as outdoor poster ratings in selected markets. The Starch organization and almost all advertising research companies—as well as many agencies and advertisers—run special surveys that employ the recognition method for advertisements in the major media. Sometimes recognition is used mainly as a preliminary to other research approaches, but often the recognition result is the chief aim of the survey.

One broadcast rating service, Pulse, Inc., shows the local television or radio program listings to survey respondents and asks which broadcasts they listened to or saw. The audience claims are supposed to be based largely upon a process of aided recall (see next chapter), in which the printed log of programs is only one cue. The result is a combination of recognition and recall, but the method is open to the same questions as to possible inflationary claims which occur when statements about recognition are permitted without controls.

A unique approach to recognition testing uses a tachistoscope to control exposure allowed for identification, although this is only a part of the interviewing procedure. The hypothesis has been advanced that inflated or distorted claims of recognition may be the result of too long or too complete exposure. The usual hypothesis is that recognition is aided by complete exposure and by inspection under conditions as nearly identical as possible to the original experience. Early experimental efforts have not indicated any increase of validity of recognition claims when exposure time is shortened.

Two investigators apparently had this same objective in their experimental work which involved the use of screens to reduce visibility of advertisements in the interview.[14] They used from one to three layers of Zip-A-Tone 080-R opaque plastic screen, removing one screen at a time; this enabled them to

[14] Gordon M. Keswick and Lawrence G. Corey, "A Sensitive Measure of Ad Exposure," *Journal of Advertising Research,* Vol. 1 (December, 1961), pp. 12–16.

measure recognition claims at four levels of visibility in what they called the Controlled Ad Awareness Technique (CAAT).

Identification of eight test advertisements was measured after the experimenters had first presented three different levels of exposure to the cooperating subjects: maximum exposure with thorough reading, moderate exposure without reading of running text, and minimum of a glance.

Each advertisement was then presented in the interviews under three screens, then two screens, one screen, and without screen. It was reasoned that if ads with greater controlled exposure could be identified through more screens, then a more valid recognition test of genuine ad noting could be achieved by interviewing with progressive increases in ad visibility. The varied levels at which identification could be obtained would also add a new dimension to recognition ratings. The experiment succeeded in establishing a median correlation of $+.72$ between exposure and identification for the eight advertisements. Application to measure recognition after normal exposure of magazine advertisements was indicated as a next step.

Various other types of recognition controls have been applied to copy in nearly all advertising media. The controlled-recognition method, applying the formula to scores obtained both before and after exposure in the vehicles, has been used to measure audiences of car cards in many leading cities in the United States and Canada. It had previously been used to measure the audiences of magazine advertisements and became the basis for the earliest published studies of the total audiences of average issues of popular magazines. Many other special studies have employed complete-recognition controls.

Limited controls of recognition have been extensively applied, and simplified methods have been advanced. One method, almost completely lacking in merit, is the use of a uniform discount on all scores. Nothing in experimental work on recognition justifies this shortcut.

The most common method of control is based on the introduction of a few spurious items in an otherwise uncontrolled interview. Respondents who claim identification of items not available to them previously are considered to be *unreliable respondents,* and their interviews are discarded. This method has some merit, although the bulk of evidence indicates that inflation is not primarily a function of a few reckless individuals.

The implications regarding motivation of reception of advertising messages are probably different for television, although awareness of commercials is usually measured through recall (Chapter Four). Arthur H. Wilkins, of Benton and Bowles, Inc., discovered important variations in

It is not recommended to go beyond this point, however. Unless controls and adequate samples are used, it is definitely unsafe to venture estimates of actual audience totals. Any figure specifying unit costs is, in a very real sense, a projection of total audience and should be discouraged. Ratings of minor advertising elements and standard details of logotype tend to have little meaning. Almost any calculation or interpretation intended to reveal degree of awareness of the identity of the advertiser or product is highly suspect. We must be content with the fact that the recognition method throws useful light on advertisement-noting and reading behavior.

The interpretation of reading behavior as evidence of interest is generally accepted, especially when the reading has occurred in natural home circumstances. One investigator has instructed respondents, mostly by mail, to indicate only those advertisements which they read *with interest.* This distinction between what was read with interest and what was read supposedly without interest is extremely *subjective and unrealistic.* If someone looks at a magazine advertisement in his own living room and pores through the details, this can only be motivated behavior. If it is done without interest, this would point to a new area not before discovered by advertising researchers.

On the other hand, recognition ratings of reading behavior—when obtained by the more accepted methods—are substantial evidence of reader *interest.* This is probably their greatest value.

While degree of interest may usually be assumed to bear some relationship to memory of advertising impressions, the actual existence of positive interest is much more likely in the process of receiving impressions from magazine advertisements than from television commercials. This may provide a partial explanation of why advertisers have been so much more concerned with recognition of magazine advertisements than with recognition of television commercials.

four

Recall and
Association Tests

AIDED-RECALL TESTS OF CIRCULATED ADVERTISEMENTS

AN EXPERIMENT BY THE ADVERTISING

  RESEARCH FOUNDATION

OPTIMIZING THE RECALL METHOD

MEASURING UNAIDED RECALL

AIDED RECALL AND ASSOCIATION

IMPLICATIONS

We turn now to a discussion of *recall,* which is the chief type of memory test for advertising not discussed in the previous chapter (which discussed *recognition* methods). We shall be concerned with aided recall, and also unaided recall and association.

The chief use of recall methods is to measure memorability or at least memorable impressions of advertisements. Adaptation of recall methods by Gallup & Robinson, Inc., for magazine and television advertising measurement occupies a large part of the present chapter.

AIDED-RECALL TESTS OF CIRCULATED ADVERTISEMENTS

Those who feel that recognition ratings do not go far enough and that they are not accurate enough may consider the merits of the more rigid aided-recall procedure.

73

Editing is also essential to evaluate the statements of points which the advertisement was designed to communicate. The largest and most dramatic score made by an advertisement is its overall proved identification— this is called Proved Name Registration (or PNR) by Gallup & Robinson.

This PNR is an *adjusted* score. That is, it is based on the per cent of readers of the issue who demonstrate that they really recall the advertisement by their "playback" of some element of the advertisement. This number is then adjusted for a number of factors, including size of advertisement, color, page placement (cover or inside pages, etc.), and the number of advertisements in the issue under study.

Gallup & Robinson also provide a Product-Class Average as well as an Issue Average as bench marks for comparison.

The chief purpose of aided-recall research is to measure total effective communication. This includes ideas conveyed and remembered, attitudes established, and possibly predisposition to act favorably. The simplest way to report and compare idea *impact* is by coding and counting the number of specific points played back by the respondents.

Consumer Impact Study

Back in 1952, the Research Department of the Leo Burnett Company designed a special service for its clients called the Consumer Impact Study (CIS), somewhat like Gallup & Robinson measures but at considerably less cost and with flexibility to cover a great many more publications than Gallup & Robinson. The CIS was a method for posttesting print advertisements immediately after their appearance in a publication; hundreds of different ads were tested until 1959, when other testing methods took priority.

CIS was primarily a measure of *impact*. It was a method for measuring the *degree of impression* made by an advertisement. This was in terms of the percentage of respondents exposed to the advertisement on whom the advertisement made a sufficiently strong impression to be remembered and recallable.

The CIS also provided "playbacks" or responses to a number of questions asked as to what was remembered about the ad and how it was remembered by those who recalled it; it thus gave information about the *kind of impression* made by the advertisement.

Analysis of these playbacks provided some indication of the effectiveness of the ad in three areas beyond mere impact:

1. The relative strength of different elements in the ad in terms of the percentages recalling each element

2. The extent to which the ad communicated its intended message, imagery, and mood

3. The reactions of respondents to the ad, especially their acceptance or rejection of the ideas

In other words, the CIS served two major purposes. It gave an indication of how well the ad performed in terms of impact in comparison with other ads for the same or similar products (or services) in the same publication. It also gave an indication of how well the ideas and imagery of the ad were communicated and received.

Problems in Recall Research

Many of the problems and questions growing out of commercial aided-recall operations relate to the difficulty of measuring a significant amount of residue. Can aided recall be applied to all persons who read a magazine issue? What are the proper interviewing dates for each publication, and are there always satisfactory dates for interviewing? To what extent are interviewers able to restrain the tendency to offer excessive clues? Can the coding of verbatim responses be made sufficiently objective to provide a true measure? What is the significance of aided-recall performance of advertisements in evaluating different publications? Assuming that an objective measurement of significant amounts of recall is possible, just how does it relate to advertising objectives?

All but the last of these questions would be far less acute if advertising impressions were sufficiently vivid and memorable to survive until a convenient interviewing date.

Most commercial aided-recall research on magazines does not use probability samples. The fact that Gallup & Robinson uses a recall test to qualify issue readers produce a survey base of readers which cannot be defined or readily duplicated. Interviewing dates have been empirically determined—apparently to achieve optimal recall performance. Coding, which is necessarily subjective, is seldom revealed to clients or other investigators. Gallup & Robinson has solved the problem of media comparisons by arbitrarily establishing a uniform midpoint for scores on all publications. Proved Name Registration scores are then scattered over approximately an equal range on the basis of an empirically developed graph. The desire to rule out media controversy is understandable, but an important by-product is the camouflage of original absolute scores.

AN EXPERIMENT BY THE ADVERTISING RESEARCH FOUNDATION

Questions of the type expressed above and a desire to compare recall with recognition led the Advertising Research Foundation to combine the two methods in a classic experiment.[1] The assignment of the Printed Advertising Rating Methods (PARM) committee of the ARF was to develop an ideal measure of readership and remembrance of printed advertisements. However, as indicated in Chapter Three, it was decided first to examine available commercial research operations, including aided-recall research by Gallup & Robinson. Another research firm was directed to reproduce the Gallup & Robinson methods in order to see how well the results would correlate. The sample and interviewing procedures were extended to permit internal analysis of certain variables.

The Advertising Research Foundation experiment was confined to one issue of *Life* large enough to permit aided-recall ratings of 96 full-page and larger advertisements. Of these, 89 were also scored by Gallup & Robinson. More than 600 completed interviews on aided recall alone were obtained from a national probability sample of individuals. Most of the recall interviews were based on issue readers qualified by describing an article or picture story, but 20 per cent of the interviews used simple cover identification for purposes of comparison.

There follows a summary of ARF findings, including comparisons between ARF recall scores and the PNR scores produced on the same issue by Gallup & Robinson. Any implied conclusions are based on data from only one issue and relate only to the gross PNR scores. Interpretations beyond the reported facts are those of the present authors.

If a final conclusion is to be based on the simple fact of correlation between the two recall surveys, it would be that the commercial findings are not fully reproducible. The correlation between ARF recall scores for women and those of Gallup & Robinson was +.82; for men, it was +.61. These correlations permit wide differences on many individual advertisements. The average ARF score for Proved Name Registration was 3 per cent, compared with the larger average score of 4.8 per cent for Gallup & Robinson.

The overall correlation in the ARF experiment may cast doubts on the stability of aided-recall scores, but an internal examination of the findings

[1] Darrell B. Lucas, "The ABCs of ARF's PARM," *Journal of Marketing*, Vol. 25 (July, 1960), pp. 9–20. Also see "How Do Starch and Gallup Scores Compare?" *Printer's Ink*, Vol. 255 (May 4, 1956), pp. 54–58.

is reassuring.[2] Since the commercial sample was not of probability design, it may be assumed that significant sample differences could be expected. ARF developed separate PNR scores for those with whom it was easy and those with whom it was difficult to start the interview. Average scores for all advertisements fell from 3.3 per cent for the more willing respondents to 1.8 per cent for those resisting the interviewers at the start. A similar comparison based on ease of completing the interview showed a drop from 3.4 to 2.3 per cent as difficulty increased. On the assumption that judgment quota samples are better represented by those easier to interview, it may be that there was a substantial influence traceable to differences between the ARF and Gallup & Robinson samples.

The most striking demonstration of the ARF experiment was the influence of the lapse of time on recall scores. The Gallup & Robinson interviewing schedule on *Life* is completed before the next issue appears, but ARF extended the fieldwork to two full weeks. ARF inquired of each respondent how long ago he last looked into the measured issue. Average PNR scores in relation to time elapsed since last reading were as below:

Days	Per cent
One	4.5
Two	3.3
Three to six	2.5
Over six	2.1

When the effects of time on aided-recall scores are graphed as in Fig. 3, they closely resemble the long-established curves of forgetting of learned material. This is significant, since one of the major problems in the application of memory tests is ascertaining what has been measured. There seems reason to conclude that this method is primarily a measure of memory of advertising impressions. It would also appear that the commercial interviewing schedule, confining the fieldwork to the first week after issuance of a weekly magazine, is based on sound judgment.

The Gallup & Robinson method of qualifying issue readers by requiring recall of an article or picture story in the issue should definitely rule out people who have not actually looked into the magazine previously. Approximately one-fifth of the ARF aided-recall interviews used the looser method of cover identification, which allows some nonreaders to qualify. Theoretically, this dilution of the reader base should lower the aided-recall

[2] *A Study of Printed Advertising Rating Methods,* Vol. 2 (New York: Advertising Research Foundation, Inc., 1956), p. 169.

operate more to the disadvantage of some advertisements than others, although this has not been demonstrated.

One advantage of the usual aided-recall procedure, which limits its valid application, is the fact that all responses are measured in association with the correct company or product name. There may be situations where recall could be stimulated from another source ultimately leading to correct name identification. Possibly there are times when conscious identification is not essential to the chief advertising objective. In all applications of this method, the measurement of identification or playback of the message is limited to what the respondent can articulate. These limitations indicate lowering of the scores and the validity of the aided-recall method, where such considerations are important.

Objectivity is one of the stronger features of the aided-recall method, insofar as it is assumed to be measuring maximum performance of respondents. Normally respondents appear to be striving for all possible recall, with little or no subjective censoring of what they are reporting. The interviewer is expected to give no direct clues in the use of probes and should exercise no bias in the recording of verbatim replies.

However, some loss of objectivity—in the broader sense in which the term is used in this book—is likely to be introduced by some field workers. Otherwise, the chief lack of objectivity is in the editing of verbatim responses for tabulating purposes. All editing has a subjective element; the decision to accept or reject Proof of Name Registration or statements of copy points is open to variations of standards. On the whole, though, aided recall is probably the most objective of the practical memory methods.

Statistical reliability of aided-recall scores, such as PNR, demands a fairly large sample size. Since it is not practical to determine just when an advertisement is exposed and to interview respondents at a fixed interval after exposure, the recall content is very unstable. Some people show poor capacity to perform on aided recall—because of faulty memory or lack of ability to verbalize or both. These considerations also call for a comparatively large basic sample. Some advertisements leave such an insignificant trace that it is not practical to use samples adequate for significant ratings. In general, there is a problem in getting stable aided-recall scores on Proved Name Registration.

Aided Recall after a Controlled Interval

Considering the problem of rapid forgetting and the uncertainty as to when magazine readers normally see advertisements, it is evident that great gains can be made where the interval can be controlled or optimized. There may be a further gain if the size of the magazine and the number of advertisements are comparatively small, in comparison with tests on thick issues of successful magazines. Unfortunately, advertisers have little interest in surveys of thin publications containing only a few advertisements.

Tests with Dummy Magazines

The early work on dummy magazines—it was first carried on independently by George Gallup when he was with Young & Rubicam, Inc., and the late Claude Robinson and led to their much larger emphasis on surveys of real magazines—has been continued on specially assembled magazines by Gallup & Robinson, Inc., and many others. The magazine assemblies have varied all the way from skillfully rebound copies of familiar publications to obviously made-up portfolios, mechanically held together. Although Young & Rubicam's present *New Canadian World* actually is a dummy magazine, respondents react to it as a real magazine.

The exposure of issue contents is usually forced—or at least controlled—within a few hours or a day. Usually the copies are put in the hands of intended respondents, often housewives, who are asked to agree to look through the magazine by a specified date. Nothing is said about advertisements. If the respondent agrees to examine the contents and to be interviewed at a later specified time, the interviewer has completed the initial step. The interviewer then returns later the same day or the next day, according to the appointment, takes the magazine into his own possession, and proceeds with an aided-recall inquiry.

This process is favorable to the measurement of recall, since exposure is forced and since the interval is short and relatively uniform. If only a few advertisements are involved, the situation is even more favorable for obtaining stable scores from relatively small samples. If housewives are used exclusively, it may be sufficient to survey less than 200.

There are arguments or situations favoring the use of altered copies of real magazines, and of dummy magazines. Familiar magazines preserve a more natural atmosphere, but must be surveyed in advance of issuance or surveyed with people who normally do not read the publication. It is also possible to select issues which do not contain too much advertising for optimal recall.

Obvious dummies or experimental magazines appear as unfamiliar synthetic publications, but they permit complete control of page location, editorial surroundings, and number of advertisements. Different inter-

experimentation at various stages in the development of a commercial, beginning with the rough storyboards or a sequence of still photographs with appropriate sound.

After two years of experimental work, Batten, Barton, Durstine, and Osborn advertising agency announced publicly in 1962 the exclusive use of an actual half-hour program in prime broadcasting time in a major market.[9] The program, a first-run adventure series, provides the agency with three minutes of commercial time to be used in any combination of time units. The program rating, in a city with only a single television station, runs from 20 to 25. Interviewing is done by telephone with samples of 1,000, which, as indicated by the rating, pick up 200 to 250 viewers.

Here are some of the special features of the method:

1. All commercials are tested as they will actually be viewed on the air under in-home conditions.

2. Each person is interviewed individually, within two hours of seeing the show.

3. A relationship between the commercial and the program is established.

4. Because of the availability of three commercial minutes each week, the cost can be carried across two or more commercials.

Not only are the viewing conditions natural but—in contrast with tests using theater projection before groups (compare Chapter Seven)—the sample may be much more typical of the program audience. The sample for the tests is systematically selected from the local telephone directory, and only one viewer is interviewed in any one home.

The first question in the interview may be "If you were to go shopping right now, what brand of (Product) would you buy?" This is asked about each of the product categories under study that night. There follows inquiry about television viewing that night, and if he indicates he had watched the show, the respondent is asked to tell something of the story line so that his exposure can be verified. Verified viewers then become the base for measures of the commercial.

Testing of awareness of the commercial begins with the unaided-recall question "What products do you remember having seen advertised?" Then aid is given in the form of mention of specific product categories under test, followed by measures of the recall of specific points about the commercial.

[9] *New York Times,* Monday, April 2, 1962, p. 32. Also, "A New Unique Way of Evaluating Television Commercials on the Air, Channel One" (New York: Batten, Barton, Durstine, and Osborn, Inc., 1962).

One question is "What did the commercial tell you about (Name of product)?"

There follows "What did the commercial on (Name of product) lead you to expect from the product? What did it promise you?"

Additional questions may also be asked regarding the believability, importance, or uniqueness of ideas featured in the commercial.

The significance of the introductory question about brand preference of products lies in the comparison between those later found to be exposed or unexposed to the commercials. Direct comparisons of this kind can be misleading, since there may be many factors involved besides actual exposure to a particular commercial. However, when the same commercial is treated in different contexts within the program, or when different commercials for a product are treated within the same context, variations of the brand preference pattern may become much more meaningful.

The complete control of commercial time within a program series on the one channel means that commercials may run anywhere from a few seconds each to the full three minutes, and two commercials may be run next to each other (back to back) or separately. As an example of the results, in testing commercial units of thirty seconds and sixty seconds, an extensive body of data indicates that evidence of penetration of consumer promise from a thirty-second commercial may be about two-thirds as great as from a sixty-second commercial.

Also, it was found that when two commercials were run back to back, it made no difference whether or not the products were related.

Since the availability of the test program occurs in units of thirteen weeks, it is possible to set up many test patterns measuring learning and attitude patterns, evaluating frequency, sequence, and other significant elements.

Aid to the creative departments is enhanced in this work because of the practicality of trying out ideas at all stages of development. An announcer can present a selling idea in live form, with or without visual aids. A series of storyboards, roughly representing various stages of an unfinished commercial, can be used with a live announcer or recorded sound. Still photos may also be used instead of storyboard sketches, and segments of motion pictures can be inserted where action is most needed.

In fact, a large part of the cost of producing finished commercials for test can be saved by using a rehearsal test film employing less expensive talent, simpler sets, and a minimum of the expensive photographic tech-

Audits & Surveys Company, Inc., has an interesting plan for covering nighttime network commercials in a pattern very similar to the above.[10] Viewer samples of up to 200 women and 150 men, depending on the product, are selected by screening systematically from telephone books in 10 major cities. The telephone interviews are done twenty-four hours after broadcast, and respondents are given the name of the program and asked whether they watched it the previous evening. The first question about the commercial merely tells when it occurred in the program and asks for the brand name. If necessary, the respondent is then given the brand name and asked if he remembers the commercial. If so, the respondent is probed for details about the commercial, what it looked like, what was pictured, what was said, what were the sales points, etc. Reports include both the unaided response to the first question on commercials and the responses made after aids are given, including verbatim comments of the respondents.

MEASURING UNAIDED RECALL

Various methods of unaided or essentially pure-recall measurement have long been used in advertising research. When exposure is controlled and the number of advertisements is not too large, it is sometimes possible to measure memory with very little aid to the recall process.

Surveys of dummy magazines and of television commercials can produce significant amounts of unaided recall. More often, the unaided method is used when the penetration of a campaign theme is to be tested rather than when individual messages are to be evaluated separately.

It is always necessary to give some direction as to interview responses, and there is danger that this may provide some slight aid to recall. The introductory question may ask "What advertisements have you noticed recently?" or "What do you particularly remember seeing in this issue—articles and advertisements?"

Seldom does the individual advertiser find such minimal guides sufficient to provide a useful copy test. If more direction or clues are provided, the procedure ultimately becomes an aided-recall process, although there is no sharp division between aided and unaided methods. When the magazine interview specifically calls for "advertisements of floor coverings" or "advertisements of breakfast cereals," it is classed as aided recall. Likewise,

[10] A Proposal for the Copy Testing of Nighttime Network Television Commercials (TV Surveys, Inc., a division of Audits & Surveys Company, Inc., Spring, 1962).

when Gallup & Robinson shows brand and company names, these provide legitimate aids to recall.

Close relation between aided and unaided recall is shown by the fact that unaided-recall interviews often are continued into an aided process. It is assumed that the earlier unaided efforts do not distort later aided responses, since the material recalled without aid would almost surely have appeared when aids are given.

There is also a significant correlation between aided- and unaided-recall responses—the advertisements which do well on unaided recall generally show superiority on aided recall. Because it is so difficult to obtain significant advertising recall without aids and because of the close relationship between the two methods, there has been a tendency to drop or minimize the unaided part of recall surveys.

Unaided Recall of Broadcast Programs

The abandonment of unaided recall for radio-program rating during World War II almost ended major usage of the method. Early in the development of radio ratings, homes were reached by telephone and respondents were asked what radio programs they listened to the previous day. A complete day soon proved to be an unwieldy unit, and there was general skepticism as to the accuracy of the ratings.

Gradually the period under inquiry was reduced, until it was confined to the two-hour period just ended. This became known as the *day-part method,* and was based on relatively unaided recall.

Responses to broadcast programs—unlike responses to most commercial messages—range from indifference to great popularity and strong loyalty in the minds of the audience. Whereas the unaided recall of a neutral or background program tends to suffer from memory failure as do advertisements, the more popular programs tend to have exaggerated audience claims. It may be that people deliberately fail to report low-prestige programs and tend to exaggerate their attention to popular prestige shows. Comparative tests with mechanical recorders have shown that some people report hearing popular evening programs even when the receiver is not tuned in! Other tests, based on comparisons of recall with coincidental calls capable of producing only an average audience rating (see Chapter Eleven), have shown impossibly low "recall" ratings for less popular shows. For such reasons, the recall method has lost the support of the broadcast advertising industry, despite the relative ease and economy of the method.

One weakness of field surveys of memory within a specified time interval is the impossibility of accounting for people not at home for the interview. Checking the audience pattern over a period of two hours just ended has shown that more people were away two hours before the call than were away only during the last half hour. This same pattern suggests that the people not available at the time of the interview are more likely to have been at home attending a program two hours before than at any time closer to the attempted call.

This makes a problem in handling data for those not at home for the call. The percentage of people not at home depends on time of day, season of the year, geographic location, and many class differences. Since the day-part method depends upon making interviews within a specified time interval, there is no opportunity to "recover" absent respondents after they have had a reasonable opportunity to return home.

Unaided recall continues to have special application to advertising and program research. To reduce the required memory span to half an hour and even to fifteen minutes gives some assurance of increased accuracy. Briefer periods imply lower economy, but some of the inherent values of the longer recall periods are lost—the "flow of audience" from one program to the next, for example. The fact that aided recall can serve most of the uses of unaided recall may account for survival of aided-recall program research after the unaided-recall method has for the most part been abandoned.

The Pulse, Inc., method of program measurement presents a program log or *printed roster* covering a recent segment of the day and asks for recall of attended programs. The method is subject to prestige claims and, like the more common recognition methods, permits uncontrolled choice of response. Pulse discourages exaggeration to some extent by asking about other activities during the same time segment, and memory loss is lessened for unpopular programs by having respondents examine the printed roster. Survival of the method, however, is based on reasons other than accuracy.

AIDED RECALL AND ASSOCIATION

While all memory depends upon associations, there are some relatively simple processes of controlled or uncontrolled association which have specific advertising-research applications.

The chief dividing point with regard to degree of control of associations is based upon *whether or not there is more than one correct answer*. Sometimes there is only one answer which may be accepted as correct. In free associations, any answer is correct, so long as the respondent gives his answer or answers in the order in which they occur to him. The chief value of controlled responses depends upon whether or not it is easy or possible to guess *right*. At best, these applications of association usually demonstrate only the association of brands or companies with specific advertising material.

Sponsor Identification

Broadcasts which have only one or a few exclusive sponsors can be checked to determine whether the audience is consciously aware of each sponsor or his product or both. Normally, this test is applied in audience measurement, since it is essential first to determine whether the respondent belongs in the program audience.

Currently, sponsor identification is being measured in connection with coincidental telephone surveys (see Chapter Eleven). After respondents report that they have the set tuned to a particular station and program, they may be asked what product or company sponsors that show. Correct answers are taken as evidence of the extent to which the audience consciously credits the program to the sponsor. There are errors and there are omissions—in fact, there is sometimes a substantial amount of identification of a program with the wrong advertiser.

Sponsor identification does not correlate highly with program popularity, except for the most popular shows. The evolution of television, with frequent sponsor changes, alternate sponsors, participating sponsors, and general separation of program format from commercials, has led to decreasing emphasis upon conscious associations of products with programs.

The measurement of sponsor identification has never been promoted convincingly. Some programs and products can be very easily associated and identified. Others, because of program type, the name of the program, previous history, or difficulty in recalling the particular sponsor's name, appear to be unduly penalized. It would seem likely that conscious sponsor identification will be rewarded by some increase in predisposition to buy.

Masked Identification

One of the print copy tests which is waning in popularity is the masking of brand and company names for the purpose of measuring association with the advertiser. The method, once applied extensively to whole magazine issues, used an opening question of whether the respondent *recognized* an advertisement. If the respondent claimed recognition of the "mutilated" display, he was then asked for the brand or company name.

years on the basis of nationwide surveys. Batten, Barton, Durstine, & Osborn ratings were obtained in 1948 and 1958 from a national urban panel of households.

TABLE 1. *Leadership of Product-brand Associations, According to Surveys* (1921, 1948, and 1958)

Product	Leading brand	Percentage of women mentioning first		
		1921	1948	1958
Cleanser	Old Dutch	79	41	10
Canned soup	Campbell's	78	85	89
Toothpaste	Colgate	53	36	37
Silverware	Rogers	48	50	36
Cigarettes	Camels	31	37	24
Automobiles	Ford	21	62	51

The 1921 measure was not identical with the 1948 and 1958 measures. Product changes—as in the case of cleansers—account for fluctuations in association levels more than advertising. Ford competed with many automobile makes in 1921, with few in 1948, but with an increasing number in 1958.

Commodity-brand associations can be reversed by presenting the brand name first and asking what type of product it represents. During an era when automobile manufacturers were identifying many models with new names, tests were made to measure associations of names with makers. There was a range from 13 to 80 per cent in the ability of selective samples of people to identify the maker when given a particular model name. Brands can be further classified as having been heard of before, having been used in the past, and being used currently or being most recently bought. Generally these tests are not adaptable for measuring specific advertisements.

Another approach to association measurement is to state a consumer want or irritation and ask for brands thought of in that connection. Some products are specifically sold to alleviate problems; for example, a mouthwash eases sore throat. Except for the tendency to list certain brands as generic names, the brand first mentioned may have some advantage of preference. The impact of heavy advertising campaigns may establish or change irritation-brand associations, but the measure is not well adapted to tests of individual advertisements.

IMPLICATIONS

Tests which depend on memory are so varied that they differ greatly in their validity and also in their application to measurement of specific advertising messages.

One common element is the fact that all of the basic methods of memory testing can be applied to advertisements after they have been circulated in a normal manner. This gives them a considerable advantage for specific purposes. It explains a large part of their popularity and why the same memory procedure is more popular if applied after normal exposure than when the exposure is forced or unnatural.

The memory techniques are not always applied primarily to measure memory, and it is not clear just what some tests measure. The fact that the objective of memory tests is almost always something other than sales or disposition to buy affects their useful area of application. The complication caused by accumulated advertising effect or confusion with other advertisements often makes interpretation difficult.

There are at least two reasons why evaluations of advertising based solely on recognition or recall scores may be misleading. First, some ideas are far easier for respondents to articulate than others. Facts, figures, and simple comparisons are more easily played back than are ideas which emphasize mood and symbolic association, even though the latter might be implanted far more powerfully.

Second, when people are asked about the remembrance of advertising—either by a recognition method or by a recall method—they easily slip from a discussion of advertising to product and back to advertising and back to product without even realizing it—or they talk about other advertisements by this advertiser or even by other advertisers. The question is: Are we getting information about the advertisement in question or what is already in the mind of the respondent? As an example, most people are so thoroughly familiar with Campbell's Soup advertising that they can talk about it without necessarily having seen a particular advertisement for Campbell's Soup.

Despite such problems as these, the memory techniques are outstanding in their popularity as measures of the effectiveness of specific advertisements.

five

Opinion and
Attitude Ratings

SIGNIFICANCE OF OPINION RATINGS

DIRECT-OPINION MEASUREMENT

SCALING AND RATING SCALES

INDIRECT-OPINION METHODS

THE DIMENSIONAL TEST OF ADVERTISING

THE PROBLEM OF BELIEVABILITY

IMPLICATIONS

On the face of it, opinion methods are among the simplest of all methods of evaluating advertisements. People will readily give their opinions about advertisements. When shown a proposed advertisement, they will state whether they think it would get their attention, how interesting they think it is, which advertising claims they believe, whether they think it will be remembered, and how likely they believe it is to cause them to buy the product or service.

Not only will they rate and compare advertisements on all of these functions, but they will also give opinions on every feaure of an advertisement at any stage of its development. This means that most applications of the opinion methods are simple, fast, and inexpensive.

SIGNIFICANCE OF OPINION RATINGS

If opinion ratings were entirely valid for every purpose to which they have been applied, there would be no need for any other copy test. The methods have been used for decades and yet have not come close to gaining universal confidence. If opinion ratings were as useful as might be hoped in a Utopia of advertising research, there would be little waste, since the opinion ratings would be available to the advertiser in time to make corrections before advertisements were circulated.

Even though opinion ratings have exerted enormous influence on the improvement of specific advertisements and advertising campaigns, we must conclude that the opinion methods do not fulfill all of the promises which appear on the surface. In a sense, the discussion in the succeeding sections of this chapter may appear contradictory on occasion because of the problem of reconciling the many favorable features of opinion methods with their limitations.

DIRECT-OPINION MEASUREMENT

Opinions may be solicited at any level from any member of the general public from the prospective consumer to the creative man to the advertising expert.

The obvious solution of going to the skilled advertising man is limited, for the practical reason that people associated with the advertising business are usually in a prejudiced position. This prejudice may be unconscious, based on allegiance to client brands—in many cases, based on conviction regarding the superiority of particular copy techniques. Even though the success of advertising leaders is largely based on their superior judgment, there have been many instances of their collective failure in attempting to judge the advertisements of others. There is a notable lack of agreement among them.

When consumers are shown advertisements and asked for their reactions, it is assumed that they are trying to report the influence of the advertising messages on themselves. This is in contrast with the judgment of an experienced advertising man who is attempting to estimate the influence of advertising messages on others who make up the intended market. In practice, however, consumers give evidence that they frequently are trying to give "expert" opinions on advertisements rather than to report their own

vertisements H, R, K, G, T, and O. If the problem is to test for interest, the six background advertisements should be chosen to represent a wide interest range, from very high to very low. If skill is used in choosing a variety of interest levels, then the differences in ranking of L and M in a uniform background should indicate their relative levels of interest.

Whenever complete advertisements are rated, there is the possibility that strong brand loyalties may prejudice the votes on advertisements of other brands. A device for avoiding the antagonisms of those who dislike the brand under test is to substitute the logotype or brand name preferred by the respondent. Tests of automobile or cigarette advertisements, for example, have begun with an inquiry into the brand owned or used regularly. The interviewer carries test materials made up to associate the test copy with each of several leading brands. If the new copy is easy to adapt, a large part of the interviewing can be done with respondents judging the copy as related to their own preferred brand.

Opinions of Broadcast Material

Early in the applications of opinion methods to commercials and broadcast programs, Paul F. Lazarsfeld and Frank Stanton developed a procedure for analysis in detail. They invented a *Program Analyzer,* by means of which the members of an audience can indicate individual and group likes and dislikes continuously throughout a program, including the commercials. A room or auditorium has each seat equipped with right-hand and left-hand switch controls for signaling likes and dislikes as the presentation proceeds. When neither control is operated, it is assumed that the person is indifferent.

Other types of mechanical voting equipment have been developed, but some investigators find paper ballots satisfactory. Schwerin Research Corporation, for example, has made extensive use of a procedure in which numbers are flashed on a screen as cues for voting reactions to points in the program. Each critical point in the script has a number assigned, and the ballot has a corresponding place to indicate favorable or unfavorable reactions. Both the mechanical system and the manual system appear to work satisfactorily in recording a full schedule of reactions throughout a program.

Program analysis, like many other test procedures, permits inclusion of more than one basic approach in the same operation. The program investigator usually goes beyond the collection of ballots. He may immediately test the memory of commercials by having each person write down all of the sales points he can remember. Then the group is likely to be invited to participate in a discussion of what they did and why they reacted to the program and commercials in a particular way at any selected point. Suggestions may also be solicited, and they are likely to be forthcoming.

There is considerable evidence that program analysis can be used effectively to guide both the construction and the selection of programs for broadcast. After all, the studio group is asked to indicate the same reactions that supposedly determine program choices at home.

One recognized problem in "voting" of likes and dislikes is what to do about a disagreeable person or unpleasant event in a program. This may be a point where interest reaches a climax, but many respondents will indicate they *dislike* the program at such a point, and it is difficult to devise instructions to overcome this inconsistency. Despite this conflict, there is much more assurance of the validity of opinion analysis of a program than of an advertisement or commercial message.

While the above procedure is definitely an application of opinion methods and in this sense might be open to question as a method of advertising research, it has some favorable features for testing commercials. Continuous voting makes it possible to dissect and examine the message in detail as well as to form a total judgment. In addition, since the commercials are usually inserted in a program format, it is possible to examine the influence of location and sequence of different commercials in the same program. It is also possible to get some idea as to the compatibility of the commercial with the program. But otherwise this analytical rating process for commercials is subject to the limitations of opinion ratings of printed advertising.

Validity of Direct-opinion Ratings

No one knows the exact degree of the validity of any method of testing the sales effectiveness of typical national advertisements. And there can be no final proof of validity because it is not possible to trace the ultimate sales influence of individual advertisements or copy themes. There is as yet no dependable sales check, either immediately following circulation or at any time thereafter. We must conclude, therefore, that there is little likelihood of developing validation tests either for pretesting or for posttesting procedures. Instead, the evaluation of test methods must be left to judgment and to the evidences of internal consistency.

Opinion methods are pretesting procedures which are completely subjective and which ordinarily are applied in advance of circulation of the advertisement. While opinion methods can be applied with some logic to certain specific characteristics, they are more often aimed at gross estimates

A popular scaling method in recent years has been the *semantic differential*.[3] The phrase "semantic differential" refers to a set of scales "anchored" at each end by polarity, that is, with words at each end of the scale as diametrical opposites. Sometimes the scale is called "bipolar." (Although polarities usually are complete opposites, they do not have to be; for example, although the opposite of "hot" is "cold," it might be more useful to set up a "hot-lukewarm" scale.)

William A. Mindak, who was one of the first to report an application of the semantic differential to advertising research problems, used a 7-point scale with assumed equal intervals between points.[4] Eight scales were applied in connection with various commercials prepared for the same product. Pretest ratings were obtained from each group of cooperating subjects, after which an interval of one week was allowed, to permit forgetting of the ratings.

Different groups were then exposed separately to each test commercial which had been inserted in a specially prepared broadcast program. The second application of the scales followed, and "differentials" were noted between the pretest and posttest ratings. Significant differences occurred, and results were then compared with consumer-jury ratings and recall playback of the same commercials. In general, the semantic differential showed agreement in rankings with the consumer jury; but the recall playback ranked the commercials almost directly opposite.

On the basis of respondents' judgments, words and brief phrases can be scaled and graphed as profiles. As a specific example, brands of beer may be compared according to how well their television commercials are liked, the attractiveness of their outdoor posters, or the neatness of their 6 pack cartons.[5]

Image studies before and after advertising impact may show whether an automobile is thought of as more or less powerful, economical, comfortable, glamorous, modern, or handsome. Advertising of a magazine may change public impressions as to whether the publication is more or less interesting, accurate, entertaining, colorful, daring, or attractive. An ex-

[3] See Charles E. Osgood, George J. Suci, and Percy H. Tannenbaum, *The Measurement of Meaning* (Urbana, Ill.: University of Illinois Press, 1957).

[4] William A. Mindak, "A New Technique for Measuring Advertising Effectiveness," *Journal of Marketing,* Vol. 20 (April, 1956), pp. 367–378.

[5] William A. Mindak, "Fitting the Semantic Differential to the Marketing Problem," *Journal of Marketing,* Vol. 25 (April, 1961), pp. 28–33, especially p. 32.

ample more closely related to immediate gains from advertising is the profile change of a brand of cold cream, as shown in Fig. 5.

It is easy to see that the cold-cream copy was impressing the ability of the brand to penetrate, cleanse, moisturize, and beautify the skin, without appearing to be any more expensive.

This type of profile can be obtained either by scaling each point for interviewing purposes or merely by using the per cent of sample associating the specified quality with the particular brand. Scaling is more precise and logical, but the judgments are often so crude that scaling adds little. Since

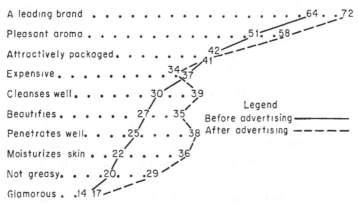

FIG. 5. Changes in profile of a skin cream, following test exposure to advertising campaign.

the purpose of the profile is to evaluate the total effect of an advertising message or to compare two advertisements, the precise rating of each item is not very important. So much depends upon the part which a particular item plays in determining a brand choice. The comparison of two profiles of changes obtained by testing two advertisements still leaves the problem of comparing and choosing between the profiles. Thus the final choice is likely to be a judgment instead of a straight mathematical outcome.

As stated above, an important principle of scaling is to establish degrees of opinions at equal intervals. Different physical weights of objects of equal size can be correctly discriminated by nearly constant majorities of test groups, provided the percentage of weight difference remains constant. If this capacity is assumed in opinion ratings, then it should be possible to separate opinion levels at equal intervals by choosing items which are rated upward or downward by similar majorities. The Thurstone-type scale employs this principle, and the following attitudes are believed to be a scale of approximately equal steps:

This is the only brand I would consider buying.
I certainly would consider this brand and probably would buy it.
I might consider this brand and maybe I would buy it.
I might consider this brand but it's unlikely I would buy it.
I might possibly consider this brand but I doubt if I'd buy it.
I doubt if I'd ever consider this brand.
This is a brand I would never consider buying.

Probably the most common scaling device is based on the assumption that rank positions are separated by equal intervals. The assignment of a value of 1 to first place, 2 to second place, 3 to third place, etc., in an order-of-merit ranking is a form of scaling.

Another simple approach is to lay out a numerical scale, such as 1 to 10, and to ask respondents to indicate a numerical value for whatever point is being rated. An electrically operated device for recording degrees of preference has a graduated spring on the manual switch which increases the current in proportion to the pressure of the hand. Strong liking or disliking by one person counts more than mild reactions on the part of others.

Louis Guttman has contributed greatly to scaling theory, and has developed logical methods for treating both the intensity of attitudes and their specific content or direction.[6] While the development and refinement of scaling are far too extensive for inclusion here, an interesting application of the method was used by Elizabeth A. Richards.[7] The application was to a change in product design rather than to advertising, but the approach can easily be adapted to a problem in advertising. The W. A. Sheaffer Pen Company had developed three mechanically different ballpoint pens, and the mechanisms affected the writing quality. There was a problem of discovering which device was most satisfactory to the users, as well as discovering the influence of the devices on the writing operation—and without confusing the two. Hopefully, the preferred mechanical device would also produce the most satisfactory writing result and belong to the pen ranking highest on an overall basis.

[6] See, for example, Samuel A. Stouffer, Louis Guttman, Edward A. Suchman, Paul F. Lazarsfeld, Shirley A. Star, and John A. Clausen, *Measurement and Prediction,* Vol 4, *Studies in Social Psychology in World War II* (Princeton, N.J.: Princeton University Press, 1950).

[7] Elizabeth A. Richards, "A Commercial Application of Guttman Attitude Scaling Techniques," *Journal of Marketing,* Vol. 22 (October, 1957), pp. 166–173.

The first part of the interview on ballpoint pens clearly established a preference for one mechanism. Next came a small group of questions about writing quality, which had been carefully pretested to ensure that the response pattern would represent an attitude. Each response was scaled on a 5-point level of intensity. An analysis of the results, following the Guttman procedure, clearly indicated that the preferred mechanical device also produced writing qualities most preferred by the respondents.

The reason for giving this example is simply to indicate that by using this same kind of approach, it would be possible to learn something about whether advertisements which respondents especially like also implant copy ideas most likely to build favorable attitudes toward the brand. Thus, the hazards of the halo effect in rating advertisements could be reduced. The chief requirements for this type of analysis are competence of the investigator and considerable extra time for applying Guttman procedures.

Irving Crespi of the Gallup organization believes that much of the usefulness of Guttman scaling can be gained in applications without excessive demands for time and special skills.[8] He would use such a scale as a 10-point range from +5 to −5. Single adjectives or phrases can then be evaluated by almost any respondent for accuracy as applied to almost any advertisement or product, and the numerical survey results can be compiled and interpreted rapidly and easily. It is not necessary to search for ranges between direct opposites or to test for the reliability of each item, as is usual in the Guttman approach. Actually, Crespi's method is similar to the semantic-differential technique.

When advertisements and copy themes are evaluated by means of scaling methods, it is common to separate each function and each element for appraisal in detail. The application of a refined scale to the gross function of a whole advertisement is incongruous at best. Nevertheless, the alternative of detailed analysis has these two basic hazards: (1) the likelihood of error in deciding just what are the significant elements determining advertising success; and (2) the confounding task of assigning appropriate values or weights to each element for the purpose of recombining them into a total value.

Systematic rating scales were slow to appear in the advertising business, but a generation ago two enterprising brothers named Townsend proclaimed the development of a 27-point rating scale which would "infallibly" determine the effectiveness of any advertisement in six minutes. One item, *atten-*

[8] Irving Crespi, "Use of a Scaling Technique in Surveys," *Journal of Marketing,* Vol. 25 (July, 1961), pp. 69–72.

tion, was assigned a value of 25 per cent out of a mysterious total of 109 per cent; other items, such as *type* and *sincerity,* had values of only 1 per cent, with other items ranging up to 10 per cent. None of the points was mutually exclusive, and the values were the same whether applied to advertisements of cold remedies or trucks—and without regard to media audiences! For a while the Townsend brothers were successful in selling their nostrum to people in advertising, but no such advertising or testing panacea has been bought by the present more sophisticated generation of advertising practitioners.

It should be recognized, however, that the development of analytical rating methods almost always has some merit. If the most improved scaling methods serve no other purpose than the application of a checklist, they are likely to contribute to improvements, and many advertising people develop their own checklists in order to avoid oversights. Such a process invariably increases the consistency with which people rate the same advertisement, simply as a result of carefully defining a limited number of specific points. If weights are assigned to each point, there will be still greater consistency and validity insofar as the weights are correct. But the questions are: Which points? What weights?

The problem of selecting points and assigning weights is only part of the problem of advertisement rating scales. Very likely the scale would have to be changed for each advertising objective, for each product, for each medium, and for many other factors. It would have to be all-inclusive and, in practical application, would surely encounter mutually exclusive features. It would also have to surmount the obstacle of combining highly rated elements into highly effective total advertisements.

Investigators have shown an awareness of the problems attached to scaled procedures, but almost always run into the bewildering task of combining the isolated test segments into an estimate of total effect. There is a strong temptation for the research man to make an arbitrary combination of rating segments into a total score, but the result would be a mathematical total of scores on such unlike functions as the communication of ideas and the stimulation of favorable attitudes! This would result in some sort of answer to the question "Which is the best advertisement?" Unfortunately, answers arrived at in this manner would not be very defensible.

Ideally, expressions of *consumer attitudes* are obtained before exposure of the test advertising messages. After exposure, hopefully without conditioning from the previous questions, the attitude questions are repeated. Conditioning can be avoided by using two carefully matched samples, one for the initial attitude rating and the other for advertising exposure and the final rating. Minimizing the likelihood that the people serving as subjects will connect the attitude questions with the specific advertising message depends upon the ingenuity of the investigator. Conditioning and consciousness of purpose may or may not be invalidating factors.

Usually an indirect opinion method is applied to a sample in a studio or by field interviews just before and again after a broadcast. An example of a test without adequate controls was one in which there was a test of a new campaign in print which began with a brand rating of several products on the 7-point scale shown earlier (see pages 113–114). The new advertisements were later exposed along with other material, and still later the brand-rating scale was reapplied. There was a significant improvement in the rating of the brand represented in the test advertisements.

The use of a complete test merely to measure changes in general approval of a company or brand is likely to be wasteful. Very likely there are specific aspects which merit individual emphasis, or distinct advertising objectives which can be assessed. For example, a manufacturer may be rated on such points as the following:

Is a leader in product research
Constantly improves products
Makes only high-quality products
Stands behind his guarantee
Gives quick repair service
Shows interest in customers
Is a good citizen in factory community
Contributes to national security

Any points which contribute to good product classification or public relations, especially if stressed in the advertising messages, may aid the appraisal of advertising effect.

Indirect-opinion evidence is likely to be more convincing than direct expressions of opinions about advertisements. Certainly there is less danger of the respondent playing the role of an "expert" judge. The inherent risks include the possibility that the respondent will connect the final rating process with the specific advertising message, and that the interpretation of results may be subjective.

The more forced the test situation, the greater is the danger of atypical reactions. If people are asked to look at the advertisements on a television program in a situation apart from normal home viewing and if the advertising exposure is concentrated, there are risks of unnatural response or degree of response.

Avoidance of the risks of conditioning appears to be impracticable. Broadcasting, in which the time factor is controlled, could be checked by a survey of the market both before and after commercials are released. Yet any attempt to increase the sample efficiency by identifying or inviting viewers or listeners in advance will tend to condition the audience. Asking attitude questions of the same people both before and after the broadcast adds further conditioning. The next step is to invite people into a studio for controlled exposure under atypical conditions. The more artificial the conditions, the greater the likelihood of a significant attitude differential. The more completely natural the conditions, the more diluted is the advertising impact and the less likely a significant differential. These are some . of the basic problems in advertising measurement of this kind.

INDIRECT-OPINION METHODS

When people are shown advertisements in a copy test and asked to rate them or the product or the company, it is possible that their reactions will be affected by awareness of the purpose of the research. However, there are methods for evaluating opinions and attitudes without openly exposing the purpose of the research.

The problem arises out of inherent factors in the *direct* solicitation of opinions. Respondents are self-conscious, they are placed in the position of feeling that they are experts, and they may be motivated to give biased responses. Insofar as opinions and attitudes can be evaluated *indirectly* and without the investigator's purpose being evident to respondents, the findings are likely to be more convincing.

The two indirect measures of opinions and attitudes to be discussed here are Horace Schwerin's measure of *brand-preference changes* and a proposal by the authors of a method of *perceptual distortion*. In the former, it is assumed that people who choose a brand of free merchandise will not be especially conscious that they are reflecting the influence of advertising. In the latter, it is suggested that the phenomenon of perceptual distortion be applied to evaluate the influence of advertising on various attitudes.

Brand-preference Changes

Under certain circumstances, the choosing of brand preferences may help to avoid some of the conditioning hazards of attitude testing. Schwerin

Research Corporation has developed skillful procedures for detecting competitive changes in preference before and after advertising exposure. Upon arrival, studio groups are invited to make a free choice of a gift package of one of a group of competing products. After the session, which includes advertising of one of the brands, the participants are again invited to select one free package. Changes between the arrival choice and the departure choice are tabulated.

As a further development which makes the testing of higher-priced items practical, the guests are told at the beginning that they are to take part in a lottery in which one will win an expensive item or a large supply of a frequently used product and are asked to indicate which brand they wish if they win. The session closes with an announcement that—as an added gesture of appreciation—a second draw will be made, and the participants are asked to indicate their choice for the second draw. Again, differences in the early and the late choices are studied for evidence of competitive brand-preference changes.

The introduction of choices of gift products serves to reduce some of the criticisms of attitude studies and may come a good deal closer to achieving a genuine buying response. It has been argued, however, that the situation is spurious, since the decision is made when the advertising arrives instead of when the need arises and that no money changes hands. It is difficult to establish a gift or lottery as the equivalent of a market sale—note that the authors have chosen to put this method in a category with opinion measures. Nevertheless, it is probably the closest approach yet made in opinion or attitude procedures to the decisions actually made in the act of buying.

In studies of changes of attitudes, Horace Schwerin has demonstrated that the changes are unrelated to previous statements regarding the influence of advertising on the individual. "It was found that people who said they were not very often led by television advertising either to buy or to inquire about something were as readily influenced by the test commercial as people who admitted to being often influenced." [9] If this finding can be generalized, it has important implications for all research into attitude changes related to advertising exposure; indeed, it is a basic element in advertising theory.

The use of studio groups (see Chapter Seven) by Schwerin has its counterpart in panel surveys made in the field with population samples. One advantage of consumer panels—those maintained by various advertisers

[9] Schwerin Research Corporation, *Technical and Analytical Review*, No. 6 (Fall, 1960), p. 6.

and advertising agencies and independently operated—is the opportunity to test attitude changes over a long period of time. Attitudes can be assessed before any exposure to advertising or to the product and again at various stages over as long a period as practicable to retain almost all the individuals in the panel.

A system for "profit-controlling television advertising expenditures" has also been developed by the Schwerin Research Corporation in cooperation with several of its larger TV advertiser-clients. A continuing three-year study revealed a high correlation between sales figures of certain products and the quality of television advertising, as measured by Schwerin's observed action measure (brand-preference changes) in relation to advertising dollar expenditures. It was further noted that there were *no* instances where increased advertising dollar pressure compensated for commercials which were less effective than competitors' commercials.

In other words, Schwerin believes that an advertiser with weak TV commercials and poor sales performance cannot buy his way out of trouble just by adding more dollar expenditures for more commercials. Thus, Schwerin's profit-controlling system is predicated on the principle of reducing advertising expenditures when TV advertising is ineffective and increasing them when TV advertising is effective. This system requires three actions: (1) continuing analysis of competitive advertising and the advertiser's own advertising; (2) pretesting of commercials in inexpensive rough form; and (3) final production and airing of only those commercials which pretesting has indicated to be equal to or better than competitive commercials.

Perceptual Distortion [10]

There is still another class of measurement which offers considerable promise to the study of advertising's effectiveness. These are measurements of how people may distort the "facts" of physical reality. Since the techniques are based on a principle that is not ordinarily discussed in the field of advertising, a few comments on perceptual distortion are in order.

Within the past fifteen years or so, psychologists interested in the psychology of perception and how we see things in our world have conducted a number of studies on distortion. They have learned that it is normal and expected for people to distend reality into conformance with their own values, attitudes, and interests. Walter Lippmann once put it: "For the

[10] The authors are indebted to Eugene J. Webb of Northwestern University for bringing this concept to their attention.

most part we do not first see, and then define, we define first and then see." [11]

The advertising researcher can take normal occurrence of distortion as a given and employ the *extent* of distortion as an indicator of effect. Here are very brief descriptions of three different studies.

Consider first the classic experiment of Bruner and Goodman.[12] Their concern was the way in which children perceptually distorted the size of coins. Working with a group of "rich" and "poor" ten-year-olds, they found that the poor children saw the coins as physically larger than did the rich children. Presumably, the coins' greater value to the poor children influenced their perceptual mechanism so that the coins *seemed* larger.

This general principle has been well documented, with most research indicating an expansion of size as the typical distortion. But the idea is not that a high value makes for bigness—it is instead that the distortion in our own minds of what objects are like will be *in the direction of our previous values.*

A fairly recent experiment showed, for example, that those who have a greater desire to own a Volkswagen perceive the car as physically *smaller* than those who are less inclined to the automobile.[13] Since smallness is more desirable than bigness for Volkswagens, the usual direction of distortion is reversed.

Consider one example concerned with advertising. One investigator used the principle of perceptual distortion while studying the relative effects of photographs and drawings in advertising layouts.[14] He duplicated a full-page magazine advertisement for a medium-priced automobile—changing the art work from a photograph to a drawing faithful to the original. Everything else in the two advertisements was the same.

The questioning was simple. The respondents were asked to guess the price of the car. One group of respondents saw the photographic (original) version, another saw the version with the drawing, and still another control group saw no advertisement at all.

The results were intriguing. For men, the median price guess for the

[11] Walter Lippmann, *Public Opinion* (New York: The Macmillan Company, 1922), at p. 81.

[12] Jerome S. Bruner and Cecile C. Goodman, "Value and Need as Organizing Factors in Perception," *Journal of Abnormal and Social Psychology*, Vol. 42 (January, 1947), pp. 33–34.

[13] Samuel E. Stayton and Morton Weiner, "Value, Magnitude, and Accentuation," *Journal of Abnormal and Social Psychology*, Vol. 62 (January, 1961), pp. 145–147.

[14] J. C. Webster, unpublished M.S.J. thesis, Northwestern University, 1961.

photographic version was about $3,250; those who saw no advertisement guessed about $3,000; and those exposed to the drawing version guessed about $2,900. Women's judgments were different—they guessed about $2,800 for both the photographic and drawing versions, and those who saw no advertisement guessed about $2,600. Even though the differences were not statistically significant, they are great enough to suggest some ideas for further experimentation along similar lines.

In addition to the sound theoretical basis for such types of studies, there are some practical advantages. The kinds of questions used are easy to ask and do not require the employment of special kinds of interviewers. The answers come in a form easily processed in tabulation. Most important, the results are easy to understand and to communicate.

Experiments of this kind are reported here simply to indicate the possibility of various kinds of research on perception of advertisements. For example, is a "good" commercial either viewed or recalled as longer or shorter than a "poor" commercial? As another example, is a "good" print advertisement perceived or recalled differently in physical appearance than a "poor" advertisement?

THE DIMENSIONAL TEST OF ADVERTISING

Finally, there is an interesting method of rating of advertisements, which we choose to call the *dimensional test of advertising*. Even though the method is not widely used and certainly is not *the* way to measure attitudes and opinions—after all, there are other methods—it will be described in some detail because of its uniqueness.

The method is based on the idea that every advertisement has many different "dimensions."

What are some of the dimensions of an advertisement that might be tested? After all, there are lots of different dimensions to an advertisement—importance, uniqueness, exclusiveness, believability, interest, likability, understanding, attitude-changing, attention-getting, memorability, etc. Is it a matter of memorability or believability or interest or likability or what in which the advertiser is interested?

The research man always needs to know what the advertisement is supposed to accomplish. If the advertiser will really define his objectives—that is, the dimensions of his advertisement—this will aid the researcher materially because he will then know what kinds of information will be useful to the advertiser.

Example of Three Dimensions

Alfred Politz says that he would write a formula for efficiency in advertising like this:

$$\text{Efficiency} = \text{importance} \times \sqrt[a]{\text{believability}} \times \sqrt[a+b]{\text{uniqueness}}$$

The three factors are as follows:

1. *Importance* of the advertising claim
2. *Believability* of the advertising claim
3. *Uniqueness* of the advertising claim

Politz continues:

> Subjective importance of your claim is most important. Then your claim must be believable (and this, too, we find out by opinion research). This is less vital, but still not to be overlooked. Then comes the third dimension in advertising: uniqueness.
>
> It can be shown that the relation between the three terms should be multiplicative and not additive. The number of people who think the claim is important has greater influence on efficiency of advertising than the number of people who think the claim is believable; and this group has a greater influence than the number who think it is unique.[15]

The Dimensional Test Itself

In describing the *dimensional test,* we shall use three dimensions as an example. It should be understood that these are not the only three dimensions and that others could be studied; but these three are major dimensions and are a convenient example of how the dimensional test is made. Certainly, many an advertiser wants a theme that scores high on many dimensions.

The basic idea for the dimensional tests grew up from work originally carried out by Dik Warren Twedt of BBDO in what he calls "trivariant analysis." [16] The discussion that follows was also influenced by conversations with him about the applicability of this method, although it is discussed here as the *dimensional test.*

[15] Also see Alfred Politz, "Politz on Copy: Make the Sales Points Stick Out," *Printers' Ink,* Vol. 250 (April 1, 1955), pp. 32–34, 38, 42.

[16] Dik Warren Twedt, "New 3-Way Measure of Ad Effectiveness," *Printers' Ink,* Vol. 260 (September 6, 1957), pp. 22–23; also see Dik Warren Twedt, "A Multiple Factor Analysis of Advertising Readership," *Journal of Applied Psychology,* Vol. 36 (June, 1952), pp. 207–215.

This is a relatively new method for "testing" three different dimensions of an advertisement—for instance, desirability, exclusiveness, and believability of the advertised claim—and each of the three subjective ratings can be compared with the other subjective ratings. Another possibility is to use the Politz dimensions of importance, believability, and uniqueness.

After deciding what dimensions are to be tested, a list of basic themes is prepared. These themes as product attributes are basic copy points.

Let us take an oversimplified example with respect to the advertising of detergents. Suppose that three different copy claims are to be tested: (1) cleansing power, (2) pleasant odor, and (3) no scum. Individual slips of paper with these phrases on them are shown to housewives, and order of presentation is randomized by shuffling the slips. The respondents are asked to rank each of the themes—first, as to desirability; second, as to exclusiveness; and third, as to believability.

The mean scale values for each of the three dimensions are then computed, and two of the dimensions (desirability and exclusiveness) can be plotted on a chart. The third factor, believability, can be shown in parentheses by each copy theme. Table 2 gives hypothetical results from the scaling of *desirability* of these claims and the determination of *exclusiveness* and of *believability*.

TABLE 2. *Hypothetical Results for Three Detergent Claims*

Claim	Desirability	Exclusiveness	Believability
Cleansing power	95	9	55
Pleasant odor	80	76	67
No scum	61	34	25

However, as pointed out in the next section of this chapter, low believability ratings or rankings for advertising themes may in fact represent either a favorable kind of curiosity or an unfavorable kind of disbelief; accordingly, such measures of believability must be interpreted with caution.

It is obvious from Table 2 that the claim judged to be most *desirable*—cleansing power—is not likely to prove an effective copy theme because consumers already believe that this is low in exclusiveness (applies to most detergents).

At the other extreme, the least desirable of the three themes—no scum—is short on *believability*.

The claim judged second in desirability—pleasant odor—is chosen as probably most effective. It is high on *exclusiveness,* but not so low in *believability* as to make it difficult for consumers to accept, and it is second in *desirability.*

This means, in this hypothetical example, that the "pleasant odor" theme is the one that "wins." Of course, no such results should be followed blindly without the use of advertising judgment. For instance, there might be times when a decision should be made to use a claim which is relatively low in believability because—if consumers can eventually be persuaded of the truth of the claim—it might then have high exclusiveness.

Evaluation of the Dimensional Test

With the dimensional test—especially if a number of different copy points are tested and on various combinations of dimensions—information can be obtained in the earliest stages of the development of the advertising for a product or service. We can even begin with the basic question as to what we know about the product or service. We can thus do "theme testing" even before copy and layouts are prepared, and this can be followed up by later testing of the actual copy and layouts in semicomprehensive form.

In these ways, we can get some subjective judgments *in advance* as to what prospective consumers may think about dimensions of the advertising that are important to the advertiser. And we can compare these dimensions with each other in a great many different ways. Of course, the greater the number of dimensions studied, the greater will be the number of comparisons that can be made.

Finally, in addition to these various stages of pretesting, we can employ techniques similar to those used in posttesting to answer the question, "How well did we do?" A comparison of certain pretest and posttest results will give us some measure of the reliability of the subjective data.

The next step is to use the "winning" themes—after proper exercise of advertising judgment—in the development of actual advertisements. When these have been prepared in semicomprehensive form, we are in a position to repeat the same sort of test—only this time we use proposed advertisements and not just statements or headlines. A comparison can now be made between the first test of themes and this second test of proposed ads.

Ideally, the final step is to run posttests after the actual advertisements selected have been run. The same process is repeated, only this time using actual tear sheets or proofs of advertisements in the campaign finally used.

One caution, however—we must always be aware of the difficulties of testing separate advertising elements or advertising themes out of context. Certainly the value of many advertising themes is dependent upon the inter-relationship of the theme with the execution of the advertisement in its many elements. Thus, headlines, graphics, and copy points can be separated out for testing purposes, but this is not the same as testing the advertisement in its entirety. In other words, the whole advertisement is greater than the sum of its parts!

THE PROBLEM OF BELIEVABILITY

One of the most intriguing problems in advertising has to do with the *believability* of the advertising. Naturally, there is concern by almost every advertiser as to whether his public will resent statements or claims that might seem excessive or unbelievable.

One famed psychologist suggested possible advantages of understatement as compared with overstatement and invented as an example the following copy for a dentifrice: "This dentifrice will not remove all the stains from your teeth. It will brighten but not whiten your teeth. It will not remove freckles. It will not straighten your nose. It will not give you the beauty of the movie stars. But we guarantee it to do a good cleaning job on your teeth and to lessen the chances of decay." [17]

Another well-known marketing researcher has pointed out that more believable advertising does not necessarily lead to sales leadership.[18] He has presented evidence that believability of advertising claims and use of the product tend to go together. In other words, the people who use a brand of any given product tend to accept the advertising of that brand as true except in the most blatant cases of exaggeration.

Some of the most useful information as to *believability* has been developed by John C. Maloney, manager of research development of the Leo Burnett Company, and the remainder of the discussion in this section is based on quotations from his work and conversations with him about believability.

Most studies of advertising believability have been based on the following assumptions:

1. Once an advertisement has been noticed and understood, there are

[17] Henry C. Link, "Why You Should Avoid Excesses in Your Advertising," *Printers' Ink,* Vol. 237 (November 2, 1951), pp. 35–37, at p. 35.

[18] Richard D. Crisp, "Believability in Ads and Use Go Together," *Printers' Ink,* Vol. 243 (May 22, 1953), pp. 37–38.

only two likely consumer reactions: the advertising message will either be believed or disbelieved.

2. A good advertisement should never leave the reader, listener, or viewer in doubt about what has been said—*complete belief of an advertisement is the only desirable consumer reaction.*

3. *A meaningful measure* of an advertisement's value is the proportion of consumers viewing the advertisement who report that *"there is nothing hard to believe."*

But John C. Maloney and Perham C. Nahl (also of the Leo Burnett Company) have taken issue with such assumptions. As Nahl has said:

> The answer, "I find that very hard to believe," may mean, "I wouldn't try that brand." But "I find that very hard to believe" may mean, on the other hand, "I don't believe it, but I'll try the brand to see if it is true"—the kind of disbelief that may be exactly what you need to jar the consumer out of the groove of familiar buying patterns into trying your product.

Many books and articles based upon research call for considerable reworking of many of the old assumptions about advertising believability. In fact, from his careful analysis of scores of studies by psychologists, sociologists, and communications researchers, Maloney concludes that *the three assumptions stated above should be completely revised, as follows:*

1. Once an advertisement has been noticed and understood, *many different kinds of consumer reaction may follow:* belief, disbelief, or a middle-ground kind of "nonbelief." As a matter of fact, if the advertisement *is* trying to change people's minds (that is, to persuade people of something), it is likely that, after a single exposure, it will be met with disbelief, or at least disinterest or nonbelief.

2. An advertisement's contribution to persuading someone that a given brand is best or that a given brand should be bought *does not depend upon complete belief of the advertisement.* Becoming sold on a brand or product—a change of attitude in favor of a product—is not likely to come about until the consumer has actually tried the product. One of the main contributions that an advertisement makes to persuasion is to make people curious—to stimulate the kind of "nonbelief" that causes them to listen to what others have to say about the product, notice if their friends use it, talk with salespeople about it, read other ads about it, or actually try the product.

3. The proportion of consumers who report that *"there is nothing hard to believe"* in an advertisement *is not in and of itself an effective evaluation of the advertisement.* Such consumer reactions to advertisements reflect both disbelief,

which stands in the way of persuasion, and nonbelief, which works in favor of persuasion.

One of Maloney's tests of these theories involved the exposure of food advertisements to several hundred different women. Most of the women found "nothing hard to believe" in the ads, and 34 per cent showed a greater readiness to serve the advertised product after seeing the particular advertisement. Some women, however, *did* report having found "something hard to believe." Did more of them or fewer of them show a greater readiness to serve the advertised product after seeing the advertisement? The results were just the same as for those who found "nothing hard to believe" —34 per cent were more ready to serve the advertised product after seeing the advertisement.

However, Maloney noticed that some of the women who found "something hard to believe" seemed to have been made curious about the advertised product. They explained their "disbelief" by talking about the product itself and implying that the advertising sounded "too good to be true"; and 44 per cent of these women showed a greater readiness to serve the advertised product after seeing the advertisement to which they had been exposed.

On the other hand, other women who reported "something hard to believe" had been sidetracked by something in the advertisement *other than the product* or felt from specific past experiences with the product that the advertising claims could not possibly be true; only 18 per cent of these women showed a greater willingness to serve the advertised product after seeing the advertisement.

Those who had been curious about the product, as compared with those who "disbelieved," were more than twice as likely to have increased their readiness to serve the advertised product—even though both groups reported "something hard to believe." The "curious" groups were even more persuaded than those who found "nothing hard to believe," presumably because the latter group included many whose reactions to the advertisements were quite indifferent.

There are three implications from Maloney's work that should be of use to advertisers:

1. Be careful any time you say or imply something which runs counter to people's present opinions, attitudes, or past experience. Do not say something strange or unusual just to be cute. Save your hard-to-believe claims for specific promises about the product—promises that can be con-

firmed by the consumer by trying the product or by talking with someone who has tried it.

2. Do not worry too much about believability, if your claims are true. You will never be completely believable to people whose minds you are trying to change and you do not have to be completely believable in order to accomplish your objective.

3. Do not be afraid of the consumer reaction "That sounds too good to be true!" if your statements are true. Although those who see your advertising may not believe you at first, if you can get them sufficiently interested in your advertising message to wonder about it, they are likely to want to try your product.

IMPLICATIONS

Opinion and attitude ratings offer an inexpensive set of procedures for investigating advertising effect from many different perspectives. They can be applied before there have been extensive expenditures of time and money in preparation of the advertising, and certainly well before major expenditures in media, and the applications range all the way from total advertising impact to minutely specialized considerations or aspects.

In addition, probably no approach has been the object of so much ingenuity and refinement. Undoubtedly some of the refinements have represented genuine improvements in methodology.

If one is to take the outcomes of these subjective methods at face value, then it is essential to overcome an ever-growing list of criticisms.

In itself, lack of objectivity is a major cause of suspicion in psychological research; naturally, the atypical conditions of advertising exposure in most tests may raise doubts about their value. Yet the fact that the conditions of testing are not the usual methods of attending to advertisements is not really a reflection on the objectivity of the methods.

The assumption that consumers can serve as advertising experts in the *direct* methods of rating is questionable. However, when these methods involve questioning about the opinions that the respondents *themselves* have, the results may be of considerable value. In the dimensional test, for instance, various ideas for points that might be made in the copy may be checked over in advance of final preparation of the advertisement.

Perhaps the most telling of the criticisms of opinion methods has to do with the apparent assumption that single messages of an advertiser can have enough impact to produce truly significant psychological changes or measurable sales effects. Actually, all of the consumer-jury methods tap the respondents' attitudes toward the advertising of a product or service, whereas the advertiser's real concern is with the consumers' attitudes toward the product or service itself insofar as these are indirectly mediated by the advertising.

In this connection, believability of advertising may or may not be an important consideration. The advertiser should remember that the immediate motivational effects of a given piece of copy, as presented in a single advertisement, are often not as important as the copy's contribution to long-term motivational effects. Many things other than the single advertisement influence people in being favorably disposed toward buying products and services. If the copy claims about the product or service are basically true and if they cause the consumer to be curious about the product or service, then the copy need not be completely believed in order to be effective.

To the extent that respondents are not representative of the kinds of respondents for whom the advertising is intended; to the extent that they are inexpert about either the advertisements or their own responses, or both; to the extent that test exposure is forced and intensified; and to the extent that the thing measured is not equivalent to a buying response, the overall implications of opinion and attitude measures must continue to be scrutinized.

Yet with proper allowance for their limitations, these subjective methods can provide useful suggestions to the advertiser, serve as a source of guidance, and give some degree of useful measurement. Certainly the various scaling methods and rating scales may often be of value simply as a check of various possible ideas, and the *indirect* opinion methods deserve careful consideration and offer considerable promise of useful results.

six

Projective Methods

EXAMPLES OF PROJECTIVE TECHNIQUES

SOME PROBLEMS

INFORMAL, UNSTRUCTURED INTERVIEWS

PROJECTIVE TESTS OF COPY

IMPLICATIONS

Answering the question as to the "why" of people's attitudes and actions has proved to be one of the most difficult of all research problems. Motives, like personal opinions and attitudes, are deeply involved with feelings and emotions. A consumer usually does not know his own motives precisely and yet may be more than willing to "explain" his own acts. He may give ready and apparently sincere explanations, even through he is reluctant to admit certain motives even to his closest friends.

The fact that an interview is a cause of some emotion and conflict merely compounds the problem of learning the true facts needed for advertisement planning. In one instance reported by Edward Battey, formerly of the ·Compton advertising agency, the purchase of a new car by a man was actually explained by interviewing his wife; then a return interview was held. On the first call, the old car was said to be in need of expensive repairs, and the needs of the children were said to require something new. Responding to a return call, however, the housewife suddenly exploded with: "Ever since Jack married me, he has bought a new car within a month of every car my father buys. He just can't let Dad get ahead of him on cars!"

In fact, emotions and bias may be so intermingled with responses from questionnaire-like interviews as to require filtering and cross-checking of replies. Not only do people deny certain motives that they have and give rationalized answers—they insist on protecting their vanity and their privacy; they relate almost all problems to their self-interests; and they tend to exaggerate minor irritations, including advertising, which they often discount as if it had little or no actual influence.

It is for such reasons that clinical or projective techniques have come into use in connection with advertising research.

EXAMPLES OF PROJECTIVE TECHNIQUES

What is meant by projective techniques? These are methods—developed for the most part by clinical psychologists—of discovering as much as possible about a person's characteristic attitudes and modes of behavior by presenting him various kinds of rather vague or ambiguous stimuli. The theory is that the individual who is being interviewed or tested will in various ways "project" his own personality traits into a situation and that, by examining the resulting data, psychologists can discover something about the individual which he might not reveal through direct questioning. Here are a few of the projective techniques, stated in capsule form.

The *Thematic Apperception Test* (TAT) uses a drawing of people, and the respondent is asked to tell a story about it. The *picture probe* shows two characters in a cartoon strip, with one making a statement, and with the respondent asked to say what the other character says. In the *narrative probe* a hypothetical situation in story form is given to the respondent for his comments. The *sentence-completion* method allows the respondent to finish each of a group of incomplete sentences any way he wishes. For *word association,* the respondent is asked to give immediately the first word or group of words that comes to his mind for each word of a series that is read aloud to him rapidly. These and other techniques, including the *depth interview* and the *group interview,* may be used separately or in various combinations.

The *thematic apperception test* is a series of pictures of individuals, somewhat unstructured. I say unstructured because there is nothing in the pictures to indicate precisely who the people are or where they are, and the respondent is simply asked to make up a story about them. Who are these people? What are they talking about? What are they saying? How will it all come out?

In other words, each person can *project* into the picture what he himself sees.

The theory, then, is that in doing this, a person will reveal something about himself. You see, the *visual sensation* is essentially the same for everybody who looks at this picture; but *perception* is quite different, depending upon your own background, experiences, aspirations, and desires. Within any such story will appear a theme which is a reflection of social pressures, personal desires, pleasant or unpleasant outcomes, social conflicts, feelings of affection, hostility, etc. And on the basis of the stories and of their structure, the motivation researcher makes his interpretations and draws his conclusions.

Another technique of somewhat this same sort is the *picture probe*. The respondent fills in the comments or thoughts of two or more people pictured in a drawing. In a study of attitudes of men toward buying life insurance for their families, each husband was shown a drawing of a husband, wife, and insurance agent. The question was—what is the wife saying and what is the husband thinking? Typical interpretations were: "She might even be saying, 'We could afford a larger amount, dear, don't you think?' And the husband thinks he is being taken advantage of in front of the agent. You can see that the man isn't too anxious to sign those papers, but he'll get worn down by his wife and the insurance man."

Another drawing showed a wife receiving a $10,000 life insurance check from the agent. Typical comments of husbands: "Boy, will she have a good time! She'll blow the whole thing in less than a year." . . . "She's thinking, 'Thank God he died while I'm still young enough to go and hook some other slob—not when I'm 60. Now I'm free!' "

To outward appearances, a husband usually seems quite calm about the purchase of life insurance. But it becomes obvious from interpretations of projective materials that he may have deep-rooted anxieties about his beneficiaries, life insurance agents, and death.

A third example is the *narrative probe*. Here you don't even need a picture or anything of this sort. You just ask the person to respond to a make-up story. In the clinical situation, the psychologist might say to an individual, "By the way, sitting in the next room is a very despicable person. Tell me the traits which this person has." The individual responding is likely to reveal, without realizing it, what he thinks are *his own* most despicable traits. Or contrariwise, the psychologist might say, "Sitting in the next room is an individual who is an unusually fine person. Tell me what this person is like." Again, the theory is that the individual responding will reveal what he regards as the finest traits of *himself*.

This technique enables the respondent to give answers with fewer self-centered implications. For example, in a study made for the State Farm Mutual Automobile Insurance Company, one of the narrative probes used was: "A friend of yours has just bought his first car. He asks you what he should do about getting insurance for it. What would you tell him?" An individual respondent makes an answer . . . another makes another answer . . . another makes another answer . . . and so on; thus, the researcher gathers together a vast array of answers, which he later reads, studies, and analyzes, trying to find out what significant points have been made.

Another projective technique is the *sentence-completion method,* in which an individual is asked to say the very first thing that comes into his mind by completing a sentence. For example, he is given the phrase, "I feel that people . . ." and is told to finish the sentence. Try this on yourself right now. Or he is told, "When things get hectic I . . ." How do you complete the sentence? Or "When given orders I . . ." Or "I am happiest when . . ." "Some day I . . ." "I become annoyed when they . . ." You can see that if you would complete sentences such as these with the very first thought that comes to mind, you might reveal some things about your personality that might not come out through more direct questioning.

Since the respondent builds a sentence from a stimulus word or words, clues may be obtained about attitudes toward various ideas or things. One examiner might start out with some very neutral words or phrases and then gradually move to the subject in which he is particularly interested In a study carried out for Johnson's Wax, respondents were asked to complete the sentences below (the answers made by one respondent are also shown).

Most floor waxes _are too slippery_____

The hardest thing about waxing is _cleaning beforehand_____

Johnson's Wax _costs too much_____

The ideal floor wax _should last a long time_____

When I am through waxing _I hope it won't get_____
_____ tracked up right away_____

The easiest way to apply wax is to _pour it on and_____
_____ then spread it around with a cloth_____

The only thing I don't like about wax is _the smell_____

Now, this set of answers by one person alone does not give complete answers as to which of the product's qualities should be stressed in the advertising and promotional work. Naturally the company wants to emphasize those qualities of its product in which consumers are most interested; and so answers from many consumers may provide material that is useful. As a matter of fact, in one of the Johnson's Wax campaigns involving the "no scuff" theme, the phrase "no scuff" actually came from women respondents.

One more instance of a projective technique is the *word-association method*. The respondent is given a series of words and asked to say the very first word that comes into his mind. As a simple example, I say to you "salt." What do you say quickly? "Pepper." I say to you "chair"; you say "table." I say "hot"; you say "cold."

There's nothing mysterious about these examples. But when a psychologist throws in some additional words that are emotionally charged—perhaps the word "love"—perhaps the name of a loved one—perhaps the name of a certain place—this can be quite revealing. This method of evaluation is based on *first* associations made to various words. The nature of the associations and the way they differ from usual responses serve as the basis for interpretation.

As an example, a motivation researcher was asked by a beer company whether this company should use the word "lagered" as one of the key phrases in its advertising. Should the word "lagered" be played up big in headlines? The method used by the motivation researcher was very simple. He read aloud a list of words, with the instruction to give the very first word that comes to mind. And then within the list he had the word "lagered" so that no special attention was directed to it. The results were that 36 per cent of the respondents gave associations like beer, ale, or stout to the word "lagered." Another 38 gave such responses as slow, tired, drunk, lazy, behind, linger, dizzy. The remaining 26 per cent of the respondents gave no answer. Need I say that the word "lagered" was *not* used in the new advertising campaign, for the meaning intended by the manufacturer was not generally understood.

Of course, you might argue that "lagered" could be built up over a period of time and sold to consumers as a meaningful word. An advertising campaign a few years ago played up "dry" beer. In questioning people, it was found that most didn't have the slightest idea what a dry beer is, but after seeing it advertised they thought it was great!

Another example is the *depth interview*. This is a very lengthy, conversational interview with an individual in order to get him to talk freely about all sorts of things that come into his mind. Almost "free wheeling." At some time in your life, you have sat in a bus station, a train station, an airport, or on a public conveyance, and some stranger has poured out to you the intimate story of his life. You just listened—and this is an important requirement in depth interviewing.

Chicago Daily News columnist Sydney J. Harris relates that he was lolling on the front porch of a resort hotel. "A man sat down in the chair next to me, and within five minutes I was told that he lived in Columbus, sold insurance, had four children, belonged to the Elks, was born in Delaware, had attended the Ohio State University, thought his wife was getting too plump, didn't like his son-in-law, and wanted me to be sure to look him up any time I happened to be passing through Columbus.

"He didn't know me from Adam's off-ox, nor did I give his confidence the slightest encouragement beyond a perfunctory politeness. I have met this same man by the hundreds, on trains and planes, in hotel lobbies and lunch counters—and the same autobiographical material starts pouring forth like a gusher that has been repressed for years."

Have you ever had that sort of experience? Or perhaps you yourself have gushed to somebody. Although this is not depth interviewing, it illustrates the *kind* of interviewing that clinical psychologists may engage in, to get an individual to talk freely about himself. This will not be a completely *free* association of ideas; that is, it isn't just *anything* that comes to the individual's mind. But it will be *controlled* association, in that the psychologist may to some extent guide the conversation. He may guide it to the extent at least that he keeps the person on the same general subject, although his role is mainly to be a good listener and occasionally to ask a question. This interview does not use a questionnaire, although it is "structured" or purposeful in that the psychologist will have in mind a series of points to be covered.

This type of interviewing technique in which occasional probing questions are asked is an attempt to uncover the motives which underlie or influence respondent behavior. The interviewer attempts to guide the discussion in certain channels.

Some years ago the editor of a leading woman's magazine wanted to know what it was that women would like most of all to read about, in stories, articles, and special features. The women being interviewed were not told the exact purpose of the interview. The interviewer went into the home and simply said: "I want to talk about women's attitudes. I want to get your views about women in the home." Then gradually she led the discussion around to women's publications, in order to find out what women would like to read in magazines. But in the process the interviewers were told the most intimate details of the lives of the wives and mothers—the extent to which they liked or disliked their husbands or children, or how much the family was in debt—intimate details of this sort. Those interviewed were willing to talk freely to a nice, pleasant, good-listening stranger, much more freely than to a friend or the next-door neighbor. What was learned, of course, about the daydreams, fantasies, wishes, and secret ambitions of women was unusually helpful to the editor in determining what kinds of things his readers would like in a magazine.

Related to this is the *group interview*. This is "depth interviewing" not just with an individual but with a whole group of people sitting together and talking on a subject. In this situation, as with the individual depth interview, the interview may be tape-recorded so that it can be played back later and analyzed precisely as to what was said. Individuals talking freely as a group may develop ideas that might not come out of an interview with one person.

For example, a group of housewives may meet and tell what they want in a certain product. This does not involve great psychological probing, but out of one such tape-recorded interview came the following factors. What the housewives wanted most of all for a certain food product was to have a container with a screw top, rather than something that is hard to pry off . . . to have a very wide-mouthed jar . . . and to have the container marked off so it could be used as a measuring cup.

A lot of different kinds of exploratory techniques have been mentioned, just to give you some slight acquaintance with them. These techniques have considerable meaning in searching for people's motives. The information obtained may affect both the product and the advertising.[1]

Although it would be a digression to go into the details of the various projective techniques, the most useful classification of them has been given by Gardner Lindzey:[2] (Because several of these methods have not been used extensively in advertising research, they are not discussed in the present book.)

Association techniques:

    Word-association technique
    Rorschach test
    Cloud pictures
    Auditory projective techniques

Here the subject is to respond to some stimulus presented by the examiner with the first word, image, or percept that occurs to him.

Construction techniques:

    Thematic Apperception Test
    Blacky pictures

Here we find a group of instruments that require the subject to create or construct a product which is typically an art form, such as a story or picture.

Completion techniques:

    Sentence-completion Test
    Picture-frustration Study

These measures provide the subject with some type of incomplete product and require that he complete it in any manner he wishes.

[1] Steuart Henderson Britt, *The Spenders* (New York: McGraw-Hill Book Company, Inc., 1960), pp. 215–222.

[2] Gardner Lindzey, *Projective Techniques and Cross-cultural Research* (New York: Appleton-Century-Crofts, Inc., 1961), pp. 49–107.

Choice-in-ordering techniques:

Szondi Test
Picture-arrangement Test

Here the respondent merely chooses from a number of alternatives the item or arrangement that fits some specific criteria such as correctness, relevance, attractiveness, or repugnance.

Expressive techniques:

Play technique
Drawing and painting techniques
Psychodrama and role-playing

These instruments, as in the case of the construction techniques, require the subject to combine or incorporate stimuli into some kind of novel production.

SOME PROBLEMS

The testing of advertisements by methods of this kind involves both promises and problems.

Advertising, even when blatant, is subtle in some of its ways of influencing the consumer. The psychological clinic is noted for its profound approach to elusive influences on motivation. Yet the typical satisfied consumer is so unlike the unhappy clinical patient that the application of similar techniques may seem both unnecessary and complex. In the past decade, most leading advertising research organizations have called upon clinically trained psychologists to aid in exploratory research in advertising, and some have also turned to clinical methods for examining proposed advertising ideas and copy.

The reasons are easy to understand. As Pierre Martineau of the Chicago *Tribune* once pointed out in a speech: "It is impossible for statistical research methods to read the human mind. Readership figures, for instance, tell how many people read an ad, but they don't tell why they read it." We also realize that in a great many situations most of us learn to conceal rather carefully our actual feelings and emotions if we know what they are—and in many instances it is difficult for us really to know what they are.

Cake Mix Example

When cake mix manufacturers were ready for their first major advertising promotion, the makers of Betty Crocker Cake Mix decided upon a campaign to emphasize the elimination of baking failures. Betty Crocker, long established as a friendly counselor to housewives, was supposed to assert, "I GUARANTEE YOU A PERFECT CAKE EVERY TIME YOU BAKE. . . CAKE AFTER CAKE AFTER CAKE." General Mills, Inc., already had in hand the scheduled early advertisements and was about to release them, but decided first to call in a clinical psychologist. Both advertiser and advertising agency were concerned about the new role in which Betty Crocker was being cast.

The advertisements went into the clinic where housewives were being interviewed, with and without exposure to the new campaign. Quickly the report came back that Betty Crocker's personality was being radically changed—instead of being a friendly, dependable helpmate, she was going to turn into a hard-selling promoter of a branded product. The investigator was given a free hand, and ultimately two additional investigators were separately handed the same assignment. All agreed that a personality was being changed, an image would be destroyed, and a valuable commercial property lost.

The fact that the cake mix advertisements were released and that Betty Crocker rapidly rose to a strong competitive position seems to contradict the analysts. They failed to consider the inconspicuous way the Betty Crocker name and picture were subordinated to the featured claim and illustration. Subsequent research has shown that she remained a friendly service personality. There are also three important questions to which the clinical experts did not address themselves. There is the question as to whether Betty Crocker had already assumed a selling role when the package took her name. A second question is whether modern cooking with readied ingredients any longer needs the type of advice which made the earlier Betty Crocker so valuable. And third, though not last in importance, is the question as to how many housewives and what types of women would feel a greater loss than gain from the commercialization of this famous food figure.

Very likely Betty Crocker's image had changed, as it should. In the meantime, her stature and identity may have given great impetus to the early sale and establishment of a successful brand. If she became associated with cooking shortcuts and with a commercial assignment, it may also be that women want shortcuts and are glad to have such a reliable shopping guide.

Actually, Betty Crocker had survived other career hazards. Earlier, when television first appeared and it became desirable to substitute a living model for an artist's ageless portrait, it became important to determine the housewives' image of Betty Crocker. Research of a conventional type was used to help select a model most likely to be accepted as a living Betty

Crocker. The Betty Crocker personality image is an asset, but an asset would surely be lost if confined to the limits of any one living mortal.

Cake mix is only one of many laborsaving and success-assuring products constantly being developed for the modern housewife. Clinical methods have repeatedly produced evidence that some women are anxious about using products which obviously require less work and less skill—less drudgery and fewer mistakes. They fear that their friends and family or they themselves will look upon such behavior as lacking in evidence of devotion, adequacy, and self-confidence. Are they shocked by the radio commentator when he says, "Sauce Arturo does it all for you. You can be a lazy-bones if you use it"? The questions are: What per cent of women have those negative feelings? How strongly do such feelings influence their actions? Do such attitudes, either in the short run or in the long run, make advertising emphasis on time-saving and laborsaving qualities and the assurance of success a liability or an asset?

Other Considerations

These illustrations are used to suggest the kind of ideas and advertising evaluation which may be developed by clinical techniques. Regardless of whether the conclusions of particular investigators are right or wrong, ideas and questions like those raised above are important considerations in making advertising decisions.

The adaptations of clinical methods used in advertising often bear little resemblance to their clinical counterparts. There is little genuine *depth interviewing* in marketing research, and the adaptation of projective techniques often differs from those used in the clinic in purpose as well as design. While there are few real depth interviews, there is widespread application of the principle of the prolonged unstructured interview. It is well to keep high clinical standards in mind in order to make maximum use of these specialized methods and to arrive at the safest conclusions.

The user of findings from projective techniques needs to realize that their value may be greater when they are used in combination with other methods.[3] Oftentimes, both qualitative and quantitative data are needed for the best solution to research questions.

Also, the user of projective data should be sure that he thoroughly understands the implications of the materials, aware of the fact that this is not the solution to all his advertising problems, have considerable evidence as

[3] Steuart Henderson Britt, "Why It's Best to Use 'Combination Research,'" *Printers' Ink,* Vol. 249 (October 22, 1954), pp. 60, 66.

to the specific methods used, and make certain that the methods are reliable and, insofar as possible, valid.[4]

INFORMAL, UNSTRUCTURED INTERVIEWS

Most clinical studies in advertising are likely to be based on unstructured interviews of some length. In such cases, the amount of exposure to test advertisements and the amount of direct discussion will vary, depending upon the judgment of the research executive. Where the advertisement is to be studied in relation to an existing image belonging to the company or product, some probing may be done both before and after advertising exposure.

The testing of a comic-strip character in a hairdressing advertisement, for example, was based almost entirely on impressions reported while looking at the display. In this instance, the "slicked down" black hair of the hero was advised against because of possible Latin-American associations in Southwestern states.

One psychologist studied copy for a breakfast cereal by getting the subjects to reenact a breakfast scene in their daily pattern. If a cold cereal stays crisp in milk, makes crackling or crunchy noises, these are good points to emphasize for vigorous, active youngsters. On the other hand, emphasis on those same qualities may repel the timid or weaker personality who seeks to enter the day in a more tranquil atmosphere.

Analysts have repeatedly arrived at similar recommendations through opposing lines of reasoning. One attempt at a Freudian interpretation of a cigarette advertisement gave approval to the copy for minimizing the irritation which smokers wish to avoid. Another, proclaiming equal knowledge of Freud, approved of the emphasis upon irritation, saying that the smoker wants this punishment for the "sin" of smoking and is reassured by having it pointed out.

Because the influences of individual campaign advertisements are so subtle and slight on most consumers, it has been expected that the informal probing of the analyst might reveal much that is not detected in more formal test methods. The immediate result has been a number of promising suggestions and controversial conclusions. Copy approaches have been revised accordingly, or in some instances formal tests have been applied to confirm or estimate the importance of the point in question. Some analysts have

[4] Steuart Henderson Britt, "Four Hazards of Motivation Research: How to Avoid Them," *Printers' Ink,* Vol. 251 (June 17, 1955), pp. 40, 45, 48.

shown great ability to arrive at convincing interpretations and forecasts. But whether these judgments have been a direct outgrowth of unstructured consumer interviews or more basically a matter of insight on the part of the investigator has not always been evident.

Certainly there has been little standardization in the approach of clinical psychologists to copy evaluation.

Panels of consumers who serve as a jury for opinion ratings of advertisements (see Chapter Five) may also contribute useful verbatim material through unstructured discussions. Both the Leo Burnett Company and Batten, Barton, Durstine, and Osborn, Inc., as well as certain other advertising agencies, use focus-group interviews of this type and find them valuable in—

1. Gaining free and uninhibited responses to a product advertisement or concept by getting more than one viewpoint and reasons why

2. Pointing up sources of confusion and misunderstanding about the product or advertisement

3. Obtaining unanticipated responses about a product or advertisement

4. Providing a source of new ideas for copywriters

5. Retaining the "flavor" of the language which people use in talking about products or services

6. Developing insights into the motivations of people's buying

7. Suggesting hypotheses for more carefully controlled, quantitative research

PROJECTIVE TESTS OF COPY

One of the greatest uses of projective tests in the clinic is that of providing insights into motivation patterns. These are the techniques which lead people to make unguarded verbal responses without awareness that they are revealing their own personalities. The respondent plays a role which can come only from his own subjective make-up, but assumes he is playing or describing the role of others. Whether these techniques are capable of providing measurement—apart from their value in leading to insights—continues to be a subject of controversy.

Word-association Tests

Probably the oldest projective procedure readily adapted to the evaluation of advertising copy is the word-association test. An example of an association test is based on an advertisement to promote the use of butter in competition with less expensive spreads. The proposed advertisement contained such words as *buttery, snack, sizzling, bun,* and *aroma.* It was not proposed to evaluate the whole advertisement, but simply to study the associations of these apparently key copy words. The five copy words were fitted into a larger group as follows:

1. table _____	5. buttery _____	9. red _____
2. orange _____	6. cold _____	10. bun _____
3. snack _____	7. aroma _____	11. friend _____
4. white _____	8. owl _____	12. sizzling _____

Every word in the list, and especially the sequence of words, has an influence on each response. This cannot be avoided, although the sequence can be varied or other background words substituted. The above pattern, used with hundreds of convenient subjects, produced such responses to the test as follows:

snack: tidbit, brunch, quick, hungry
buttery: smeary, fatty, greasy, yellow, heavy
aroma: smell, pleasant, odor, perfume
bun: roll, bread, gravy, oven
sizzling: hot, sputtering, spattering, meat

One peculiar feature about words associated with food is that the English language is so lacking in adjectives to describe taste. There were few taste associations with *buttery,* possibly for lack of vocabulary. An association test of this kind may quickly raise doubts about particular words and may influence the copywriter in his choice of words, but it does not directly provide an evaluation of an advertisement. Like all of the projective approaches, it leaves the investigator with verbatim responses to be *interpreted.*

One important element in association tests, which seems of less significance in copy research, is delay or blockage in responses. At best, the association test is only a guide for testing copy. In the above example, slight delays in some of the responses appeared to have no connection with whether the concept was pleasant or otherwise.

Sentence-completion Tests

Sentence completions are easily adapted for copy research, especially with regard to headlines, slogans, and claims. A simple approach is to mutilate the statement and ask subjects to fill in. Here are some hypothetical examples:

YOU GET A LOT TO LIKE _____.
(This is a cigarette slogan ending
"WITH A MARLBORO.")

MEN WHO WEAR THE OLYMPIAN HAVE _____
(This is a headline for Esquire socks ending with
"THE BEST LINES.")

SHE'S SMART! SHE'S THRIFTY! SHE _____.
(This is a display line on an S&H Green Stamps advertisement and ends
"SAVES AMERICA'S MOST VALUABLE STAMPS.")

Examination of completions may indicate that the form of expression works favorably or in opposition to the intended point. The third headline, because of associations with a well-known cosmetic, may not lead effectively to Green Stamps. On the other hand, the form may speed and intensify the acceptance of the advertised idea. The significance of suggestions derived from this approach will depend a good deal upon the test sample and the method used for interpretation.

A scientific analysis of sentence-completion methods in the testing of advertising material was carried out by Jennifer S. Macleod.[5] The experiment involved nine automobile advertisements and a probability sample in one community. The chief purpose was to assess the value of sentence completions, as well as direct attitude questions, in predicting the content of appealing advertising copy. The material from the nine advertisements was mimeographed, and fictionalized brand names were substituted as part of the procedure for concealing true brand associations. Although the outcome of the published tryout was negative for both sentence completions and direct attitude questions, the procedure is worthy of further consideration.

The first step in the Macleod survey was an attempt to obtain, from male heads of 368 households, their brand choices of the fictitious car makes as described in the nine mimeographed pieces of copy. Two to three weeks later a different interviewer, under apparently different auspices, asked the same people to respond to 40 incomplete sentences and also to a direct attitude questionnaire. Both techniques were to be checked against the brand

[5] Jennifer S. Macleod, *Predicting the Responses to Advertising Themes from Sentence Completions or Direct Attitude Questions about an Advertised Product* (New York: Advertising Research Foundation, Inc., 1958).

choices expressed in the first survey. Some of the 40 incomplete sentences were as follows:

The best kind of car is one that _____
The most enjoyable thing when you go to buy a car is _____
Driving very fast in a car is _____

All sentences were written in the third person, and each respondent wrote in his own completions. Since the other part of the test included direct attitude questions, the sentence completions were finished before direct attitude questions were asked in one-half of the 116 completed second-wave interviews, and the order was reversed in the other one-half of the sample.

A quantitative comparison between the sentence completions and the actual advertising copy was obtained by means of *content analysis* (see the next chapter). There were 98 specific categories set up for classifying each whole sentence in the advertising copy and for each completion response given on the incomplete test sentences. Favorable, neutral, and unfavorable sentences were assigned weights of +1, 0, and −1 respectively. Advertising headlines were triple-weighted and subheads were double-weighted. Three trained judges worked independently in rating all of the sentences in all nine advertisements. One judge or coder scored the sentence completions.

The next step was to group the 98 categories into 18 broader indexes for purposes of comparison. "Desire for economy," for example, included such specific categories as "low price range," "good value, high trade-in," and "operating economy." The sum of the scores on these specific categories less scores on such opposites as "high price range" became the score for the "desire for economy" index. The 18 index scores for each of the nine advertisements were then divided at the median into *high* and *low* groups. The index scores on sentence completions were similarly divided for the purpose of comparison with the advertisements. Tests of statistical significance were also applied, and the data were subjected to thorough internal analysis for consistency.

In analyzing the Macleod study, it is desirable to consider the objective, which was concerned with what advertising appeals will influence people to buy. Actual buying behavior was not the criterion, but rather the expressed choice of a fictitious make of car as described in the written copy of a real advertisement. One of the two methods under test was that of sentence completions, and content analysis was used in order to arrive at quantified comparisons. Comparison of the scores on sentence completions with those for the "most appealing" advertisements failed to produce important correlations. The investigator suggested that the negative results may have been the fault of procedures adopted, but it seems unlikely that practical applications would ever be as thorough or more astute.

The Macleod report refers to the sentence-completion method as having been adapted from clinical use for the purpose of revealing a respondent's attitudes even (1) if he is not consciously aware of them, or (2) if he is not willing knowingly to reveal them. This is the chief reason for applying projective techniques, although they also operate much faster than depth probing in the clinic.

The above experiment is an adaptation of the clinical approach, with a minimum of modification for advertising research purposes. If it failed to demonstrate quantitative proof of validity, clinical applications in general are not noteworthy for quantitative validation.[6] Perhaps the chief gain from their use will continue to be the ideas suggested and the insights revealed.

Picture Techniques

Picture techniques, resembling the Thematic Apperception Test (TAT), are adaptable to the testing of display advertising illustrations. The most obvious use is to take the illustration in isolation from verbal copy or caption and invite subjects to talk about it or "tell a story" about it.

A very considerable trial of this approach has been made by clinical psychologists, but for the most part the interpretations of responses have been arrived at somewhat intuitively. A more systematic quantitative approach, as described in the Macleod experiment, can also be used with picture responses.

Each copy test is concerned with a particular advertisement or copy idea. The responses to projective tests of visual elements may often be determined so much by the personality of the respondent that the comments of individuals have to be discarded. Other responses may clearly reflect practical implications for the creative man—favorable, unfavorable, or neutral in relation to the advertising purpose. If too many responses are unrelated to the ideas and atmosphere intended by the visualizer or are unfavorable, it may be desirable to change the visual treatment. Informal unpublished studies of scores of advertising illustrations removed from their captions

[6] Darrell B. Lucas, "Can the Clinical Techniques Be Validated?" in Robert Ferber and Hugh G. Wales (editors), *Motivation and Market Behavior* (Homewood, Ill.: Richard D. Irwin, Inc., 1958), chap. 12, pp. 122–132.

have indicated frequent lack of relevance or lack of positive contribution to the copy message.

An example of a possibly detracting illustration was a photograph of a large herd of horses—intended to show the horsepower of an automobile. Almost no test responses to the picture gave any hint of power or speed; in fact, many respondents referred to the milling around of horses in the photo and the confusion and danger of injury to the animals. The headline caption clearly stated that the car had enormous horsepower, but the particular scene seemed to detract from that idea in the minds of many readers.

One of the specialized applications of the picture technique to advertised ideas and products is the presentation of a scene in which a customer appears to be making a choice. For example, the scene may show counter cards in a store featuring two or more copy claims, with a potential customer apparently about to make a choice of products. Skill and pretesting are required to develop a visualization which will prompt the respondent to deal with the decision process without having the picture too obvious and directive. However, comments relating to how the customer is arriving at his choice and the choice he finally makes may throw light on the efficacy of the varied counter displays.

A test such as the picture technique is useful to the extent that it produces evidence not as easily or as accurately obtained through direct questions. The setting up of a picture test, the time required to introduce it in an interview, the time required for the nondirective responses, and the work of subjective interpretation—all add to research time and costs. Investigators have tried the same picture both in a projective setting and in a direct question context and sometimes have found the results the same. When this has occurred, the projective approach usually has been dropped. Projective methods should be used only when they add enough to the findings to justify the time required for the tests.

An example of practical research, to determine the appropriateness of an illustration, involved whether or not to use a photograph of a man's face as the dominant feature in an advertisement.[7] The advertiser became concerned over whether the man would be thought of as sad or cheerful, as worried or unworried. Respondents were shown the picture and asked to rate the man in the picture on several pairs of opposite characteristics: rich-poor, worried-unworried, cheerful-sad, etc. Since the majority rated the

[7] Perham C. Nahl, "Speedy, Inexpensive Pretests of Ads: Capsule Case Histories," *Proceedings of Fourth Annual Conference of Advertising Research Foundation* (New York: Advertising Research Foundation, Inc., October 2, 1958), p. 55.

man in exactly the mood that was intended, the picture was recommended for use with the headline PEACEFUL OUTLOOK PICTURED HERE.

Cartoon Technique

The cartoon technique, used in the psychological clinic, may be used to test advertising ideas and copy claims. James F. Engel has made interesting comparisons of responses to cartoons and to direct questions.[8] One question, easily adapted to testing of a copy theme or advertisement, dealt with alternate prices of 67 cents per hundred and 27 cents per hundred for aspirin.

The cartoon used by Engel shows a woman talking with her druggist, who states (see Fig. 6):

FIG. 6. Cartoon as projective technique.

This widely known brand of aspirin gives you 100 tablets for 67 cents, and this brand gives you 100 tablets for 27 cents. Which would you like?

The verbal question was worded as follows:

Let's assume you needed some aspirin and went to a drugstore to buy some. If you had your choice between a widely known brand of aspirin giving you

[8] James F. Engel, *A Study of a Selected Projective Technique in Marketing Research,* Ph.D. dissertation, University of Illinois, 1960. Also, James F. Engel and Hugh G. Wales, "Spoken versus Pictured Questions on Taboo Topics," *Journal of Advertising Research,* Vol. 2 (March, 1962), pp. 11–17.

100 tablets for 67 cents and another brand giving you 100 tablets for 27 cents, which would you choose? Why?

Matched samples of 150 housewives were obtained from the lists of patients of 17 physicians and two public health nurses in Champaign-Urbana, Illinois. One group responded to cartoon presentations of six topics pertaining to physician-patient relationships. The other sample responded to direct open-end questions on the same topics. It was hoped the doctors knew their patients well enough to provide a validating basis for both survey techniques, but Engel discovered that they "did not know their patients well enough to make an accurate rating."

Accordingly, the results of the study depended on comparisons of the two test methods. The two survey groups' product choices expressed in per cent were as follows:

Survey groups	67-cent aspirin	27-cent aspirin	No choice
Cartoon respondents	48	30	22
Respondents to questions	74	18	8

Since the direct questions clearly asked for a choice, it is logical that they would produce more decisions, and 92 per cent made a choice. Of the cartoon respondents, 38 per cent called for further information, whereas the direct questions discouraged all but 6.7 per cent from deciding solely on the basis of price.

According to both methods, it would appear that the advertiser would realize greater gross profits by using the higher price. It also is clear that if the two methods produce such widely differing results, the cartoon method might recommend a lower price in medically associated products for which direct questions might show higher price to be superior. The two methods produce significantly different results, and which is more valid or more reliable cannot be assayed.

Interpretation of cartoon responses requires that each element be coded according to established categories. Setting up the categories and assigning weights is largely a subjective process, although coders can consistently sort the responses according to any prearranged pattern. This and the fact that these two survey methods are not logically designed to evoke responses in the same area lead to rationalization of the differences in findings.

Engel feels that the cartoon responses on brand choice may have provided more accurate evidence because the housewife was under less implied pressure to show that she was concerned with aspirin quality. Quality was mentioned as a reason by 65 women on direct questioning, but by only 40 of the cartoon respondents. Of the cartoon respondents, 57 threw the burden back on the druggist to provide further information, whereas only 10 such responses were made to the direct questions. A multiple-choice response to the direct questions might have produced more similar results if limited to the following categories:

(   ) Would buy 67-cent brand
(   ) Would buy 27-cent brand
(   ) Would ask the druggist for more information
(   ) Would buy neither

These and other types of projective tests have been used in a variety of situations.

Role Playing

Role playing is another method which may be rather easily adapted to the study of advertising copy. The most direct approach is to present an advertising message or a part of it and to ask respondents to describe the type of person who would choose that product. This does not work well when the product is already familiar or when the advertisement depicts its own buyers.

It is better suited to a situation such as that when revolutionary designs of automobiles are being introduced simultaneously by several leading manufacturers. Extensive study of responses to advertisements of the Falcon, the Corvair, and the Valiant when compact cars were first announced revealed varying contrasts among expected buyers. A considerable amount of research involving various clinical methods was done by the manufacturers and their agencies on both the cars and their advertisements. Some advertisements were tested even before authentic pictures were available for exposure to respondents, with some useful results.

Role-playing tests can help to ensure that advertisements are appropriate for the actual or desired class of buyers of the product. Many advertisements, especially when trying to lend prestige or to upgrade a market, are too obvious or contradictory for their purpose. It is not enough for the advertisement to depict or make claims for a particular kind of buyer.

Role-playing studies of separate elements of such advertisements can help to show whether the whole copy message contributes to the desired class impression, or whether some aspects tend to cancel others. Such tests should expose the more subtle influences, such as "lowest cost per mile" and "exclusive car models," as well as obvious contradictions.

IMPLICATIONS

The problem of adapting exploratory findings is well illustrated by projective or clinical methods. They depend upon the respondent being unaware that his responses suggest hypotheses as to his real motives.

His completion of a cartoon situation, for instance, may suggest to the research executive that some hitherto ignored motive plays a prominent part in buying a particular product or brand. However, if the survey plan attempts to probe directly in the same area, it may only raise resistance and defeat the survey purpose. It then becomes the responsibility of the research executive to design a total interview which covers all required areas and which contains the needed elements for measuring the point or points in question. This is a complicated combination of art and science.

It is difficult to decide whether or when to use clinical techniques in testing advertisements or their elements. Unstructured, informal interviews are adaptable to almost any problem, but are likely to consume great amounts of time in relation to specific outcomes. Projective techniques are varied and have to be selected or adapted according to the particular problem. Nor is it essential to adhere to the clinical purpose of each technique, so long as the only objective is to obtain unguarded responses revealing hidden or subtle reactions. It is not the personality of the respondent that is under scrutiny, but rather the impressions that advertising may make upon him.

The projective methods are cumbersome in comparison with direct questioning and have the further disadvantage of producing results which are difficult to quantify. Often it is extremely difficult to adapt the advertising problem to a projective test, to ensure responses which are consistently relevant, and to obtain cooperation from a representative sample of people. All of these factors add to the difficulties of interpretation, especially to reaching positive conclusions.

Critics have vigorously challenged the validity of clinically determined advertising decisions, at times using cases of failure of clinical research to produce or identify the best advertising design. Yet such attacks are paradoxical, for the cases chosen to prove the point must assume a knowledge of actual advertising effect. The approach to all psychological tests of copy rests on the assumption that the sales performance of typical individual national advertisements is lacking. Certainly no copy test of known validity exists for application to the problems of most national advertisers. The point is that projective tests are used to discover indicators and not to displace judgment in advertising.

The values of projective techniques in forecasting human behavior can best be understood by admitting that reliability is likely to be low, and that validity is unknown. Even in the clinical applications for which these methods were invented, projective analysis is not the most precise predictor of subsequent behavior.

In advertising, projective techniques can be applied with some quantitative interpretation that leads to suggested actions. Lack of self-consciousness on the part of respondents may help to reveal authentic reactions. Favorable responses will reassure the advertiser, and negative reactions may call for reconsideration of copy design in whole or part. The fact that reactions are both specific and general may clearly point to those elements most in need of change or emphasis.

seven

Laboratory Testing
and Analyses
of Content

TESTS IN AUDITORIUMS

GROUP LABORATORY APPARATUS

GENERAL EVALUATION OF LABORATORY EXPERIMENTS

ANALYSES OF VERBAL CONTENT

IMPLICATIONS

Very little exposure of media advertising occurs under conditions such that the advertiser knows both the time and the place of exposure for most of the advertising. One exception is the advertising in a theater program, sold largely on its promise of exposure in the theater. It is relatively simple to select locations in a theater for objectively observing a sample of the audience and judging the degree of advertising exposure and involvement. Most other general advertising, however, depends primarily upon exposure in relaxed home situations inaccessible to the research man.

The fact that advertising exposure is mostly a private matter imposes a hard task on the researcher. There is no practical way for observers to get into a broadly representative sample of homes and study the natural reception given to advertising. If it is sufficient to use memory-test methods, it is possible to call on consumers after normal advertising exposure. Otherwise, test conditions have to be set up which will limit the sample or will condition the advertising response in some way.

These are the problems which lead the investigator to invite the public to come to his "laboratory" for certain advertising tests; and once the people in the test sample come to the laboratory, it is possible to apply methods and apparatus not easily used in field surveys. Both Gallup & Robinson, Inc., of Princeton and Schwerin Research Corporation of New York have adapted regular theaters for exclusive use in advertising research. They attempt to assemble definable market samples and to obtain evidence of responses to advertisements. Others have equipped special laboratories with devices designed to aid in measuring such advertising responses as attitudes, ocular reactions, and psychogalvanic responses. Actually, nearly all testing equipment can be made portable and taken into the home or another convenient meeting place.

Laboratory evaluation of advertisements without test subjects includes the Flesch method of grading text material and other content analysis methods (see pages 165–170). In this sense, we might even say that there are laboratory tests of advertising that do not require people as subjects!

TESTS IN AUDITORIUMS

An auditorium or studio is convenient for presenting film recordings, simulating a television or radio broadcast. Visual presentations tend to be free of social interchange within the audience; since eyes are directed toward the screen, it is possible to insert numerical cues for opinion votes for the purpose of program analysis (compare Chapter Five).

Burke Marketing Research, Inc., of Cincinnati uses a small studio, called the TV Laboratory, in order to bring people together and obtain information about commercials in the following ways:

1. *Ten-second enjoyment rating.* A measure of the first reaction of the viewers to the commercial, reflecting its attention-getting and holding power. It is based on the electronic recording of viewer attitudes.

2. *General interest rating.* An overall rating of the commercial as to its viewer interest, based on the questionnaire.

3. *Persuasiveness rating.* A measure of the relative influence of the commercial in creating a desire to buy the product advertised.

4. *Believability rating.* A measure of the degree of disbelief.

5. *Good-taste rating.* A measure of the extent of disagreeable or offensive attitudes created by the commercial.

6. *Per cent recalling a sales message.* A measure of the number of viewers able to recall sales points or ideas concerning product advantages.

7. *Number of sales messages recalled per 100 viewers.* A measure of the quantity of sales ideas penetrating the audience.

8. *Sales-message penetration.* A completely detailed content analysis of all sales points recalled by all viewers.

9. *Irrelevant recall.* Primarily video recall and extraneous comments about the commercial that cannot be classified as sales messages.

10. *Reasons for unbelievability.* An explanation of why some viewers did not believe what the commercial said or implied.

11. *Reasons for saying the commercial was not in good taste.* An explanation of what was offensive or objectionable in the commercial.

12. *Enjoyment ratings for specific commercial elements.* A measure of the enjoyment or interest of the viewers in various elements of the commercial, based on the electronic recording of attitudes.

In its Mirror of America auditorium, Gallup & Robinson, Inc., has arranged the seating to resemble a theater full of box seats. Although the advantages of large audience size are retained, it is also possible to subdivide the audience into many smaller clusters for purposes of effective group discussions on one or many topics. Groups of friends or groups with common interests can operate in a relaxed atmosphere without the disadvantages of discussion in large assemblies. Attractive, comfortable furnishings, combined with catering facilities, contribute to informality. When the occasion demands it, the attention of the whole audience can be directed toward the main stage or screen.

The gathering of samples of consumers in an auditorium makes possible all of the advertising pretests ordinarily conducted in field surveys. Television or radio commercials can be screened and, without the haste of individual field interviews, it is practical to present full programs with commercials fitted in. Printed advertising material can be put in the hands of individuals or "blown up" on a screen. Reactions may be measured as opinions, attitudes, comprehension, immediate memory, or some other psychological function. People who are willing to come to a studio, especially if assured of a reward, are usually willing to stay through a lengthy session devoted only partly to "work."

The theater or laboratory has limitations, of course—one being that not all kinds of people in a market or universe are willing to come. If advertisements are to be tested, the exposure is in a situation unlike the normal circumstance in the home. The audience does not happen upon national advertisements in a typical way, and the showing of advertisements is forced —far from ideal for ascertaining audience cooperation and response under normal motivation. Yet forcing has an advantage in that it almost guarantees that the advertisements will be observed—and without this, tests of attitude change and memory are hard to interpret.

There may be a further serious limitation of the theater or studio for testing commercial messages if the commercials concern intimate products or copy references. The Center for Research in Marketing, Inc., which operates a closed-circuit television test panel in a sample of homes based on the use of community antennas, demonstrated this possibility.[1] Women responded with disapproval to the presentation of a certain commercial in a theater, whereas women in their homes gave favorable reactions. The closed-circuit test with a normal television screen is assumed to have further advantages as compared with a large screen for theater projection.

GROUP LABORATORY APPARATUS

Copy research does not lack for mechanical apparatus. Many instruments have been conveniently developed for group measurement. This combines the processes of measuring and tabulating responses. The speed of summing group reactions sometimes adds to the studio session the possibility of oral discussion of findings. Most group-measuring instruments have evolved from designs for individual measurements, although some equipment is not well adapted for group use.

The Program Analyzer, mentioned in Chapters Two and Five, will integrate responses of a number of persons in a test studio, voting their continuous pattern of likes, dislikes, and indifference to the program and to the commercials. Individual reactions may be examined also.

Other voting equipment has been designed to punch tabulating cards continuously, while the respondent watches a program or commercial message. Still other apparatus is calibrated to take into account the intensity of finger pressure by the program viewer so that "degree of enthusiasm" can be recorded. These opinion voting machines do not actually add to the objectivity of the measurement as do most other test instruments. However, they are advantageous in saving time, by bringing together people who can be tested in a relatively short period of time, as contrasted with the time that would be necessary in field surveys.

The *psychogalvanometer*, which keeps a record of changes in galvanic

[1] News bulletin, The Center for Research in Marketing, Inc., Peekskill, N.Y.

responses, has also been developed into a group-testing instrument. Each participant has one hand or finger attached to an electrode, but is free to observe and react to advertisements. Excitement is known to increase sweating activity and thus reduce electrical resistance on the skin surface; it is also possible that nerve activity, which is basically electrical, contributes to the measured changes recorded by the instrument.

In any case, reactions indicated by a psychogalvanometer are amazingly fast, considering that they represent somatic effects of ideas. Within two or three seconds an initial response to a test advertisement is indicated, and this may be followed by ten to twenty seconds of more steady reaction. If the advertisement is kept exposed for a minute, it is unlikely to provide much more evidence of continued reaction, although the copy may lead to more than one peak reaction.

Unlike the opinion voting machines, the psychogalvanometer is a completely objective measuring instrument. The question of validity, for advertising research, is another matter. Certainly interpretations of the meaning of galvanic patterns have not become definitive. Extreme fluctuations of the record may indicate excitement, attraction, repulsion, perplexity—or what? Each test subject has a different basic level at the start of every test and, considering the atypical conditions of advertising exposure, it is difficult to know how the galvanic record relates to normal advertising response. It can be said with assurance, of course, that advertisements producing little galvanic change are probably too neutral to cause much reaction or response under normal circumstances.

Other instruments, sensitive to changes in pulse rate, blood pressure, and respiratory rate, reflect changes in feelings and have been adapted for uses similar to the psychogalvanometer. Many other reflexes also indicate states of feeling; dilation of the pupil of the eye is a notable example, and has even been proposed as a means of testing interest in TV commercials.

In an effort to relate somatic responses to advertising stimuli, the hypothesis was once advanced that the initial reaction might correspond with initial attention. Twelve Chicago transportation advertisements, already measured for audience size, were tested with a psychogalvanometer.[2] The evidence of attention in the market survey correlated moderately well (+.51) with the laboratory results from the galvanometer, but the corre-

_____

[2] *The Continuing Study of Transportation Advertising, Study No. 7, Chicago, Ill.,* Advertising Research Foundation, Inc., Study No. 7 (May, 1946). Also, Darrell Blaine Lucas and Steuart Henderson Britt, *Advertising Psychology and Research* (New York: McGraw-Hill Book Company, Inc., 1950), p. 468.

but motivated perusing and selective reading are usually ruled out. Eye movements within a particular layout may remain somewhat normal in front of a camera, but a normal choice of which layouts to look at and for how long is not likely.

The recording eye camera appears to be objective in a technical sense. With a broader interpretation of objectivity, though, two points may be questioned. One point relates to the naturalness of eye movement within a layout—does a person being tested follow his personal choices in locations and sequence of examining a pictorial display, or does he try to impress the investigator? Insofar as the reader consciously diverts from his preferred reading path, he reduces the objective value of the test. The second point has to do with the interpretation of the record in relation to the exposed material. Ordinarily, there is opportunity for at least a 2-inch error in determining the actual area perceived, and the investigator has this margin within which to exercise his own personal bias (even though unconsciously) in reporting his findings.

Photographic records of actual audiences of "billboards" have been employed by Alfred Politz Research for the practical purpose of estimating media audiencess (see Chapter Twelve). Traffic studies made with cameras concealed near outdoor posters reveal the number of people within sight over a given period. The camera is set to make a systematic sample of time through properly spaced exposures. Measures of audiences of traveling displays on the outside of buses are made by having a camera "looking out" of the bus window and systematically taking pictures of pedestrians and other traffic. In this application, it is assumed that people on the same street with both eyes visible to the camera are potential viewers of the traveling displays.

A laboratory method for *pretesting* outdoor-advertising designs consists of an instrument that "resembles a driver-trainer device used to train beginning drivers. The driver's hands are on a steering wheel while he peers through a viewer. His job is to keep a miniature car on the road—the posters going by are just part of the passing scene. After he has completed his drive, he is asked to recall what he saw." [5]

Direct observations of test subjects, without their knowledge, can be achieved with nothing more complicated than a small peephole in the wall near the displayed material. A much more satisfactory device is the *one-way*

[5] Edmund W. J. Faison, "Pre-testing Outdoor Advertising Designs," *Outdoor Advertising Association of America News,* Vol. 51 (November, 1960), pp. 22–23, 34–35.

mirror, which permits easy viewing through a special window that does not expose the observer. Subjects may be brought to a room and asked to wait briefly; during the waiting time, they are supplied with reading matter, including the test material. One or more observers behind the one-way windows can then keep a record of reading behavior in a relaxed atmosphere.

This method has been used considerably by the Curtis Publishing Company. For instance, when a person is brought into a reception area, he may be given a copy of *The Saturday Evening Post* and told to take as long as he likes in reading it (up to perhaps an hour and a half). While he reads, a hidden observer records the amount of time spent between page turnings. By employing comparative treatments, the relative effectiveness of headline placement, type of pictorial material, etc., may be checked. The legal problems of hidden observation by an observer located in another room are said to be solved by placing a receptionist who works busily on her own affairs at a desk in a far corner of the room. This method is less precise than the eye camera, but it is more natural, as the person wears no gear and does not even realize that he is being observed.

Ocular equipment which throws competing images before the two eyes offers a unique test of selective attention. After ruling out the possibility that the dominant eye is the determining factor, it has been possible to demonstrate that some stimuli will effectively dominate over others. Such tests of two possible covers of *The Saturday Evening Post* have shown which one tends to be perceived when both have equal stimulus advantage.

An improved design of binocular equipment has been developed by HRB-Singer, Inc., called VISTA. A VISTA unit was used by the manufacturer in experimental work conducted for the Advertising Research Foundation.[6] The binocular test was applied along with controlled tests of distance, illumination, and time of exposure of advertisements. The combination of all four tests showed multiple correlations of less than +.50 with available recognition ratings and recall scores on the same advertisements (compare Chapters Three and Four). However, each of the four tests was used to isolate factors in advertisements which seemed to be related to high ratings. When these factors were developed in new advertisements, the binocular and distance tests proved consistent; the illumination and time of exposure test did not.

[6] Robert E. Stover, "Can Visual Effectiveness of Advertisements Be Controlled?" speech presented at the Seventh Annual Conference of the Advertising Research Foundation, Inc., New York, October 3, 1961.

The binocular test has to do with *visual dominance*. So that this concept will be clear, compare it with the loudness of sounds in the following situation—if a person were to wear a set of earphones, with one tune being played in one ear and another in the other ear, the louder or more dominant tune normally would be the one that would "come through" to the listener. It is the same way with the "loudness" or dominance of visual stimuli measured in binocular tests.

Whatever may be the limitations of the binocular test, it appears to be remarkably independent of the factors which normally motivate advertisement noting. The totally atypical advertising situation in which people look at two advertisements simultaneously through an optical instrument produces an effect that is largely out of the control of the viewer. He does not consciously select which advertisement to see and will continue to see a dominant advertisement unless he closes the eye viewing it. The phenomenon is so consistent that it is largely independent of usual eye dominance, even though one eye may strongly dominate in direct viewing under ordinary circumstances.

The binocular test demonstrates the selectivity of both attention and perception and their important roles in sensory experience. There is an implication that when advertisements occupy facing magazine pages, one advertisement may register with the reader somewhat to the exclusion of the other. If this is the meaning of binocular tests, the early HRB-Singer experimental studies of physical advertising designs may lead to important principles of effective display.

Visibility meters which test a printed display without the need for human subjects have been developed and proposed for certain uses. A meter which is calibrated to measure contrast in a printed surface has been used to estimate legibility of type. A similar principle is used in other equipment designed to estimate the visibility or vividness of illustrative material and other attention incentives of printed advertisements.

Here are two thumbnail case histories, derived from the experience of one of the authors, which show how laboratory methods have helped to solve specific advertising problems.

Case History 1: Comparing the Effectiveness of Two Ads. For a well-known advertiser, a four-color, full-page advertisement was developed for use in *This Week* magazine. Although this was obviously powerful advertising, several of us wondered whether a black-and-white ad, using somewhat larger space, wouldn't be more effective. (This larger black-and-white advertisement would cost approximately the same as the four-color ad.)

To test this idea, another ad was prepared in which the left-hand page was identical with the one in color (except, of course, that it was in black-and-white) and two-fifths of a page were added on the right-hand sheet, immediately adjoining. Continuing photographs were made of the eye movements of two comparable groups of women as they individually read magazines in which the two ads had been inserted. It was found that the black-and-white advertisement *was looked at for twice as long* a period as the four-color advertisement; in addition, it was determined that the women *could recall twice as much* of the content of the black-and-white advertisement.

The decision was obvious: namely, to use the black-and-white advertisement. (It should, of course, be pointed out that no generalization as to the relative merits of color or black-and-white advertising is intended here; the recommendation was limited to the specific advertisement being studied.)

Case History 2: Testing a Copy Phrase. A new package was developed by a food company, and a new copy phrase was to be used to describe a special feature of the package so that it would be easy to remember and request at the store. Before the final advertising copy was prepared, the company wanted to know whether this new copy phrase would be immediately understood in print advertising. Accordingly, a "rough" ad which featured the copy phrase in its headline was shown in a special flash-exposure box to a number of individuals. The advertisement was flashed on for six seconds. After this, each person was asked to describe what he had seen. As a control—that is, for purposes of comparison—the same procedure was repeated with another advertisement which played up the package features themselves rather than the copy phrase.

The results of this test indicated that the copy phrase was not quickly understood. It became meaningful in the first advertisement only after the package feature had been explained by the second advertisement. On the basis of these findings it was decided to use television commercials instead of print advertising to introduce the new package. Thus, after the superiority of the special package feature had been clearly demonstrated, the copy phrase used at the end of the commercial would be more meaningful.[7]

GENERAL EVALUATION OF LABORATORY EXPERIMENTS

All of the methods and instruments discussed thus far in this chapter—except visibility meters—require the availability of test subjects, usually coming to an appointed place. An exception is the measurement of ad-

[7] Steuart Henderson Britt, "The Application of Social Science Findings to Advertising," *Aspects of Modern Marketing: Tools, Techniques, and Market Trends,* American Management Association Report No. 15 (1958), pp. 94–100, at pp. 98–99.

vertising opportunity in public places, such as the highways and streets exposed to various types of posters. Another is the limited amount of print and broadcast advertising exposure occurring in waiting rooms, libraries, and places of refreshment or entertainment. Otherwise, the methods discussed in this context may be suspect in that the auditorium or laboratory circumstances restrict survey samples and affect responses to advertising.

Auditorium and laboratory tests generally have a considerable advantage, however, in the opportunity to set up controlled conditions. This equalizes the test situation for the purpose of making comparisons or copy choices. Generally, the methods and instruments available in the laboratory offer a high degree of objectivity, minimizing the influence of deliberate bias on the part of either the test subjects or the investigator. The problem of stable sample size is usually no greater than in field research, and frequently smaller samples can be used.

The crucial consideration in evaluating these test methods—in comparison with either pretesting or posttesting in the field—is largely centered on the quality of the samples and on the naturalness of advertising exposure. Sometimes, as in the case of the psychogalvanometer, there is a question as to just what the instrument measures. One cannot safely take findings from the studio or laboratory and use them for practical advertising decisions without considering whether the test measures the intended quality under sufficiently normal advertising circumstances and with a reasonably representative sample. As Draper Daniels, formerly executive vice-president in charge of the Creative Departments of the Leo Burnett Company, has well said:

> The primary idea of such devices is to help creative people determine the probable effectiveness of new advertising approaches, the speed and clarity with which an advertisement or commercial communicates to the consumer, or which of two or more solutions to a creative problem seems to offer the most promise. In other words, the principal purpose is to provide assistance to judgment, which can help to make more effective advertising.

This means that these kinds of devices are not used as a means of *finally evaluating* the effectiveness of given advertisements. The limitations imposed by the sample biases involved in such research and the obvious artificiality of such measures preclude any completely sound evaluation. Nevertheless, even though the resulting data are in general not projectable, they may provide an invaluable feedback from consumers to creative people *while* the actual creative process is under way.

ANALYSES OF VERBAL CONTENT

Three important methods have been developed for evaluating verbal content without the use of special mechanical equipment. Two of these methods, the Flesch method and content analysis, do not even require the use of people as subjects; the third method, the cloze procedure, does require people. The ease and accuracy with which words may be used to communicate ideas and to motivate the audience may be estimated in a general way by the creative writer or by the research executive. But such judgments are open to human bias, preconceptions, and other limitations.

This has inspired a considerable effort to devise ways of making more refined estimates, either by introducing greater objectivity or by improvement in basic validity. Two such procedures will be discussed here.

Flesch Method

A method developed over a period of years by Rudolf Flesch assumes that difficulties of reading level are largely based on the number of words per sentence and the average number of syllables per word.[8] It is also assumed that reader motivation, which contributes to a reduction of reading difficulty, is related to the frequency of appearance of personal references.

At one time Flesch combined all three factors into one formula score, but he has since evaluated motivation separately. The levels of reading difficulty have been standardized against grade levels for reading in schools. Since detailed description and examples of the Flesch method are found in his own writings, they will not be elaborated here.

The point is, for our purposes, that advertising copy can repel readers if the difficulty of reading is too great. Traditionally, the advertiser has used short sentences to increase persuasive power. He has implied a good deal of personal reference, more to motivate the purchase than the act of reading. But the use of long technical words and invented word combinations sometimes has tended to offset the advantage of short sentences. Meanwhile, the number of consumers able to read easily above the eighth-grade level has steadily increased, although it should also be said that about one-fourth of the adults in the United States read no magazines regularly. Obviously, copy can best be geared to the audience of a particular medium.

It is true that the Flesch procedure can be challenged. Big, concrete words

[8] Rudolf Flesch, *The Art of Plain Talk* (New York: Harper & Brothers, 1946). Rudolf Flesch, "A New Readability Yardstick," *Journal of Applied Psychology*, Vol. 32 (June, 1948), pp. 221–233.

in a rich context may be read easily, whereas little, abstract, unfamiliar words may make reading difficult. Also, long sentences, used by a popular or controversial personality, may not discourage people from reading. Style itself may do much to offset violations of mechanical form.

Nevertheless, Rudolf Flesch and various magazine editors have demonstrated that the same article may have its reading audience increased as much as 50 per cent by being rewritten according to Flesch standards. Regardless of whether there can be exceptions or whether the seasoned copywriter has much to learn from Flesch, the beginner would do well to study his principles. The copy tester may find his chief use of Flesch scores in demonstrating that greater readership goes with simpler writing.

Cloze Procedure

Some of the criticisms of the Flesch method are overcome in a unique testing procedure called the "cloze procedure." [9] It is related to the term "closure" in gestalt psychology.

The method, which uses human subjects, takes into account the familiarity of words, of content, and of pattern of prose. The test consists of dropping out a sample of words from a context and having the subjects guess the exact words which have been deleted. The recommended steps are as follows:

1. Drop out various single words, without regard to the size of each word, selected to be representative of the entire composition.

2. The sample of words can be selected at random or systematically from the whole piece, but the dropouts can be as close as every fifth word. (This would limit the number of words selected from short selections and reduce the reliability of such tests.)

3. Leave a standardized blank space for each omitted word. (The standard length of space indicates that the size of space is not intended to suggest the length of the missing word.)

4. Choose a sample of people to represent the intended audience. Actually, convenient samples may be used, since the results are interpreted on a comparative basis.

5. Have each respondent fill in the blank spaces with what he thinks is the most likely word.

[9] Wilson L. Taylor, "Cloze Procedure: a New Tool For Measuring Readability," *Journalism Quarterly*, Vol. 30 (Fall, 1953), pp. 415–433. Wilson L. Taylor, "Recent Developments in the Use of Cloze Procedure," *Journalism Quarterly*, Vol. 33 (Winter, 1956), pp. 42–48, 99.

6. Count the number of precisely correct answers and determine the average for the sample. Each composition or copy unit can be tested with the same group of subjects and the scores compared.

Little experience with this method on advertising has been reported, but it has promise comparable to the Flesch method, with some indicated advantages. Actually, the two methods have been demonstrated to agree on conventional prose, but only the cloze procedure will detect the difficulty of reading or understanding unconventional writing. Cloze procedure measures comprehension as well as ease of reading, and can be used to test the abilities of individuals as well as the readability of the material. It can be applied to spoken words as well as written matter. In essence, cloze procedure takes account of the fact that language is not a simple function of words, but depends heavily upon context and pattern as well.

Content Analysis

A phrase applied to procedures which, like the Flesch method, can be used to evaluate written material by examining its content is "content analysis." No test sample of people is required, although more than one judge or analyst may work as a check on another. Definitions and standards are set up at the outset and then applied systematically to all or a sample of the material to be evaluated. The application may be directly to the headline and text of advertisements or to any kind of verbatim responses related to advertisements. For example, playback or attitude responses or any other kind of verbal responses to advertising copy may be examined in this way. The interpretation of the Macleod study (discussed in Chapter Six) was based on content analysis.[10]

The value of content analysis is based largely on the assumption that generalized estimates of what a body of words communicates are likely to be inaccurate. The writer of an advertisement may reread the copy and conclude that it tells the audience what he wants it to tell. An investigator may glance over verbatim remarks in a survey, such as responses to attitude questions, and conclude that they are favorable or otherwise. Even the unbiased observer may read material and form early judgments of such a positive nature that his final conclusion merely confirms his early impressions.

Content analysis avoids or reduces these pitfalls of general evaluation by

[10] Jennifer S. Macleod, *Predicting the Responses to Advertising Themes from Sentence Completions or Direct Attitude Questions about an Advertised Product* (New York: Advertising Research Foundation, Inc, 1958).

examining minute details at every stage and by compiling a total score for the communication. The score may be actually a group of scores on separate aspects.

Since the Macleod report shows a meticulous and skillful application of content analysis, its procedures will be used to illustrate the main steps of content analysis. Three distinct applications of the method covered the written copy in the advertisements themselves, the scaled responses to attitude questions about the products, and the completions of projective sentences used as copy tests.

The first step in content analysis is selection of a basic verbal unit; in this case, whole sentences or sentence completions were chosen. Words, phrases, or larger units are sometimes made the basis for evaluation.

It was important in the Macleod experiment to determine the kinds and intensities of ideas communicated by the automobile advertisements. Since the attitude responses and sentence completions were used to evaluate the advertisements, it was desirable to determine whether these verbatim responses reflected the attributes and consumer benefits alleged in the advertisements. In order to do this, it was necessary to make another preliminary step, which is the defining of practically every specific content category related to the problem. This requires some examining of contents—not to evaluate but solely to discover the variations of ideas, appeals, features, and other elements which can be defined as categories. This can be done by one or several investigators and is necessarily subjective. The Macleod study defined 98 specific content categories relating to the automobile advertisements and the test responses.

The next step in content analysis is for one or more coders or judges to classify the units according to the established categories. As a precaution, Macleod used three judges to classify sentences in the advertising copy. Sentence completions were simple enough to be done consistently by a single judge. The attitude responses were coded in the process of development and required no further coding. All of the advertising copy and all of the test responses were classified for the purposes of this study. Long compositions may require only a systematic sample of parts to be analyzed.

The next step may require somewhat subjective decisions or processes. Weights may be assigned to categories, and even the assumption of equality or unity of all values amounts to weighting. Macleod gave each copy sentence a weight of 1, but arbitrarily assigned weights of 3 and 2 to headlines and subheads, respectively. Completions had a weight of 1, but since they might agree or disagree with a category, the values ranged from $+1$ to 0

and on to —1. This scaling method, applied to attitude statements, established five levels; the values could be anywhere from +2 on through +1, 0, —1, and —2. It is desirable to use judgment to the extent of assigning weights for evaluation in content analysis, but this must be classified as a subjective step.

The algebraic summation of scores for each defined category is likely to result in an unwieldy numerical finding. This can be offset largely by the further step of grouping related categories into a smaller number of indexes. The 98 defined categories in the Macleod study were grouped into 18 broader indexes. The algebraic sum of the plus and minus scores was then determined for each index. Internal tests, or retests for consistency, were then used, with the result that some of the indexes had to be dropped.

Procedure beyond the establishment of scores on index grouping may vary considerably. Macleod arbitrarily divided the general indexes at points which would put equal numbers of respondents in "high" and "low" groups. This was an ingenious means which made it possible to set up fourfold tables for comparing the two copy-research methods on each index. It also provided quantitative comparisons which could be tested for statistical significance.

This is one of the impressive features about content analysis—as compared with gross subjective evaluations of verbal material, together with intuitive judgments of significance. The discussion here concerning content analysis should not imply that there is any stereotype of methods, but rather that there is an opportunity for each investigator to devise an approach well suited to his particular problem.[11]

As an example, one researcher has developed a procedure dubbed the "Content Response Code," which could be used with respect to advertising.

Subjects make small marginal plus and minus marks directly beside printed material to which they have positive or negative reactions. Instructions, which emphasize spontaneity and candor in marking, explain the marking procedure in terms of such "good/bad" word pairs as fair/unfair, true/untrue, and valuable/worthless.

Marks made by subjects are coded into a master copy of the communication which has been divided into content units. . . . Response-profile results are used to select units for presentation in a follow-up session in which the units

[11] For a detailed treatment of content analysis, see Bernard Berelson, *Content Analysis in Communications Research* (Glencoe, Ill.: Free Press, 1952). Also see Ithia de Sola Pool, *Trends in Content Analysis* (Urbana, Ill.: University of Illinois Press, 1959).

are projected on a screen and the subjects' original responses are reinstated by returning to them their own marked [materials].

Respondents then fill out answer booklets in which, for each reinstated unit, they record the nature of the original response, the specific words or phrases (if any) responded to, and their general feelings about the reinstated material. Tabulation and thematic analysis of these written responses complete the procedure.[12]

Such a method, of course, does involve the use of people, but it is mentioned here to indicate that there are various methods of content analysis. The advantages of systematic, detailed content analysis are most striking when dealing with discussions involving intimate or socially conflicting motives. This would be the case with advertising which might suggest the substitution of margarine for butter, artificial sweetening for sugar, or synthetic fibers for linen. If the manufacturer turns the problem over to the people in his advertising department or research staff, they will have difficulty in forming unbiased judgments. If a preliminary survey uses a direct approach, the respondents are likely to distort their replies according to their own prejudices. If unstructured interviews are used, the advertising or research administrator is likely to see in them confirmation of his own established prejudices. Even if the investigator attempts to read verbatim comments with an open mind, there is a serious danger of arriving at early conclusions tentative and then proceeding to confirm them with the balance of the responses.

This means that there is an ideal opportunity for content analysis. Even the trained investigator is likely to find content analysis leading him to conclusions or evaluations different from his first or general impressions.

In one instance, research on fibers for products used in contact with the human body seemed generally favorable to a new substitute. More as a precaution than because of any serious doubt, the investigator decided to employ thorough content analysis. The findings led to a reversal of conclusions in the report, and test marketing later demonstrated low acceptance for the substitute. Those who participated in the study frankly stated that their own conclusions were changed by content analysis, although none would say that the numerical findings of this procedure would dictate decisions. The findings merely furnished additional guidance to the forming of decisions.

[12] Roy E. Carter, Jr., "The Content Response Code: a Pre-testing Procedure," *Journalism Quarterly,* Vol. 32 (Spring, 1955), pp. 147–160, quoted material from pp. 159–160.

In other words, there is much to recommend the application of content analysis as a direct test of copy. The copywriter quite naturally feels that an advertisement communicates what he intended. Headline writers and illustrators or visualizers also aim at communicating intended ideas and impressions, and yet projective methods (see Chapter Six) may indicate that visual and verbal displays are not adequate. The running text may also be inadequate because those who write are sometimes too close to their own work or aiming at the wrong audience level.

Content analysis offers a means of more objectively assessing the effectiveness of communications. Almost every writer can gain by having some experience with this technique.

IMPLICATIONS

All testing of advertising in the laboratory may seem at least partially invalid because of the conditions involved. The limited types of people who can be gathered together and the forced conditions of advertising exposure set immediate limits to the usefulness of the approach. The artificial atmosphere may place even more limitations on the validity of certain types of findings.

Nevertheless, the studio and the laboratory make it possible to apply procedures not practical for population-sampling surveys under normal conditions of advertising exposure. They permit intensification of advertising exposure and immediate measurement, before time and conflicting impressions have eroded intended effects. Obviously, the abnormal conditions of testing must be taken into account, but in the absence of better research, the findings of the studio and the laboratory may greatly aid the judgment process.

Those evaluating methods which do not require people as subjects—such as the Flesch method and content analysis—are quite specialized. The cloze procedure serves a similar purpose in evaluating either written or spoken words, but it does require a sample of people.

Measurements of visibility, legibility, readability, and communication by laboratory methods and analyses of content permit of many exceptions and revised conclusions, but their chief value is in their relative objectivity and as sources of confirmation or unique information. Advertisement builders may sometimes find such evidence extremely helpful. They may reject this kind of information, but when this is done knowingly and for clearly understood reasons, the hazards are likely to be small.

eight

Inquiries and Sales Measures

INQUIRIES

MEASURES RELATED TO SALES

INTERVIEWING CUSTOMERS

CORRELATION OF ADVERTISING AND SALES

PRETESTING IN SELECTED SALES AREAS

FUTURE BUYING BEHAVIOR

IMPLICATIONS

Many advertisements aim at ultimate response in the form of buying behavior or some intermediate step, such as making an inquiry. Advertisements that explicitly request such overt responses are relatively easy to evaluate, assuming that the solicited response is immediate and is the only major objective.

The evaluation is further facilitated if the advertisement contains an order form or coupon or if the responses are in any way keyed to specific advertisements. Most order forms and coupons bear some identification of the specific advertisement and medium.

INQUIRIES

The reasons for soliciting inquiries vary. Usually the inquiry is intended to aid the selling process directly, but sometimes inquiries are solicited primarily to test the effectiveness of the advertising message. Sales may be aided by using inquiries as leads for salesmen, or by following up directly with literature and samples designed to convert inquiries into sales.

If, on the other hand, inquiries are sought primarily for the purpose of testing copy, the strategy is quite different. The number of inquiries is often a very small fraction of the total number of people the advertiser expects to stimulate. A few thousand inquiries may become the basis for estimating advertising impact upon millions of prospective buyers. This discussion is chiefly concerned with soliciting inquiries for the purpose of testing copy.

How Inquiries Relate to Advertising Effect

When a national advertiser invites inquiries primarily to test copy, it is assumed that he does not expect to make a profit solely from sales to respondents. Instead, the overt actions of those who respond are taken as evidence that some useful impressions were made on a much larger audience.

If the responses appear to reflect genuine interest in the product, the advertiser probably assumes that a great many more people were at least partially interested, but not enough to make an inquiry. If returns from two or more advertisements are compared under similar circumstances, the advertiser may assume that the advertisement producing more inquiries has also done a better job with the whole audience, but this is not necessarily true.

One of the determining factors in any response is the attractiveness of the offer. If the offer is too good, people will tell others about it. This may lead to requests from people who had no contact with the advertisement at all. When this happens, it gives little evidence of the merit of the advertising message under test.

At the opposite extreme is the offer which is so unattractive that practically no one responds. When response is too low, the advertiser finds himself without adequate data to make a decision. If inquiries are to be meaningful at all, it is first necessary to design an offer which is relevant and which is neither too attractive nor too unattractive.

Logical offers include small product samples, additional product information, and gifts. Novelty gifts should be used only when their intrinsic value is small and when it can reasonably be assumed that the respondent made thorough examination of the advertisement. Only inquiries requesting additional product information are likely to ensure that the response is motivated by genuine interest aroused by the advertising message. It is quite difficult to obtain a substantial number of bona fide inquiries for additional information on most products, although a return coupon is usually helpful.

The Return Coupon

Mail order advertisements or those seeking immediate sales leads make regular use of boxed-in return coupon forms in order to make responses easier and more numerous. Advertisers interested in testing broader copy appeals may also use return coupons, but this may give too much emphasis to the offer. The number of replies is likely to be more than doubled, but the evidence of impact of the copy is less clear. There are several reasons why return coupons increase responses to an offer, even though the copy may not be basically designed for direct action.

The psychological advantages of a coupon form begin with the fact that the coupon draws attention to the offer. It is not even necessary for the reader to go through copy details in order to discover the coupon. Many coupon-carrying advertisements include captions and visual devices directing the reader to the offer. The normal attention-getting power of the coupon, coupled with extra emphasis in the copy, helps to explain the great increase in inquiries to offers accompanied by coupons.

The coupon not only draws attention to an advertising offer, but also suggests that the reader take action. To a degree, a reader must psychologically reject the offer in order to pass by the coupon provided for his response. Frequently the advertiser compounds his suggestion by means of captions and copy, urging the reader to mail the coupon. In this way, the inherent suggestive influence of the coupon is heightened by the suggestions made in the surrounding copy.

Another psychological factor favoring response to a coupon form is present when the respondent is relieved of further obligation. When an advertiser invites an inquiry, he assumes any related obligation. Very often, the advertiser explicitly relieves the respondent of obligation, using such words as, "Without obligation, please send me . . ." The word "free" may also be featured in the headline, in the copy text, and in the coupon itself. The relief from obligation, inherent in a coupon response, is fortified by these explicit assurances given by the advertiser.

The most obvious psychological advantage of the return coupon is its convenience for making the proper request. It provides both the physical form and the exact verbal instructions for obtaining the thing offered to the reader. The advertiser may further simplify the response by suggesting that it be pinned to the reader's letterhead or pasted on a postcard. Some publications make it possible simply to tear off a franked self-addressed coupon after inserting the reader's address and to drop it in the mailbox. Another possibility is to invite readers to telephone or telegraph collect.

The theory of measurement through coupon returns may be stated quite simply. If two advertisements for the same product are identical except for a headline or lead element designed to attract attention and to "get people into the ad," then the number of returns of the coupons from one advertisement as compared with the returns from the other advertisement provides useful information. In fact, this is quite a sensible method of determining the relative value of a headline (or lead illustration) as compared with a different headline (or lead illustration).

On the other hand, the use of coupons for measurement would be undesirable in many, if not most, advertisements; they would get in the way of the basic advertisement itself. It would be out of place to add a coupon to the usual advertisement for cigarettes, automobiles, and most other commodities.

Inspection of coupon returns on consumer magazine advertisements will quickly reveal the techniques used to draw attention to the offer, to urge the response, to relieve the respondent of obligation, and to make the response as easy as possible.

Relationship of Inquiries to Reading Interest

Inquiries from single advertisements run in thousands, whereas an advertisement may be directed toward millions of people. The attachment of a coupon, reinforced with every justifiable inducement, is not likely to bring inquiries from more than a small percentage of the people whom an effective general advertisement must influence. Accordingly, since the noting and reading audiences of advertisements can be measured, it is logical to compare coupon returns with estimates of total reader interest.

Daniel Starch, whose readership research service bears his name, has made extensive comparisons of inquiries with Starch scores on noting and reading.[1] While there is some general tendency for advertisements with high Starch scores on noting to obtain above average returns from offers or coupons, there is no justification for relying upon inquiries to reflect

[1] Daniel Starch, "An Analysis of 12 Million Inquiries," *Media/scope*, Vol. 3 (January, 1959), pp. 23–27; (February, 1959), pp. 38–43; (March, 1959), pp. 40–44.

Starch ratings or readership. Even when the Starch analysis was restricted to the coupon part of the advertisement, there was no consistent relationship between Starch ratings and replying to individual advertisements. Copy which interests many readers and supplies wanted information may, by that very fact, reduce the motivation for further inquiry. This may explain why so little correlation has been observed between inquiry returns and readership ratings of informative technical advertisements in industrial publications.

Generalized interpretations of the meaning of a large volume of responses from a coupon are complicated by the fact that most consumers *never* clip any magazine coupon. They prefer to consult other sources for information or to buy and try new products. The readers of some publications are extremely unresponsive to coupon offers, although they may prove excellent customers. There are also seasonal differences in coupon returns for most products, as well as general seasonal differences in coupon flow—February and October normally bring much higher responses than June and December. Economic slumps are likely to stimulate responses to free offers, and new products may bring more inquiries than well-established ones. When these and other factors are added to the variable influence of the specific offer, there can be little justification for projecting a few thousand inquiries to the response of the whole audience of an advertisement. Nor can the effectiveness of advertising media be safely judged on this basis alone.

Split-run Inquiry Tests

Much of the confusion in evaluating inquiries from advertisements—with or without coupons—can be resolved through the use of split runs in the same issue of the same publication. Many publications permit an advertiser to use the same space for two or more copy variations in systematic rotation throughout the entire circulation. If it is desired to test two advertisements, every other copy coming off the press will carry the same insertion. This permits simultaneous circulation of two or more advertisements in identical editorial surroundings with comparable audiences.

If inquiries or mail orders are the only objective of two advertisements and if there is a statistically important difference in returns, the interpretation of a split run is simple. If, however, the aim is to test different copy elements or to estimate impact on the whole audience, many more precautions are needed. Variations of basic appeal, displayed in dissimilar layouts with varying emphasis upon the offer or coupon, become too complicated for ready analysis. If there are also variations in the nature of wording of the offer or structure of the coupon, little analysis is possible.

On the other hand, responses to offers buried in the running text, where only one copy element has been changed, may provide convincing evidence of direct action and possibly of general reader interest. Conclusions should never be drawn before a thorough appraisal of all internal and external factors has been made.

Broadcast Offers

Solicitation of inquiries through broadcasting can be used for some of the same purposes as printed offers. The tendency has been to insert offers in broadcast messages more for sales promotion purposes than as actual tests of particular commercial messages.

There have been some spectacular responses to offers on television and radio. Spoken suggestions to respond by letter or by telephone are more persuasive than those in print, although the convenience of a coupon is lacking. The split-run idea is not easily adaptable for broadcasting, but groups of similar markets can be used for experiment and comparison, and within a single broadcast medium a "staggered" sampling of time units might be arranged.

MEASURES RELATED TO SALES

Since nearly all advertisements are intended to facilitate sales, it is clear that any direct measurement of selling influence is of interest in copy research. If the national advertiser had a practical procedure for measurement of the sales influence of individual advertisements, he could quickly achieve mastery over his advertising techniques heretofore enjoyed only by retailers and mail-order advertisers.

Basically, there are three approaches to sales evaluation of specific advertisements and of entire advertising campaigns. Although no one of the three methods has proved to be a complete evaluator of the sales influence of general national advertisements, all three can contribute helpful evidence.

The *first* method is a direct questioning approach, in which customers are asked to report the influence of advertisements on their purchases. A *second* approach attempts to relate product purchases or ownership to advertising exposure or expenditure, and this includes the application of mathematical analysis and the technique of correlation. A *third* method is the application of controlled experiments to limited markets or areas as a means of estimating later sales impact on the total market, and sales area tests will be discussed in the latter group.

Each of these methods will be discussed in the following three sections.

INTERVIEWING CUSTOMERS

There are many reasons why it is difficult to get comprehensive information from customers which will reveal the influence of specific advertisements on their purchases.

One obstacle which we immediately encounter is that most people believe they generate their own decisions and will actually deny the influence of advertisements. Social barriers to the admission of certain influences have arisen, and it has become popular to disavow the acceptance of advertising. Since the accumulated advertising contribution to any single purchase may go back over a period of years, it is understandable why direct probes of the consumer's motivation have tended to be so fruitless.

Much advertising expenditure is assumed to help hold loyal customers, but the effects are more dynamic when people are induced to try new products or brands. Consumer-purchase panels, wherein families report a continuous record of purchases, provide information on changes of brands. If an investigator is quick to follow up brand changes with an interview, there is an increased likelihood of learning the underlying causes of change. Even under these favorable conditions, direct questions about the influence of advertising on the purchase of small items have revealed little to justify advertising costs.

George Gallup, whose contributions to recognition and recall research are recounted in Chapters Three and Four, has reported success with a different approach for obtaining testimony from new buyers of brands and products.[2] Women in a probability sample of households were asked in detail about circumstances surrounding recent product brands purchased for the first time. They were asked to try to recall where they got the idea leading to the new purchase. Questioning goes *from* the purchase *to* the advertising, instead of the more traditional method which tries to go from the advertising to the purchase. Advertising is treated as a cause for action, and hence the name *Activation* research, as used by George Gallup.

Much of the Gallup & Robinson activation interview is devoted to documentation of the initial testimony as to advertising effect. Respondents

---

[2] George Gallup, *ACTIVATION: a Major Development in Advertising Research* (Princeton, N.J.: Gallup & Robinson, Inc., June, 1957).

are required to recall what the advertising looked like and said and where it appeared. If television was the medium, people are probed for program name, date, content, and other means of verification. Physical proof of the possession of products is also requested. If a product is missing from the shelf because it has already been consumed, the housewife is asked to give a detailed account to support that fact. Elaborate inventories, especially of pantry and bathroom articles, are sought in order to ensure maximum coverage of possible purchases of all related products.

Activation surveys lead to the development of an index number for each reported product brand; and the relationship between index numbers and sales is studied. There has been notable success in tracing brand switches and new product introductions, especially where heavy television advertising has been used. Results for magazines and other national media are also reported.

According to George H. Gallup, more recent activation explorations have aimed at measurement of advertising influence on three major categories of customer. Not only is the new brand buyer studied but also the repeat buyers and those who fluctuate in their choices of brands. Mathematical analysis is applied to the survey data in order to establish the weights of these three categories in evaluating the total advertising effort.

While Gallup & Robinson have reported a considerably higher level of advertising effect by these methods than have other investigators, people in the advertising industry have been somewhat cautious in their acceptance of the method and the findings. It is difficult to assess the promise and the value of consumer testimony on the sales influence of advertising. One basic objection is that the method seems to measure change in buying, but if a woman has been buying Kellogg's Corn Flakes (for example) for her family for a good many years, she is not nearly so likely to answer that she was influenced by the advertisement to buy this product as would another woman who is buying the product for the first time.

Most research investigators in this area of buying behavior have given up before finding sufficient evidence to justify more than a small part of advertising costs. Others have obtained such a disproportionate advantage of broadcasting over other media as to suspect their own findings.

Certainly television is a dramatic medium; and when a commercial message is closely associated with a program, it is relatively easy to recall and identify it in an interview. High television scores may reflect poor interviewing technique, but may also simply reflect the strength of the broadcasting medium.

Paul F. Lazarsfeld of Columbia University has expressed a strong belief that interviews made with customers can identify those who bought a product brand as a result of advertising or of advertising in a specific medium.[8] It would first be necessary through a process of detailed questioning to bring out references to advertising influence and then to trace and confirm each influence. This means that the respondent would have to be capable of recalling advertising impressions. Lazarsfeld has recommended a procedure for gathering actual sales data or experimenting. His plan calls for comparison between people exposed and not exposed to advertising, for application through comparative evidence obtained by treating major sales territories differently, and for mathematical analysis of the data. All these factors will be brought into the discussion in the next section.

CORRELATION OF ADVERTISING AND SALES

While most national advertisers find it extremely difficult to measure the sales impact of specific advertisements, it is comparatively easy to obtain evidence of the exposure or penetration of their advertising messages. It is also possible to find out what brands of products people have in their homes. These types of evidence and the manufacturer's own knowledge of advertising expenditures and product sales may be studied to see whether there are logical relationships between advertising efforts and sales responses.

National advertising typically operates over extended periods and in combination with many other types of promotional activity. The simple relationships between advertising cost or opportunity and accomplished sales can seldom be taken as proof that specific advertising caused the observed sales. Nevertheless, the correlation between advertising exposure and product possession is a useful type of evidence, when interpreted with caution. In this context, correlation refers to relationships, varying from those which can be directly observed in the data to those requiring complex mathematical analyses of many variables. Precautions need to be stressed as much as procedures.

Since media are responsible for providing advertising with opportunities for exposure of ideas for prospective buyers, media have a considerable

[8] Paul F. Lazarsfeld, "Evaluating the Effectiveness of Advertising by Direct Interviews," in Paul F. Lazarsfeld and Morris Rosenberg (editors), *The Language of Social Research* (Glencoe, Ill.: Free Press, 1959), pp. 411–419.

incentive to provide evidence of sales effects. One of the earliest correlation studies was made—although not published—by a major magazine. Readers and nonreaders were compared on possession of products advertised in the publication. More importantly, people claiming to have seen from one to five advertisements in a campaign series were compared with issue readers who claimed to have seen none of the advertisements. In almost every instance, those reading the issues and those seeing one, two, or more of the advertisements showed progressively more product possession than nonreaders of the issues. The gains were extremely favorable in relation to advertising costs.

When it comes to assessing increases in product ownership as direct effects of seeing or reading printed advertisements, one basic question has to be settled. As compared with the extent that people buy products because they have read advertisements, to what extent do they read advertisements because they have already purchased the product? It is a common experience, especially after having made an important brand choice, to feel a heightened interest in advertisements of that brand.

Actually, a high correlation between product purchase and advertising readership may result from either of two kinds of cause-effect relationtionships—readership may help to lead to purchase, or purchase may help to give rise to readership.

High correlation coefficients may also result from a third kind of causation—probably the most important of the three possibilities. If a person is interested in and "sold on" a given product (or service) for whatever reason or reasons, he is inclined both to look for the product (or service) and for advertisements about it simply because he is interested in the possibility of purchasing it. Thus, there would be a high correlation between the eventual purchase of a product and readership of the advertising, since both kinds of behavior are concomitants of being interested in and sold on the product. In other words, both purchase and readership may be the results—without either being the cause—of some of these high correlations.

There is far less likelihood that new purchasers of particular brands will give attention to product-sponsored broadcast programs than that they will read printed advertisements because of recent product purchases. This may explain the long procession of correlation studies in the field of radio and then television, with their implied measurement of advertising effects. Broadcast media have sometimes claimed direct sales evaluation and have, on other occasions, made more modest claims of attitudes built up through communication of advertised ideas. Two decades of such correlation surveys have met with skepticism and often rejection on the part of technically trained research people.

An example of a simple division of viewers and nonviewers of sponsored broadcasts, where product possession is also known, is presented in Table 3.

TABLE 3. *Per Cent of Viewers of Sponsor's Program Possessing Brand*

Brand and product	Frequent viewers	Occasional viewers	Nonviewers
R brand of razor blades	11	8	7
M brand of mouth wash	13	11	8
T brand of toilet soap	27	22	19
C brand of cake mix	21	18	16
B brand of breakfast cereal	9	7	4

These typical margins of difference in product ownership at first appear to be exclusive outcomes of advertising on particular programs, but internal analysis of the survey data may reveal that brand ownership is only one of the differences between viewers and nonviewers of a sponsored program. The nonviewers may have less money or less need and may be further from store outlets. Many other factors may contribute to the situation.

Anyone who believes in the power of advertising usually assumes that some sales advantages reported in correlation studies are genuine advertising effects. The great problem is that of controlling the influence of variables, many of which are probably not even known. Investigators have tried to match samples on many characteristics, including exposure to all major media. The advent of television, with stations opening up one market at a time, permitted additional controls based on observations before and after stations were built. This provided more of an experimental design, disturbed chiefly by the fact that television stations came first to the most promising markets.

Following are a few of the recognized factors which should be considered when interpreting correlations of television advertising penetration or product possession among exposed and unexposed population groups:

The broadcast signal may be better for homes in areas where the product is also most accessible.

Viewing a program usually involves staying at home, and this same tendency may favor product use.

Size of family is one factor related to both program viewing and usage of many products.

Viewers, as individuals, may normally be faster or slower consumers of the advertised product.

Advertisers usually try to advertise their products by using media which are most likely to reach people who are most likely to buy the products. A correlation of advertising exposure and product use may simply reflect a degree of success in selecting media on this basis.

Nonviewers include many types of nonprospects, such as those too poor for the sponsored products.

The early owners of television sets or color sets are venturesome or prosperous people who may be more responsive to advertising of all kinds.

The ownership of a product brand should make it easier to remember both the brand and the program which it sponsors.

People who are inclined to make excessive claims of product possession may also tend to overclaim familiarity with programs and with advertising messages.

Despite the competition of various media for audience time, the viewers of a particular program may be "consumers" of more other media than are nonviewers.

When manufacturers increase their media expenditures to buy television in selected markets, they may step up the whole program of sales promotion at the same time.

When comparisons are made before and after television stations or programs enter a new market, there are opportunities for independent changes in the responsiveness of the market during the measuring interval.

While many of the above variables can be controlled by matching survey samples, this process often destroys the projectability of the results to a whole population.

The problem of matching samples and establishing a defensible basis of comparisons between exposed and unexposed populations has been dramatically attacked by Irwin M. Towers, Leo A. Goodman, and Hans Zeisel in a proposal to measure the effects of *nonexposure!* [4] They would simply draw two parallel random samples of the population. Each sample would include the normal percentage of viewers of a particular program. One sample would continue without change, while the second sample would be *denied exposure* to the program and its commercials. Just how to control this nonexposure is, of course, a problem; but the two samples would then

---

[4] "Nonexposure: What It Can Tell the TV Advertiser," *Printers' Ink,* Vol. 278 (March 30, 1962), pp. 64–66.

be comparable except that one would no longer be exposed to the particular advertising messages. The influence of nonexposure could thus be measured under scientifically comparable conditions. No other published proposal has heretofore provided for truly comparable test groups, but it should also be said that the proposed study is theoretical at this time and has not been carried out.

Media have not been alone in the attempt to establish meaningful correlations between specific advertising efforts and sales or possession of products. Independent research operators have worked out ingenious systems of sales measurement, even for single insertions of an advertising campaign. Daniel Starch, in particular, set up elaborate controls in an attempt to sift out exclusively advertising influence on sales.[5] Purchases of products by magazine readers—both before and after issuance—divided according to claims of reading or nonreading of brand advertisements were offered as evidence of sales effects. This approach logically represented an advance in control of related variables, but slow acceptance by the advertising industry may have been caused by the problem of obtaining accurate field data on advertisement reading and on dates of product purchases. Certainly the method has not been generally accepted as a sales evaluator of national advertisements in magazines.

Daniel Starch has presented additional evidence that readership of advertising is closely related to the attracting of prospective buyers.[6] He discusses the assertion that high-readership ads tend to attract nonprospects for the products and services advertised. This is not so, he says, and he presents a good deal of evidence indicating that the more readers an advertisement has, the more the actual number of prospects. (Also, the more prospects, the greater likelihood there is of more readers.) "The data clearly show that as advertising (either for your own brand or for competition) is stepped up, reduced, or stopped, there are marked effects on the number of buyers and current users."[7] There is the likelihood, of course, that advertising appropriations often are either increased or decreased largely in anticipation of what sales trends are expected to be.

[5] Daniel Starch, "Advertising's Sales Power Can Be Measured," *Advertising and Selling,* Vol. 41 (February, 1948), pp. 33–68.

[6] Daniel Starch, "Ad Readership Scores Can Be Equated with Attracting Prospective Buyers, Starch Asserts," *Advertising Age,* Vol. 31 (October 31, 1960), pp. 77–78.

[7] Daniel Starch, "Do Ad Readers Buy the Product?" *Harvard Business Review,* Vol. 36 (May–June, 1958), pp. 49–58, at p. 58.

In 1961 Starch added to his analyses on the correlation method of esti-mating the sales influence of advertising.[8] By comparing the findings of several of his approaches to this type of analysis, he was able to demon-strate a degree of consistency which he felt confirmed the relatively simple "Netapps" (NET Ad Produced PurchaseS) method. This requires maga-zine issue readers or television program viewers merely to report on whether the advertisements were seen and whether the product had been purchased within one week after noting.

If 15 per cent of 30 ad-noters bought the product, this would account for 4.5 purchases. If 10 per cent of 70 non-ad-noters bought the product, this would account for 7 purchases. The total number of reported purchases is known to be 4.5 + 7.0, or 11.5.

However, if the 30 ad-noters had not seen the ad, and if 10 per cent would have bought as did the non-ad-noters, this would account for 3 of the 4.5 purchases they did make. Thus, only 1.5 purchases seem direct out-comes of ad-noting or reading, which would be 1.5 out of a total of 11.5, or 13.04 per cent. In this case, the advertising would be credited with 13.04 per cent of the reported purchases within the week after publishing or broadcasting the advertisement.

The present authors find insufficient consideration given by Starch to certain factors which he treats too lightly or not at all. There is the possi-bility that noters of specific advertisements are generally better ad-noters and buyers of advertised products. In fact, the Advertising Research Foundation has demonstrated that prospective buyers were 50 per cent better noters of advertisements in *Life* magazine than the nonprospects were.[9]

It is also possible that noting of advertisements makes it easier to re-member and report products purchased or that purchase of a product makes it easier to remember noting the advertisement. Perhaps more important is the fact that Starch Readership Service data are not sufficiently accurate to justify such precise analysis. As with other correlation studies, there is always the possibility that other factors which are not isolated or identified may vitiate the entire approach.

The work of Harry Deane Wolfe of the University of Wisconsin in

[8] Daniel Starch, *Measuring Product Sales Made by Advertising* (Mamaroneck, N.Y.: Daniel Starch & Staff, 1961).

[9] Darrell B Lucas, "The ABCs of ARF's PARM," *Journal of Marketing*, Vol. 25 (July, 1960), pp. 9–20, at p. 14.

isolating the influence of advertising also deserves comment.[10] Wolfe discusses his explorations with this precautionary statement:

> It is doubtful that complete advertising measurement is likely to be attained.
> There are too many variables, complicating factors, and uncontrollable influ-
> ences acting on the mind of the consumer. But an "all or nothing" complex in
> research seems childish; a combination of 50% fact and 50% hunch seems a
> far better basis for decision than is 100% hunch.[11]

His final estimate of how much of sales ads "produce" depends upon a
comparison of latest brand usage among those who could recall that brand's
advertising messages and those who could not. His correlation analysis
indicated that slightly over 25 per cent of $15 million in sales bore a
relationship to knowledge of present advertising. One of Wolfe's most
interesting contributions is the summary of other factors which contributed
to the total sales of $15 million:

1. Consumers like the product.
2. Consumers know it is a nationally advertised product.
3. Consumers know the brand name.
4. Consumers *once* knew the advertising.
5. Consumers can find the product in their favorite store.
6. Consumers took advantage of a special promotion such as mailed coupons, in-box coupons, off-price sales in store.
7. Consumers were influenced by store advertising and store display.
8. Consumers bought it on impulse.
9. Consumers bought it because of *communal influence* (or word of mouth,
if you will) exerted by parents, relatives, friends, dealers, professional people
(doctors, dentists), and others.[12]

The correlation approach, with respect to these and other factors, may
result in the assertion: "But all of these factors were the same for both the
exposed and unexposed groups." And the response is: "If there are all of
these and possibly more factors influencing the sale, then how can correlation evidence be more than a crude estimate of advertising's effect?" Wolfe
has met this rebuttal by his statement that 50 per cent fact is better than no
facts at all.

[10] Harry Deane Wolfe, "A New Way to Measure Advertising Effectiveness,"
Tide, Vol. 32 (February 14, 1958), pp. 51–57.
[11] Page 52 of citation in footnote 10.
[12] Page 57 of citation in footnote 10.

However, it needs to be pointed out that if people abandon judgment which is 55 per cent right in favor of leaning on research which is 50 per cent right (and this often does happen at one accuracy level or another), there has been a loss in decision-making efficiency. Moreover, this is usually done with an overt acknowledgment of the research inaccuracies. The poor research is often set forth as being "at least as right as it is wrong." But the real difficulty is to try to balance the likely accuracy of the research with the likely validity of judgments made *without* the research.

In any case, it is more conservative to evaluate whole campaigns than to rate each advertising insertion. Sales trends over a period of months or years may show a parallel with advertising expenditures or readership ratings.[13] When magazine readers are separated into those noting and those not noting particular brand advertisements, the differential may show a convincing pattern.

But there remain possible influences other than advertising. People who do not see the magazine advertisement of a particular brand, for example, must obviously include those who noted few advertisements of any kind. The people who read few advertisements may act quite differently as consumers in comparison with people inclined to read a great many advertisements. This does not deny the importance of the evidence, but raises a serious question about crediting *all* sales advantages to advertising alone.

A Direct-mail Method

A great difficulty in evaluating advertising in terms of sales effectiveness has been that of finding an acceptable criterion. But the criterion might well be sales—if we can find a "pure" measure of sales directly related to advertising!

An ingenious way to control most of the extraneous variables which might influence sales (other than advertising) has been proposed by Dik Warren Twedt of BBDO. The method has not been used, and would be very expensive if used. But it is of considerable interest from a theoretical standpoint.

In a direct-mail split test, evaluation of different appeals can be objective and immediate. If the subsamples are unbiased and if the differences in returns are significant, we can usually safely attribute obtained sales differences to the differences in the advertisements.

Accordingly, Twedt suggests that we develop 10 different advertising

[13] Page 58 of citation in footnote 7.

layouts for a product, for example. In each layout, the product and the price are exactly the same, but the layouts are purposely constructed to maximize difference in responses, therefore, including some ads which we believe will "pull" rather poorly.

At this point we need a known, relatively homogeneous population for the test. Suppose that a department store in a large city has a mailing list of 45,000 charge customers. A mailing of each of the 10 forms of the advertisement could be made to every tenth name on the list; that is, each advertisement would be mailed to 4,500 potential buyers. The order would be:

	Advertisement
	and possible appeal
Customer	
1	A (quality)
2	B (protection)
3	C (ease of use)
4	D (curiosity)
5	E (service)
6	F (scientific)
7	G (announcement)
8	H (how this product came to be)
9	I (testimonial)
10	J (snob appeal)

The cycle would then be repeated throughout the list.

The department store mailing would be in the form of an enclosure of a flyer with the monthly statement. Since a large department store would already have a regular schedule of statement enclosures, the additional expenses would be in the preparation and production of 10 layouts instead of 1; the collating of outgoing envelopes so that bias in the 10 subsamples is minimized; and perhaps additional postage.

If each layout offered the same price inducement, and of a sizable sort, it seems reasonable to assume at least a 5 per cent return on the mailings. On this basis, the average return per layout would be 200 or more orders. Differences in return would provide helpful evidence as to the most promising appeal to be used for advertising in a national medium.

Other Mathematical Techniques

Mathematical models for partial and multiple correlations of all factors that might influence sales may make a growing contribution to the evaluation of advertising. The first decade of extensive application of high-speed computers to assess the sales influence of advertising has made some research analysts optimistic.[14] Using controlled advertising situations in which intensity and type of promotion varied, the results of one study suggested that by use of a mathematical model the quantities needed to evaluate and compare alternative promotional campaigns could be computed. But there are reservations and limitations.

E. I. du Pont de Nemours Company has pioneered in the application of mathematical operations research models to advertising. Some of the basic considerations are worth quoting:

> Simplified, the general idea is to identify and isolate all the separate factors involved in sales, then compare the contribution each makes in getting people to buy the product.
>
> The first step, identification, is relatively simple. Most of the factors contributing to sales—weather, salesmen, dealers, buying power, to name just a few—are obvious and fairly common everywhere. Isolating and comparing the effects of each of the sales factors is far more difficult.
>
> The patterns and data that emerge from an analysis of the product's previous sales are used to build a mathematical model. Once the mathematical model is built, the job of isolating and comparing all the factors affecting sales begins.
>
> How is this done? Ideally, you hold all the factors constant except one. By doing this with every factor involved, you eventually get a pretty good picture of how each one affects or relates to the total sales problem under analysis.
>
> Unfortunately . . . some factors affecting selling, such as weather, population and the consumer's buying power, are completely beyond the advertiser's control. Others, the salesman's personality, for example, are generally not even ascertainable.
>
> Can you manipulate the advertising factor to determine its effect on sales? With a product that has never before been advertised this is feasible . . . a product that's been previously advertised obviously doesn't lend itself to this pat method of measurement.   /
>
> As the next best thing, du Pont's advertising research section uses a technique called evolutionary operations. . . . By varying the advertising expenditures year by year in some planned fashion . . . and by equalizing out the other factors by controlling them or at least by measuring their variability, you isolate the advertising factor.[15]

Essentially there are two ways of obtaining marketing data for mathematical evaluations of advertising expenditures. The practical, unrefined

[14] Marcello L. Vidale and Harry B. Wolfe, "An Operations-research Study of Sales Response to Advertising," *Operations Research,* Vol. 5 (June, 1957), pp. 370–381.

[15] "How du Pont Measures Ad Results," *Tide,* Vol. 32 (September, 1958), pp. 61–66.

approach is to take the company records of sales and of all promotional expenditures and analyze their relationships. While this approach is centered upon wholly normal advertising conditions, it is beset with the many variables in promotional efforts and marketing conditions. As a measuring approach, it is also blurred by the fact that business management guides its promotional moves according to judgments of opportunity for gain. Thus, a highly rewarding advertising allocation may reflect the judgment of management quite as much as the quality of the copy.

The alternative to retrospective study of company marketing records is to permit some control of promotional efforts for the purpose of making advertising research more definitive. Control may take such forms as holding other promotional efforts fairly constant while varying the application of advertising—or setting aside selected marketing areas or segments for experimental advertising study.

A more extreme concession to research purposes is to turn all promotional decisions over to the demands of experimental design for a period of exploration. While it is next to impossible to set up a controlled experiment which meets all practical requirements, it is even more difficult under normal operating conditions to abstract definitive evidence on the sales influence of most national advertising.

The limitations of correlated evidence of the sales influence of advertising are complicated. The normal promotional activities of a company are opportunistic, interrelated, and at times erratic. If a new merchandising man or advertising manager happens to come on the scene while data for advertising analysis are being collected, his impact may completely overshadow ordinary advertising changes. New personnel, new product models, changed consumer demand, and an endless array of other factors may make evaluation of advertising extremely difficult and tenuous.

Also, as soon as research is permitted to control promotional activities, other problems arise. Usually there is no such thing as holding other promotional activities *constant,* since they are not normally constant! If sales territories are assigned to research, there arises the problem of comparability between territories; and there is also the question as to whether knowledge learned presently in one territory will have valid application later in the whole market.

In other words, there still may be advantages in the partially controlled market study, but the practical solutions and applications are decidedly limited.

The ideal research, based on correlation of variables, calls for complete experimental design in which all variables are accounted for or actually controlled. Such experiments, usually local, make it possible to study the effects of varied advertising and to compare different advertising copy and strategies in selected markets. Some of the problems include variations in the operations of competitors, basic variations in test markets, changes related to time, and completely controlled promotion. Decisions must be objectively scheduled—never to play a hunch or to exploit an opportunity, as in normal business. The experimental approach is certainly the best way to obtain data on advertising influence, but the ideal advertising experiment has not yet been worked out.

Computers

Despite the limitations and precautions indicated for mathematical analysis of advertising effects, the development of electronic computers has brought a promising approach to advertising research (and also to media research—see Chapter Sixteen). The derivation of mathematical models for which the computer is the only practical counterpart is too specialized a subject for detailed treatment here. But it would appear that as fast as man can evolve models or formulas for advertising analysis, computer technology will progress to make solutions possible and practicable. These twin techniques represent tools which may eventually enable research to move step by step toward more complete and more valid estimates of the sales influences of all marketing forces. But the goal is still far away.

All mathematical explorations of relationships between national advertising and sales are subject to a number of restraints. Computers have mechanical precision, and it is usually possible to set up and solve appropriate mathematical models. Restraint begins with the fact that models require the correct selection of the right variables and the assignment of appropriate and proper weights.

Models also involve assumptions, some of which cannot be tested readily for their validity. Traditionally the data relating to advertising have lacked precision, and fine instruments or analysis do not improve the data.

For these reasons and others which may not be as obvious, our summary regarding possible mathematical analysis of the effects of advertising on sales response is as follows:

Levels of accuracy in advertising research are lower than in most other areas of application of these techniques.
The procedure does not correct for faulty or inadequate assumptions.

Weights and relationships included in design of the model are not validated or corrected.

Computations cannot overcome the limitations imposed by poor data. (A computer is not a "brain" but just a good "right arm.")

Deviations from normal advertising operations for the purpose of obtaining the data must be allowed for in applying the findings.

It is easier to assess the influence of gross advertising expenditures than the effects of campaigns or individual media; and it is easier to evaluate a campaign than to isolate individual advertisements or insertions.

PRETESTING IN SELECTED SALES AREAS

The possibility of testing out advertisements in limited markets was suggested in the previous discussion.

This method of *sales-area testing* has long been a part of advertising research. Groups of cities or markets are selected, using some cities as controls without advertising changes. The sales pattern for the product is checked through store inventories for several weeks before the test. Then new advertisements are introduced, each variation being tried in several cities and checked for sales results in many stores. Inventories of stock are kept during the test period and may be extended some weeks thereafter to study the normal sales pattern. If certain advertisements are followed by sales increases well above the normal fluctuations in the same markets, they have an increased prospect of proving effective in later national coverage.

No two cities or markets are actually identical, and the selection of test cities is extremely important for sales-area tests. Cities should be comparable in such population characteristics as economic levels, occupational distribution, national origins, and permanence of residence. Types of industry and everything related to the purchase pattern for the product should be matched. Naturally, the selection of cities should be aimed at matching the characteristics of the total market in which the product is sold.

Dealers play a crucial role in the test, particularly if they keep the stock inventories necessary for measuring sales. Since all competing products should be checked, it is possible to keep the dealers from knowing the identity of the brand under test. Otherwise, they may be *too cooperative* and "push" the product.

Even if the investigator keeps track of inventory, which is the wiser procedure, he must keep account of all stock coming to the shelves from elsewhere within the stores, from warehouses, wholesalers, drop shippers, wagon distributors, the manufacturer, and even through loan from other sources.

Ready availability of stock at all times is also highly important. Two or more inventories before the test period, frequent inventories during the test, and two or more inventories following the test are recommended. The final inventories, especially in control cities, can help to ensure that the effects of the test advertisements are not confused with normal sales variations.

The timing of a sales-area test, the selection of media, the schedule of insertions, and the advertising plan must all be well coordinated. The test should be scheduled at such a time that the results will be most significant for the particular time at which the advertising is to be released generally. Buying trends for the product and its competition, as well as general business trends, should be considered. The local media being used should relate as closely as possible to the national media for later use. The rate of insertions should not be speeded up to a point which might distort the relative normal performances of different test advertisements. Even more important, the test copy should not be designed exclusively for immediate sales unless this is the strategy intended for the national campaign, and this last point clearly limits the kinds of advertising for which sales-area tests are adapted.

Sales-area tests always produce differences. The problem, then, is to evaluate the differences and to estimate the sales effectiveness of each advertising design.

Early applications of this method led to unsupported conclusions, because normal sales variations by store and by community were not examined. There was little internal analysis of the data. After "winning" advertisements were selected and extended to national markets, there was often reason to believe that results were poor. Reexamination of the sales-area test data, in the majority of such cases, showed that the differences obtained under test were smaller than the usual sales fluctuations in the same markets!

Sales-area tests should be used mostly for new products which are frequently purchased. If the product is purchased after long intervals or if the purchase pattern tends to be erratic, it is not practical to measure the effects of ordinary changes in advertising. Since sales-area tests necessarily cover brief periods, the results cannot be helpful in evaluating the campaign buildup and cumulative effect typically sought through national advertising.

An interesting idea was used by a manufacturer who was willing to be

or other inquiry responses are a reasonably sure sales guide. There are other circumstances, campaign strategies, and product categories which seem to call for serious consideration of a properly executed sales test in comparable areas or markets. New convenience products, designed for frequent repeat purchase in a mass national market, are likely to fit into such a program. Many other products which are already widely advertised through national media seem almost incapable of adaptation to sales-area tests in single city markets that cannot be separately covered by most national media.

It is to be observed, of course, that successful application of a valid sales measurement of most national advertisements would obviate the need for the many test methods discussed previously. Even though readership ratings, attitude research, and the many specialized approaches might give a more direct gauge of success in attaining some of the intermediate goals of advertising, the ultimate objective is usually related to the sales process. As is the case with much retail advertising, a true sales measure would provide most of the required basis for intelligent planning and selection of advertising materials.

The fact is that little has yet been learned about the actual measurement of the sales influence of most national advertisements. This is especially true in trying to predict future buying behavior.

Much advertising works so slowly and shares with so many other sales influences that the national advertiser is unlikely to succeed in isolating the effects of each individual unit. Only a scientifically conceived program of genuine advertising experiment, supported by favorable policies over long periods, seems likely to contribute materially toward the solution of the problem of sales evaluation.

Meanwhile, many useful approaches are available for probing specific areas of advertising effects, for establishing the degree of success in attaining certain intermediate objectives, and for reinforcing the process of decision making at almost every stage. Preceding chapters have dealt with the most prominent and most promising of these techniques. The more direct attack through inquiry testing and actual sales evaluation has met with greater obstacles, but none of the evidence needs to be wholly rejected. Rather, every method included in this chapter can be used to throw light on the sales productivity of advertising, providing it has the benefit of the best available procedures combined with intelligent interpretation of the meaning of the results.

part two /

Measurement
of Advertising
Media

nine

Basic Media Concepts

CHARACTERISTICS OF VARIOUS MEDIA

SOME TERMINOLOGY

QUALITY AND QUANTITY OF RESPONSES TO ADVERTISING

A BROAD MEDIA CONCEPT

RESEARCH IN RELATION TO CONCEPTS

PROSPECTS AND NONPROSPECTS

REPEAT ADVERTISING OPPORTUNITIES

IMPLICATIONS

Advertising messages and advertising media are inseparably intertwined. This means that every piece of advertising copy should be designed to fit specific media audiences.

After all, most advertising money goes to buy media space and time, and it is extremely important that messages reach large numbers of the right kinds of people in the right frame of mind at the right time.

The media which bring advertising messages to consumers account for the bulk of national advertising costs. Television, radio, newspapers, and magazines—four leading avenues of entertainment and information— had advertising expenditures in 1961 of over $6.9 billion—approximately 58 per cent of all advertising dollars spent that year (see Table 4).[1]

[1] "1962 Ad Volume Will Break the $12-billion Barrier—At Last," *Printers' Ink,* Vol. 280 (August 10, 1962), pp. 12–13, at p. 13 for final 1961 figures.

"copy" is used here and throughout this book to refer to *all features* of an advertisement, either print or broadcast, that distinguish it from all others.

As to economy—an advertiser can deliver messages to a mass audience at a fraction of a cent per person. As to speed—an advertiser can get a message to masses of people within hours, if necessary. As to control—an advertiser decides what he wants to say, to whom he wants to say it, and when he wants to say it. As to responsibility—an advertiser signs his message, becomes completely responsible for it, and cannot disclaim it.

SOME TERMINOLOGY

Ask an advertiser why he buys the media he does, and he will probably give you these reasons:

1. *Cost.* It's the cheapest per thousand persons reached.
2. *Coverage.* It covers the territory I want.
3. *Impact.* It seems to help make the reader or listener remember longer.
4. *Prestige.* It carries more weight with the customer.[3]

Note that *cost and coverage are both quantitative* in nature and that *impact and prestige are more qualitative* in nature. On the more qualitative side can be added such factors as emotional appeals and reactions to various media. On the more quantitative side can be added such factors as coverage, penetration, composition, cumulative audience, and frequency. Seymour Banks and Ronald B. Kaatz of the Leo Burnett Company have provided some useful descriptions of these terms.

1. First of all, we come to a word called *coverage*—the ability of a medium to generate audiences at a criterion level within a designated market segment. What we mean is simply this: If you look at the data on the circulation or the audiences of a medium, you decide, for this particular market segment, whether there is sufficient advertising being delivered into it to say whether or not you will count that area as receiving the medium.

It is an all or none phenomenon. You say either Cook County is covered by the *Chicago Tribune*, or it is not. You are not interested in the relative level, just in whether or not you have coverage.

The only problem is that in print one uses the word "coverage" as we want to use it in penetration. We want to use it consistently in all media: broadcasting, print, outdoor, etc. Coverage tells you whether or not you have sufficient advertising coming into a territory so that you feel that it receives

[3] Ray Lapica, "III. Psychology of Media: Why Admen Buy What They Do," *Sponsor*, Vol. 8 (May 3, 1954), pp. 34–36, 82–94, at p. 34.

satisfactory weight—that it can be counted as lying within the confines of a given effort.

2. From coverage, we move to the next area, *penetration*. We want to know the level, the degree, to which a given market or market segment is exposed to a medium, so that we have some indication of advertising penetration.

The simplest measure, or the one which is probably most frequently used, is the broadcast rating. A rating simply means a percentage of homes in a program station area—within the coverage area—which, in fact, do listen or watch a program. In other words, it says that if a program has a rating of 20%, then 20% of the homes in the coverage area watch the program.

We have such figures, also, in print where the data are often stated in terms of penetration. For instance, the Politz studies of *Life* showed that 22% of the people, 10 to 14 years of age, were readers of *Life* magazine.

Penetration helps us to answer a question, such as: In a single insertion, how many people can we reach in this market segment?

3. *Audience composition* helps us to answer the following question: Of the people we reach, how many are in the right segment?

Whereas penetration is a function of audience size, audience composition is based upon the kinds of people who are in the audience and is *not* affected by audience size.

We should be quite clear that these are two different kinds of measures, and that they should be used when they are appropriate.

All three things we have been talking about—coverage, penetration, and composition can apply to single insertions or single media buys. The next two—cumulative audience and frequency—however, are based upon campaigns or combinations of media.

4. We do not particularly care what term we use to describe *cumulative audience*—whether we say "cumulative audience," "net unduplicated audience," or "reach," the basic idea is the same: Given a "bunch" of media, how many people are reached one or more times?

5. *Frequency* is the number of repeated messages being delivered or exposed by campaigns to the members of the audience. Frequency is really a figure based upon actual exposure to the net audience. It is not an overall figure; it is not a gross audience. It answers the question: Of the people reached by the campaign, how many messages did they receive?

To summarize:

1. *Coverage* is the simplest measure. It tells us whether or not we have media in a given area.

2. *Penetration* says how many people in a given market or market segment can be reached with a single message.

3. *Composition* deals with the makeup of the audience—of the people we reach, how many are of a particular kind?

4. *Cumulative audience* [or *reach*] says for a given campaign how many people are reached or how many households are reached one or more times.

5. *Frequency* says, of the people reached, how many times we have reached them.[4]

QUALITY AND QUANTITY OF RESPONSES TO ADVERTISING

Whether any advertisement will succeed depends upon both the *quality* and *quantity* of impressions it makes upon the right kinds of people.

Qualitative factors, such as attitudes and motivations, are primarily responses to advertising copy, although media have considerable bearing on attitudes and motives. The quantities and classes of people reached are also affected by advertisements, but they are more the responsibility of the media which carry them, and any evaluation of major national advertising media must put chief emphasis upon quantity or numbers of the desired kinds of people to be reached.

The distinction between *quality* and *quantity* of responses to advertising is largely a matter of convenience. Most scientific research is aimed at quantitative measurement, but some dimensions of advertising are more difficult to assign numerical values than others. Attitudes, images, and motivations that result from advertising or that affect its reception in media are not measured very precisely, but are likely to be described in such broad terms as "favorable," "unfavorable," or "indifferent." It would not be very accurate to say that the attitudes engendered by advertisements in one magazine are X per cent more favorable than in another publication.

The attitudes established by advertisements in a particular medium are partly determined by the attitudes toward the medium itself. People may like television in general more or less than magazines, and they may like certain TV programs more or less than certain features in certain magazines. The attitudes are also related to the acceptability of advertising in the particular medium. The same people who like one medium more may happen to like advertisements in that medium less. One may like television, but at the same time dislike television advertising. There are other factors, such as the company and its advertising message, which affect attitudes resulting from particular advertisements. The *qualitative* influences of media on advertising response will be discussed in Chapter Fifteen.

The simplest *quantitative* dimension of advertising as related to media is

[4] Seymour Banks and Ronald B. Kaatz, *Media Analysis Principles and Practices* (Leo Burnett Company, Inc., 1961), unpublished.

the number of different people reached by the message. Media must take the ideas created by skilled writers and bring them to millions of prospective buyers of the product. Obviously this process of projecting messages must be aimed at prospects of good market quality.

Of course, media are also as responsible for the *quality* of the audiences reached as for their total numbers. In that sense, even the quantitative measures are qualitative.

Physical Aspects of Media

All forms of advertising media, broadcast or printed, affect the physical presentation of advertisements. Some of these physical features are of great advantage to the advertiser. Color, motion, the human voice, and attractive surroundings are usually helpful in making advertisements interesting, dramatic, and compelling. Other features may limit display or reduce the possibility of communicating much more than the product identity.

It must be apparent, therefore, that simple quantitative comparisons between different media are extremely difficult to make. The physical form of the advertising message as it reaches the consumer is different for each medium.

Media are also bought in physical units. Since 1914, the Audit Bureau of Circulations has certified to the number of copies of the major magazines and newspapers sold under specified conditions. When a publisher makes a contract to circulate advertisements, he is responsible for distributing a specified number of *printed impressions* in the scheduled issue.

Likewise, every television network is responsible for the number of specified broadcasting stations on which a program or message will appear within a fixed time schedule. Outdoor advertising also has specified numbers of panels in stated locations, with insurance of visibility to traffic.

These are some of the physical items which media sell to advertisers, and media can be held to their contracts. Even so minute a physical thing as shrinkage of the *mats* from which newspapers cast their printing surfaces may become the basis for a refund to the advertiser. These same physical factors are essential to maximum performance of the functions of advertising.

The major national advertising media—television, radio, newspapers, and magazines—perform their advertising utility as a subordinate function. The primary functions of entertaining and informing audiences are scrupulously guarded by publishers and public commissioners. Advertising, the source of all television and radio revenue and most publication revenue, is

space or time units in an advertising vehicle is a realistic gauge of media performance, two important considerations must be added.

One is the fact that media differ in their capacities to capitalize on the same size of audience; the response from a television audience will differ from the response of a radio, magazine, or newspaper audience. Advertisers feel that they can use the features of one medium to better advantage in a particular situation—even though a different medium may have equal audience. Even if advertisement noting means essentially the same thing in different media, the opportunities for successful advertising impact may differ greatly.

In the attempt to measure media values through advertisement noting, a second major consideration is this: Noting is very much a function of the attractions of the advertising message. Advertising audiences in the same media vehicle are known to differ enormously, even though the exposure opportunity may be nearly constant. If media values are to be assessed on the basis of advertisement noting, then it is important to obtain some kind of average which will neutralize the differences in advertising copy. In fairness to the media vehicle, it may well be argued that the rating should be based on only the best performances; any lesser performance reflects the weakness of the copy appeal rather than failure of the medium to provide the opportunity, assuming that effect of position is controlled.

Communication and Playback

The ultimate advertising function cannot be performed merely through advertisement noting. While some messages are designed to do a much more effective job of communicating selling ideas than others, it is also true that media may differ widely in providing and encouraging this opportunity. A vehicle which equips the advertiser with better basic tools and which brings audiences to him in a more favorable circumstance should be given credit for better performance. While the part played by copy and the part played by media may be inextricably interrelated at this stage, it is logical to evaluate media in the light of advertising communication.

Yet communication is not something which is easy to define or which can be objectively observed by anyone. Presumably it includes ideas, concepts, attitudes, and motivations which are reflected in later behavior. If an advertisement implants specific sales points or related ideas, the ability of an audience to "play back" these ideas later is evidence of communication. Recall research, as discussed in Chapter Four, is based on this assumption.

Likewise, attitudes and motivations favorable to the product may be measured after exposure.

This type of measurement usually picks up only residue of the most vivid impressions, and it is difficult to express the total impact with any single absolute figure. The total number of members of the audience who can play back some minimum evidence of communication does not represent a very meaningful yardstick for differentiating the performances of different media vehicles. Certainly the amount communicated to each person should also be considered.

Sales and Profits

As with copy research, the ultimate goal of the contribution of a media vehicle is to influence the sales or profits resulting from advertising expenditures in that vehicle. But this goal is so difficult to assess and it represents so completely the "teamwork" of copy and media that it remains only the broadest general guide to media selection.

It would hardly deserve mention in this book were it not that every advertiser makes just such an evaluation every time he allocates a single dollar to one medium in preference to another. Therefore, the consideration of sales and profits is not in any way unrealistic—the only weakness is inability to measure these profits for advertisers and to tell them exactly what part of the gain may properly be credited to a particular media purchase.

Reflect for a moment on how profits are made by companies. Is the fact that a company spends a certain amount of money to advertise its products the sole reason that the company ends its business year with "black" income figures? Hardly.

Businesses are really people. These people work together with their hands and minds and machines and materials—and all people are different from each other. There are also varying external business influences. Markets are constantly in a state of flux, and it is always difficult to say what are "normal" economic conditions.

The point is simply this—*each way in which businesses differ within, and each changing force that acts from without, can have a bearing on the profits of a business.*

The important variables are everything from the nature of the product . . . to the nature of the market . . . to sales volume . . . to general economic conditions . . . to costs of production . . . to selling costs . . . to amount of competition . . . to governmental regulations . . . to quality of management . . . and so on, and so on. Certainly advertising—in terms of both quantity and quality—is but one part of the total marketing mix.

Yes, there are statistical techniques in existence to measure the relationships between advertising and profits. But these techniques are not used in this connection, for the very simple reason that there are too many factors which cannot be measured.

RESEARCH IN RELATION TO CONCEPTS

Research technology has already made possible the measurement of total numbers of individuals reached at each stage in the preceding concepts. Information about projectable national magazine audiences was introduced by *Life* magazine in 1938; data as to nationally projected broadcast network program audiences were announced by the A. C. Nielsen Company in 1948; and more comprehensive data on both magazines and television were set forth by the A. C. Nielsen Company in 1961.

Advertisement exposure information for broadcast commercials has been available through analysis of electronic records of receiving set operation since the beginning of the A. C. Nielsen Company projected audience reports in 1948. Exposure estimates for magazine advertising pages were reported by *Look* magazine and jointly by *Reader's Digest* and *The Saturday Evening Post* in 1959 and 1960, respectively.

Reports of projected advertisement noting for broadcast commercials are uncommon, although private surveys have long inquired as to whether specific commercials were noted. In the field of publication advertising, limited sample surveys of advertisement noting (see Chapter Three) have implied national projectability by reporting *ad-noters per dollar*, but are not widely accepted for this purpose. The earliest published projections of advertising audiences were those of the transportation advertising industry, summarized in 1950.[6]

The chief research organization measuring advertisement playback, Gallup & Robinson, Inc., uses a limited sample and employs procedures which discourage media evaluations. They have developed techniques for producing projectable totals of audiences capable of playback of advertisement features, but the problems of using such information to evaluate media vehicles were described in Chapter Four.

[6] *The Continuing Study of Transportation Advertising,* conducted by the Advertising Research Foundation in cooperation with the National Association of Transportation Advertising, *13-Study Summary, 1950.*

There remains the problems of securing data on sales resulting from single insertions of an advertisement in media vehicles. Serious attempts have been made to furnish such data to the advertising industry, but acceptance has been slow (see Chapter Eight). Such a solution, if ever found, would obviate the need for all other considerations in media concepts.

PROSPECTS AND NONPROSPECTS

Most media choices are made by advertisers for the purpose of reaching limited markets instead of the entire population. Advertisers may reject children too young to influence buying or to be reached by the medium and may care little for men or for oldsters or for apartment dwellers or for others who do not want their products. More media choices are selective than aimed indiscriminately at gross totals. There is usually more concern with those who are prospects at present than with those who might later become prospects through acquired wealth or husbands or houses or dogs or whatever increases their likelihood of buying various products.

Some media vehicles fit an advertiser's market better than others, although all media reach some people who are not really prospects. The shaded area in Fig. 7 (page 208) is intended to indicate the less productive part of the population or group available to an advertising medium.

The experimental study by the Advertising Research Foundation (discussed in Chapters Three and Four) showed that prospects claimed nearly 50 per cent more recognition of related advertisements than did nonprospects.[7] The respective percentages of issue readers of *Life* claiming to have seen particular advertisements were 25.5 and 17.5. Communication, as measured by aided recall, showed more than double performance by prospects over nonprospects, with scores of 3.8 and 1.8 per cent, respectively.

Since the magazine probably allowed equal opportunity for impressions on prospects and nonprospects alike, it would appear that the further the advertising process progresses, the more the advertising message contributes and the less the media vehicles contribute. This assumption is implicit in the discussion of media concepts.

When advertisers select media, it is clear that vehicles with more prospects not only reach more potential buyers, but also deliver substantially more of the sales message to these people. On the other hand, there is no

[7] Darrell B. Lucas, "The ABCs of ARF's PARM," *Journal of Marketing*, Vol. 25 (July, 1960), pp. 9–20, at p. 14.

sharp distinction between those who are likely to be prospects and those who represent "waste" coverage. Some who are not currently prospects may later patronize the advertiser, and some who do not at first consider themselves in the market are later converted into customers. Some pick up advertised ideas and pass them along to others, regardless of whether they themselves have personal need for the product.

In reality, there are many different levels of advertising prospects. Few advertisers have sufficient knowledge of their own customers to define just which of the available media audiences are absolutely best for their own use.

REPEAT ADVERTISING OPPORTUNITIES

Repetition in advertising means exposure or noting of the same insertion of an advertising message repeatedly by the same audience of an advertising vehicle.

One unique feature of broadcasting is its momentary quality, permitting only one exposure of any particular element of the broadcast (except in the case of reruns). Printed advertisements and their media are more permanent, making it possible for readers to return to an issue repeatedly and even to review the same items and advertisements. It is known that an average issue of some magazines is read on several different days by the typical reader. The *Reader's Digest* conducted research showing that the average reader looks into the same monthly issue on 5.3 different days.[8] This compared with an average of only 1 to 1.8 days for another leading magazine, *The Saturday Evening Post,* which was published weekly at the time of the study.

While it is true that a reader may pick up a magazine issue on several different days, his main purpose may be to examine areas not already looked over. But people are not always systematic about their magazine reading or about marking where they left off. Repeat reading of the same issue may lead to much skimming of areas covered earlier and possibly to some deliberate rereading of things of special interest. The result of this extensive issue exposure is a heightened assurance of exposure of advertising pages. Not only is there greater chance of a first exposure, but there is also a chance of two or more exposures of the same advertising message. All of this adds value to print media from the viewpoint of advertisers.

Actual measurement of exposure days for advertisements was explored

[8] "A Study of Seven Publications," Report No. 1, *Reader's Digest* (October, 1956), p. 11.

by *The Saturday Evening Post* in 1957, followed by a study of advertising page exposure days in four magazines in 1960.[9] This study showed that the average advertising page in *The Saturday Evening Post* and in *Reader's Digest* had 1.3 and 1.7 exposure days, respectively, for the average issue reader. Some competitive publications exposed their average advertising page on only one day to the average issue reader. It may be argued that the value of more than one exposure day for a periodical advertisement is greater than a single exposure day. However, advertisers think there is a limit to the value of multiple exposures. Otherwise, it could be argued that the same outdoor panels, confronting the same audience day after day for an entire month, or even longer, would be best.

Not only is it possible for an advertisement in a magazine or newspaper to be exposed on several days, but it also happens that a reader may look at the same advertisement more than once and actually reread it. Thus, advertisement noting may be repeated in the same vehicle, and the process of communication may be extended or intensified. Rereading of advertising messages may reflect an extremely high interest level or perhaps an attempt to gain a fuller understanding of the message. It seems likely that advertising copy is much more responsible for this phenomenon than the medium carrying the copy.

Figure 8 is adapted from a model designed by Paul E. J. Gerhold of Foote, Cone and Belding to represent stages of the media function from the purchase of physical units to the ultimate sales. Prospects for the particular advertiser are indicated above the line, and nonprospects below. Stage I indicates the number of copies or receivers or whatever makes possible the transmission of the advertising message. Some publication copies and some receiving sets may be owned by people who are not in the market for the particular product of any one advertiser. In this sense, the physical units of the media vehicle in the first stage are evaluated in terms of the *kinds* of people who are exposed to them.

The next stages in Fig. 8, like those in the preceding Fig. 7, are concerned only with people in relation to media vehicles and the advertisements they carry. Stage II shows vertically the total number of individuals in the audience of the vehicle, with prospective customers above the line. The steps in Stage II, beginning with one step at the top, indicate the number of times the same individual is exposed to the same issue; obviously, there is only one exposure to a broadcast. The increasing horizontal spread,

[9] "Ad Page Exposure in 4 Magazines," sponsored by *Reader's Digest* and *The Saturday Evening Post* (Philadelphia: Curtis Publishing Company, 1960).

toward the middle of Stage II, indicates that some individuals may return to the same issue two, three, or even more times.

Stage III shows the same dimensions for the exposure of advertisements or advertising pages; again, a single broadcast of a commercial can be exposed but once.

Stage IV has to do with the perception or noting of advertisements, showing that even the nonprospects may see and take note of a message more than once. The tendency of nonprospects to examine or read the message repeatedly may be lessened by the fact that they lack motivation.

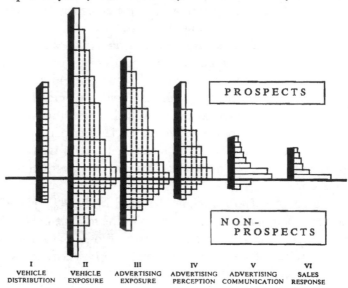

PROSPECTS

NON-
PROSPECTS

I	II	III	IV	V	VI
VEHICLE DISTRIBUTION	VEHICLE EXPOSURE	ADVERTISING EXPOSURE	ADVERTISING PERCEPTION	ADVERTISING COMMUNICATION	SALES RESPONSE

FIG. 8. A model for evaluating media. Courtesy of Advertising Research Foundation, Inc.; Source: *Toward Better Media Comparisons* (New York: Advertising Research Foundation, Inc., 1961).

Measures of the playback of copy points have confirmed this pattern, as depicted in Stage V. The final stage, in which purchases of the advertised product are made, naturally is confined to prospects. Purchases may be repeated, although it seems unlikely that the same person would repeatedly see the same advertisement and respond repeatedly with product purchase.

The case for repetition of the advertising message has been well stated by Alfred Politz:

> Why do buyers and sellers of advertising time and space agree so closely on the value of repeat presentations to the same person? This confidence obviously goes back to a multitude of daily observations reinforced by observations in the field of marketing. Advertising is a special form of learning, and *adver-*

tising generally represents a special case within the general law that learning progresses with repetition. Very few, unusual persons can remember a poem after reading it once. The normal human being has to read the poem again and again until it finally "sinks in." It is this general reinforcement of learning by repeat teaching which operates in mastering a language, walking upright, and buying the brand suggested by the advertiser.[10]

As a matter of fact, there is factual evidence that an advertisement in a magazine may be repeated one or more times without significant variation in readership. This is borne out by research studies as to repeats in industrial advertising and by studies on consumer advertising.

A number of reports in the McGraw-Hill Laboratory of Advertising Performance indicate the effectiveness of repetition of industrial advertisements.[11] Also, in a classic study advertisements were repeated in the weekly publication *Steel* according to eight different survey schedules and in the monthly *Product Engineering* according to five different schedules.[12] The eight weekly surveys were conducted to cover the following time cycles for repeating ads: every week for four weeks, every other week for four insertions, every fourth week for four insertions. The five monthly surveys were conducted to cover additional repeat patterns: every month for four months, every other month for three insertions, every third month for two insertions. Observations and readership figures for *all* advertisements in the two publications were obtained, not just the figures on the repeated advertisements. The study revealed that—on the average—each time an advertisement is repeated, it attracts an equal number of new readers, as well as a number of old readers (the number varies according to the repetition pattern) who recall the advertisement from the original or previous insertion.

Effectiveness of repetition of the same advertisement has also been demonstrated for consumer advertising by Steuart Henderson Britt and by Daniel Starch.[13]

---

[10] Alfred Politz, "What Is Essential to Know from Magazine Media Research?" *Media/scope,* Vol. 3 (April, 1959), pp. 3–8, at p. 5.

[11] McGraw-Hill Laboratory of Advertising Performance, Nos. 3041, 3042, 3042.1, 3043, 3044, 3045, 3047, 3047.1, 3050.

[12] McGraw-Hill Laboratory of Advertising Performance, No. 3040.

[13] Steuart Henderson Britt, "Study Indicates Effective Magazine Ad May Be Repeated without Loss of Readership," *Advertising Age,* Vol. 27 (May, 14, 1956), pp. 53–64; also reported under title "Effects of Repeating Advertisements in Magazines," *Tested Copy* (published by Daniel Starch & Staff), No. 79 (November, 1956); Daniel Starch, "How Does Repetition of Advertisements Affect Readership?" *Media/scope,* Vol. 3 (November, 1959), pp. 50–51.

The results of the experiment by Britt imply that it is possible for exactly the same advertisement run again to be more effective than by variations in the presentation of the sales message. In the study reported by Starch, high-scoring advertisements, when repeated, continued to score high; and low-scoring advertisements, when repeated, continued to score low. Starch has also presented data that suggest that observation scores for outdoor posters may improve with repetition.[14]

Work done by Alfred Politz for *The Saturday Evening Post* also indicated that exposure of the same magazine advertisement to the *same* individuals resulted in approximately 50 per cent more value than the first exposure alone—as measured in terms of (1) knowledge of the product or its claims, and (2) expressed willingness to buy the brand.[15] (For further information about this study, see Chapter Twelve, especially page 277).

It should not be surprising that there is growing evidence that repetition and frequency in advertising may add to its efficiency. To argue otherwise is to assume that every advertiser should get his highest return from his first advertising dollar and then suffer a decreasing efficiency in returns from all dollars spent thereafter. *Media/scope* has compiled a large body of evidence showing that both frequency and repetition may pay off at an increasing rate.[16] It can be reasoned that introductory advertisements or infrequent advertisements make too weak an impression to initiate much interest in buying. Succeeding advertisements may sometimes be more effective by building up already established weak impressions to the action level.

Finally, there has been some speculation that there might be a "sleeper effect" with respect to advertising; that is, there might be a greater change in attitude following a slight passage in time after exposure to the advertising, as compared with a change in attitude at the time of exposure to the advertising. But there is some evidence that *repetition* of advertising is more likely to reinforce the original effect of the advertising message than to produce a sleeper effect.[17]

However, it might be argued that there *is* a sleeper effect for most advertising that is not likely to be overcome by repetition of the same or similar

[14] Daniel Starch, "Should Outdoor Posters Be Repeated?" *Media/scope,* Vol. 3 (December, 1959), pp. 40–41.

[15] "The Rochester Study," *The Saturday Evening Post* (1960), pp. 54–61.

[16] "Frequency in Print Advertising: Part 1," *Media/scope,* Vol. 6 (April, 1962), pp. 60–62, 64, 66, 68, 70, 74.

[17] Martin Weinberger, "Does the 'Sleeper Effect' Apply to Advertising?" *Journal of Marketing,* Vol 25 (October, 1961), pp. 65–67.

advertising. This is likely to be true because the sleeper effect really shows up at the point of purchase—where message *content* is important and where attitudes toward the product itself hold sway. The question of sleeper effect is not so much a matter of how long it has been since the person was last reminded of the nature of a product's advertising as how much difference there is between a person's frame of reference while seeing or hearing the advertisement and while actually buying it.

IMPLICATIONS

In order to deal intelligently with measurements and attempted measurements of advertising media, it is essential to understand what is meant by such concepts as coverage, penetration, audience composition, cumulative audience (or reach), and frequency. These concepts were discussed briefly at the beginning of the present chapter.

A review of the stages leading to profitable advertising in a media vehicle shows that the audience of the vehicle represents a maximum potential of individuals or households which a specific advertising insertion can reach directly.

However, the advertiser has assurance of getting his message across to more of the audiences of some media than others. Also, as will be shown in the next two chapters, the audiences of different media (such as magazines and television) are defined differently, and comparisons are made difficult. Advertising exposure definitions are more comparable for different media, and exposure represents the final advertising function for which media can claim full credit.

On the other hand, exposure measurements are usually independent of the costs of media advertising units such as are sold by magazines. There is no safe way to make intermediate comparisons with regard to dollar values!

There remain two definable psychological stages in the media function which precede actual sales. These two, *advertisement noting* and the *amount of communication,* are extremely involved with copy content and design in addition to media effect. Advertisement noting is relatively easy to define and measure in a single dimension, although it gives only minimal assurance of actual delivery of the sales message. Communication, on the other hand, and the result in playback of ideas and attitudes, is much more dependent upon the quality of advertising copy than on media performance. It is further complicated by the fact that measurement requires dimensions

reading, convert only part of that advantage for the advertiser. However, a part of this advertising interest accrues to all copy in the daily paper. The newspaper advertiser has a further opportunity in that he is permitted to pay for and specify some choices with regard to location and surrounding editorial content. Newspapers traditionally charge the nonlocal advertiser substantially higher rates than the local business operator. Problems of price, physical limitations, and intricate scheduling for national coverage tend to keep truly national advertising in a minor role in the daily press.

Broadcast network programing, especially on television, is far more intimately associated with advertising than is the case with either magazines or newspapers. Sponsorship of a program enables an advertiser to eliminate all commercial competition on that network for the time period in question and a specific amount of time before and afterward and, under certain restraints, to choose content and format favorable to his messages. There are network and Federal restrictions to be considered, but sponsored programs give advertisers greater influence over media and messages than in any other major medium. Programs are definitely chosen to attract prospective customers or at least to ensure that the content will be compatible with commercials and products (or services). Broadcasting can be "consumed" only at the rate and in the sequence with which it is released; and the sponsor must try to make sure that the program audience is also his audience.

The present chapter deals with the audiences of printed media. Historically, *Life* magazine was the first major media vehicle to estimate and describe for advertisers its own total issue audience and those of its nearest competitors.[1] This survey and the reporting of it were unique in several ways. Not only was it the first projectable media audience study, but it also reported reading audiences of a size unheard of until then, representing more than nine readers per copy. It introduced new definitions and techniques. It measured and reported the audiences of competitors, and designated them by name. All of this was new in media research and, indeed, in the conduct of most business promotion.

AUDIENCES OF MAGAZINES

Evolution of a technique for magazine audience measurement stemmed from the acute need for such information in the advertising business and

[1] *Continuing Study of Magazine Audiences,* Report No. 1, *Life* (December 1, 1938).

from the incredibility concerning the kinds of information first obtained through direct inquiry about magazine reading.

Difficulties of Measurement

The act of reading, including the reading of most popular magazines, carries with it a degree of prestige. Some magazines enjoy more prestige than others, but the number of people claiming to read any magazine appears likely to be inflated. The number claiming to be readers, even *regular* readers, of a well-known publication may be more than fifteen times as many people as there were copies printed! Claiming of reading of a specific issue of the same publication may run close to the same number.

Following are the results of three different studies that demonstrate the difficulties of precise measurement, if measurement is based upon direct-questionnaire techniques.

1. H. P. Longstaff and G. P. Laybourn made comparisons of the relative standings of a number of publications as determined by three different readership-study techniques.

In the "orthodox" type of study employing a questionnaire which asked, "What magazines do you read?" only 47.3 per cent of those replying mentioned Magazine A even though practically everyone to whom the questionnaire had been sent was a "known reader" of Magazine A. On the basis of this original questionnaire, Magazine A ranked third in readership, Magazine C ranked second, and Magazine B ranked first.

When a follow-up questionnaire was sent to those who, in replying to the original questionnaire had failed to mention Magazine A, Magazine B, or Magazine C, asking "Do you read this magazine (Magazine A, Magazine B, or Magazine C)?" the relative readership standings obtained in the original questionnaire were reversed.

When the comments made on the follow-up questionnaire were taken into account, the readership of the three publications in question were changed still further.[2]

2. Hans Zeisel has reported three different magazine preference studies which gave three different answers, apparently due to what specific question was asked.

In Magazine A's survey, the question was, "Which one is your favorite?"; and Magazine A won over B and C. In Magazine B's survey, the question

[2] H. P. Longstaff and G. P. Laybourn, "What Do Readership Studies Really Prove?" *Journal of Applied Psychology,* Vol. 33 (December, 1949), pp. 585–593, at pp. 592–593.

whether he *happened to have read the issue yet,* with only sure readers being counted in the audience. Words like those in italics further devalue the importance of previous reading. Following is a more detailed description of the interview.

The editorial-interest interview on any magazine issue is prefaced by a general question as to whether the respondent has looked through any issue in recent months. If a person has not had enough interest to look into an issue in, say, six months, it would appear that he would have little desire to advise the editor on how to improve the magazine. Admitted recent readers, however, seem logical candidates to advise the editor, and the interviewer holds out an issue, saying:

> Here is an issue of (Name of magazine) that you may not have happened to read yet. While I quickly leaf through it, would you give me your first impression of which articles look interesting?

This approach, with some slight variations, is the means of orienting both the interviewer and the respondent to an inspection of the issue— aimed at information on attitudes, not historical facts about reading behavior.

The *editorial-interest technique* originally allowed for a reading check on each item. After the respondent indicated his interest or lack of interest in the item, the interviewer asked if this was the first time he had seen it. The question is an ingenious one, since a "yes" answer amounts to an admission of never having seen it. However, Alfred Politz considered single-item identification too burdensome and possibly inaccurate and proceeded through the entire issue before mentioning previous reading.[7] If the respondent interrupts to mention that he has seen something, he is asked whether he would say it looked interesting if this were the first time he had seen it.

While wording may vary slightly, the above procedure is a widely approved method of conducting respondents through magazine issues in audience research. After the major editorial features have been noted, the respondent is cautioned about the fact that articles and pictures in different magazines are often similar. He is then asked what appears to be a logical closing question:

> Just for the record, now that we have been through this issue, would you say you definitely happened to read it before, or didn't read it, or aren't you sure?

[7] *A Study of the Accumulative Audience of Life, Life* (May 1, 1950), p. 106.

The question is designed to be explicit about the particular issue, with emphasis upon the issue as a whole. At the same time, it is carefully worded to attach no prestige to claims of reading an important publication, and to imply no loss of status for admitting the reading of a low-class magazine. *Just for the record, happened to,* and *before* are words and phrases which guard the respondent's ego, no matter which final response he gives. In survey supervision, however, the field workers must be trained to handle this closing question with extreme precision, for it represents the most important purpose of the interview.

Magazine audiences measured by the editorial-interest method have been shown to match those measured by the application of recognition controls. Extensive prepublication interviewing has shown little evidence of false reading claims for most consumer magazines.

By way of contrast, a direct approach to issue reading, including thorough inspection of prepublished issues after the respondent knows that the purpose is to verify the fact of reading, will produce fully one-fourth as many spurious reading claims as there are people in a properly measured audience.

Age of Issue

A magazine, unlike a broadcast program, may lie on a table for weeks or be passed on to one or more other households before it is discarded. While advertisers may be chiefly interested in what happens in the first few weeks, it is well known that the same copy of a magazine may be opened and read a year or more after issuance. In other words, the total audience of a magazine issue is something which grows for years; certainly the practical period of audience accumulation for the issue is likely to extend for several weeks or months.

The advertiser may lose interest in late readers because they are so few, because the season is far gone, or because he cannot wait indefinitely for research evidence. Research, on the other hand, may discount the later readers not because they are unimportant, but because early readers forget the issue before the last person has read it. As a result, a survey of issue audience may show a declining measured audience, even though the real audience is still growing.

Life magazine is considered to be read and passed along relatively fast, and a special tabulation of interviews in the accumulative study showed the pattern of estimated total audience of Table 5.

The issue ages at time of interview are averages for interviewing periods.

any higher number of regions to match his product's distribution. Accurate information on reading audiences to fit all possible regional combinations would require far more extensive samples than are presently contemplated. Note also the trend toward regional editions for regional markets at a time when geographical differences in markets seem to be getting less and less important!

With further reference to audience surveys for magazines, their great attraction lies in the fact that they supply the advertiser with information not available from other sources. They discover who reads magazines, how many read them, and where they live, in addition to many facts about their living and reading characteristics.

The number of copies sold, as reported by the Audit Bureau of Circulations, tells little about reading, but is an actual count of copies sold under specified conditions. The importance of these audits remains undiminished and furnishes assurance to the advertiser that the publisher has carried out his obligation in good faith. As a sound basis for advertising contracts, it is unlikely that sampling estimates can supplant the copy census.

Primary and Nonprimary Readers

Magazine audience surveys include people who read copies passed along to them and copies available away from home. Interviewers make no effort to find a magazine copy in the home, but only try to discover whether each person in the sample has previously read or not read any particular measured issue. Readers belonging to the household originally owning the copy are commonly designated as primary—to distinguish them from "pass-along" or incidental readers. There is a tendency in advertising to use the total reading audience, although sometimes the quality of nonprimary reading is challenged.

While it is not easy to identify primary homes which have purchased single copies, there is some evidence of reading quality based on approximate separation of primary and nonprimary groups.[10] Experimental work by the Advertising Research Foundation showed that advertisement noting by readers of *Life* in primary homes exceeded noting in pass-along homes, as indicated by average scores of 20.0 and 17.3 per cent respectively of those reading the issue. The average score for those picking up the issue outside of the home was 17.9 per cent. There was also evidence of slightly better average recall of advertisements by primary readers, whose score was 3.2

[10] Darrell B. Lucas, "The ABCs of ARF's PARM," *Journal of Marketing*, Vol. 25 (July, 1960), pp. 9–20, at p. 14.

per cent, compared with scores of 2.8 and 2.5 per cent, respectively, for pass-along readers and incidental readers.

The relative proportions of primary and nonprimary magazine readers can be deduced to some extent, in spite of the difficulty of identifying these groups clearly. The audience of *Life* magazine, for example, is more than double the reading population of the households of original owners. If some members of these owner households do not read *Life*, then it is evident that the proportion of nonprimary readers is even greater. Most other publications have a smaller proportion of nonprimary readers than *Life*, ranging down to an almost negligible proportion for some Sunday newspaper magazine supplements.

In terms of the known biases of "noting" measures, it is possible (and perhaps probable) that the evidence discussed here is not so much a reflection of differences in the "quality of readership" of primary versus nonprimary readers, but more a difference in the "noting bias" of primary versus nonprimary readers. To the extent that primary (and presumably more regular) readers of a magazine are more familiar with what to expect of a magazine's advertising than nonprimary readers, they would be more likely to think, "Yes, that looks like an ad that I would have expected to appear in Blank magazine."

Differences in the characteristics of primary and nonprimary readers are certainly difficult to measure, but rough classifications indicate that nonprimary groups include increased proportions of teenagers, people in large families, and members of households on the lower end of the economic and occupational scales.

The pattern of male and female reading does not appear to vary between primary and nonprimary households for the general magazines edited for both sexes.

The total significance of the known and estimated facts regarding primary and nonprimary reading would indicate that the nonprimary audience is somewhat lower than the primary, both in the quality of the reading and in the quality of the readers from an advertiser's viewpoint. These deficiencies are significant, but they are probably so small in relation to the size of the nonprimary audience as to make that segment highly important for most leading publications. Since total reading audiences are normally described in terms of the quality of primary and nonprimary readers combined, *it is recommended that advertisers follow the total-audience concept.* The totals may be expressed either as individuals or as households in which at least one person qualifies as a reader.

Newspapers of standard size, unlike magazines, have such important reading content on the exposed front page that it can be digested only by an act of reading. The fact that there is seldom any front-page space available to advertisers is compensated for in part by the continuation of news items on inside pages. The reading incentives of such inside features as sports, society, and cartoons also ensure heavy inside traffic.

Since by its very nature news motivates quick reading and rapidly loses interest, there is little need to wait more than a few hours or a day before measuring total audience. From a research standpoint, however, news develops so rapidly that the same publication may have several different editions every day, and this tends to "foul up" test procedures.

Measuring Daily Newspaper Audiences

The prestige of reading a newspaper—especially certain prominent publications—poses a threat to any direct approach for audience measurement. A further complication is the fact that people honestly think they are *regular* readers of a paper even when they actually miss a good many issues.

As with magazines, it is more objective and satisfactory to measure average issue audiences than to attempt to define and measure some degree of regularity of reading. And, as with magazines, it becomes necessary to divert the respondent from the true purpose of an audience interview in order to obtain unprejudiced information. Following is a description of a technique which has produced generally acceptable audience information on newspapers in such a complex market as New York City.[11]

The first effort at diverting the respondent comes with introductory questions dealing with various activities, including exposure to such other media as television, radio, and magazines. The interviewer may then say:

> I would like to ask you a few questions about newspapers. Some people like to read the papers for news, and some like to read the papers because of the columnists and features. Others like to read them for the ads.
>
> Which paper do you like best to read for the news?
>
> Which paper do you think has the best columnists and features?
>
> Which paper do you look at most frequently for the ads?
>
> Do you read the same paper or papers every day? Or do you like to change around sometimes to see what other papers have to say?
>
> We would like to know what papers you ever read or look through. Which of these (give printed list of local papers) weekday papers have you read or looked through at any time *in the past week?* We mean at home or any papers

[11] *Profile of the Millions*, 2d edition (New York: *The News*, 1958), p. 271.

you might have looked at somewhere away from home. Will you include the ones you usually read as well as the ones you just happened to look at in the past week. For instance, have you read or looked through (Name of paper) at any time in the past week?

This series of questions gives the respondent a chance not only to list papers of high status but also to admit casual looking over lower-status papers without too much ego involvement. Much of the question design is intended to aid memory and to encourage mention of any paper which happened into the respondent's hands. After the mention of one paper or more in response to the last question, the interviewer asks:

It is very important for us to know when different papers are read. When was the last time you read or looked through a weekday copy of the (Name of paper)?

If the respondent answers that he has read a paper "today," there follows the question:

When was the time before today?

While respondents have no way of knowing that yesterday is different from any other day, it actually becomes the crucial day for measurement. Only the "yesterday" answers to the last question are counted as a part of the daily newspaper audience. It is logically a fact that all the people reading a particular daily paper *yesterday* are equal to the total audience of the daily paper. This gets around the question as to whether an issue is dated the day it arrives and whether the respondent reads it on the same day. Only the people who read some issues on more than one day and who also miss reading at all on some other days might distort the audience measure. The number of such people is considered negligible.

An added feature of the above method is that it is not necessary or desirable to show a particular issue. This avoids the complications of varied editions and dates. The average audience is, of course, based on an average of numerous interviewing days, including the six weekdays in proper balance.

Measuring Sunday Newspaper Audiences

The weekend or Sunday newspaper differs from the daily paper in that it usually includes several special sections with varied reader appeal. Some sections, such as the magazine supplement, may have distribution in many markets, with patronage chiefly representing national advertisers. There may be many readers of one or more sections who do not see the rest of the paper.

The nature of the contents of the newspaper and the interval between issue dates may encourage reading beyond the first day or two. This suggests a longer delay before measuring the issue audience than is required for the daily paper. This is especially important if the total audience is defined to include all persons who have read any part of a Sunday paper.

The New York *Sunday News* and other weekend papers have asked about Sunday papers in surveys in which questions about daily papers had already been asked. In order to minimize any commitment the respondent may have attached to his report on dailies, he is reminded that people do not always read the same papers on Sunday. He is then asked if he read or looked into any part of the Sunday (Name of paper) within the last four weeks. He is reminded of the news section, magazine, comics, or any other special parts of that particular paper. Only if he says definitely "No" to all parts is questioning dropped on that paper.

Those who answer "Yes" or "Not sure" about the last four weeks are then shown a kit containing pages from each of the main sections of the previous Sunday paper. All edition dates are eliminated, and questioning about each section continues without reference to issue dates.

Regardless of whether or not the respondent remembers having seen any of the items shown, he is asked, "When was the last time you read or looked into any part of the Sunday (Name of paper)?" Only people who remember specific items and also claim reading relative to the previous Sunday's paper are counted in the measured audience.

Because of the difficulty of carrying all items from all editions of the available Sunday papers, respondents who fail to recognize items are asked, "What was it you saw in the Sunday (Name of paper)?" Any authentic item recalled is accepted as evidence of reading. Audiences measured by this process may be broken down according to the various identified sections of the Sunday paper.

Samples for Newspaper-audience Measurement

Individual newspapers commonly concentrate on localized markets, and audience surveys are restricted to the areas served. The specific area may include any circulation territory which is of interest to the publisher or to advertisers. Cities having more than one independently published newspaper especially require known-probability samples for newspaper-audience surveys. Even a "monopoly" paper with nearly 100 per cent penetration of households may not be read by all members of the family on an average day.

Each qualified reader must be measured separately. Projected audience totals—especially where competition is keen or where newspapers differ strongly in reader appeal or in reading habits—can be safely accepted only when the sample is representative and the measured universe can be clearly defined.

AUDIENCES OF OUTDOOR PANELS AND CAR CARDS

It is common to weigh the audiences of outdoor poster panels along with those of other print media in estimating advertising opportunities. However, since outdoor-panel audiences are the audiences of advertisements exclusively and since the medium has no other primary function than advertising, outdoor audiences are discussed only as advertising audiences in Chapter Thirteen.

Likewise, the audiences of car cards are considered to be advertising audiences. Both outdoor advertising and car cards will be considered in relation to advertising exposure in Chapter Twelve.

IMPLICATIONS

Accurate measurement and clear description of magazine audiences are highly important to national advertisers, who are the main buyers of magazine space. Newspapers, which normally sell space primarily to local advertisers, can be used more intelligently if audience information is known.

One of the unique features of printed media which complicates audience measurement is the prestige associated with reading and the resulting tendency to overclaim reading. Unusual also is the fact that so many skilled research experts have expended so much time and effort to devise techniques adequate for audience measurement under this handicap.

Measurement of both magazine and newspaper audiences is based on the same principle of diverting the respondent from the main purpose of the interview. It is assumed that most readers of either medium can recall long enough and discriminate well enough to give accurate information. By appearing to generalize the area of inquiry and emphasizing the subject of interest instead of behavior, research technology has succeeded in producing total-audience estimates acceptable to the advertising industry.

These audiences are not census counts, but are projections of sample percentages to total eligible populations under survey. The usefulness of such information is attested to by the conversion of print media planning, within one generation, from the basis of physical copies of publications sold to that of reading audiences and their economic and psychological characteristics.

eleven

Television and Radio Audiences

The broadcasting industry recognized the importance of measuring advertising opportunity in terms of people almost as soon as radio networks were created to reach national audiences. By 1930, the Association of National Advertisers had organized the Cooperative Analysis of Broadcasting to measure program popularity in telephone homes of many cities.

The early method of measurement, based largely on unaided recall, has been replaced by concurrent measuring methods less subject to memory errors. But the process of measuring advertising opportunity in terms of people in the audience continues, with improvements of sample and extension to national projections.

The universe within which measurement of broadcasting can operate is the population living in television or radio households and located in areas adequately served by station signals. Radio receivers were available in approximately 95 per cent of all households in the United States before the advent of network television. The expansion of television reduced the percentage of radio households slightly, and the probable saturation limit for

243

both television and radio—with adequate broadcast signals—is about 90 per cent of all households.

Network television, like earlier network radio, extends to almost the entire national market. The leading networks can reach approximately 95 per cent of all households equipped with television receivers. *Coverage,* actual program reception from a particular network at least once a week by someone in the household, includes the great majority of television households. The leading networks and their affiliated stations combine optimal numbers of stations in optimal locations with generally popular programs to achieve maximum national *coverage.* If a network has coverage of three-quarters of all television households sometime during the evening and weekend hours, then a sponsor has the opportunity to aim for substantially this audience by making his program sufficiently attractive. The practical audience limit of a program is somewhat smaller, but the network can offer an opportunity to reach its *coverage* through one or more weekly broadcasts.

From the standpoint of viewers, network evening television—the dominant broadcasting activity of national advertisers—includes sponsored programs and would seem to include spot commercial announcements. Actually, spot commercials are not a part of network advertising since they are purchased on an individual station basis, as contrasted with network time purchases of a group of interconnected stations.

Many national advertisers are called participating sponsors, but realistically their only connection with the program is the fact that their commercials occur during its broadcasts. The advertiser, who either sponsors a program or knows that his message will be broadcast in conjunction with a particular program, is chiefly interested in the program audience. This has given great impetus to the measurement of program audiences, both nationally and locally, and several types of measurement are available to the industry. Definitions of what is measured and the accuracy of measurement are both closely related to the method used.

Measurement of television and radio audiences is simpler than measurement of magazine and newspaper audiences because of the fixed reception time. A network television show covers the entire United States at approximately the same time or on approximately the same clock schedule—there is a small but significant amount of program audience that comes from delayed telecasts, and delays can run as much as fourteen days.

Anyhow, for the most part, there is no waiting to allow for the program and the commercials to reach the total audience. In fact, with the instantaneous reception to be measured, most television audience methods depend upon concurrent checking at the moment of viewing. All methods discussed in this chapter are of the *concurrent* type.

MECHANICAL RECORDING OF RECEPTION

Reception of television programs at a fixed time by means of receivers in a relatively fixed location makes the mechanical or electronic recorder an ideal instrument for measurement of sets or households tuned in. In 1942,

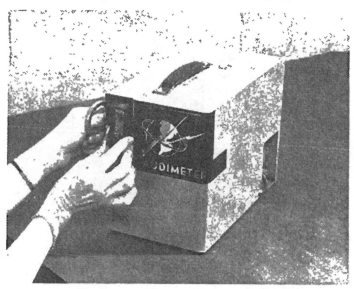

FIG. 9. Nielsen Audimeter. (*Courtesy of A. C. Nielsen Company.*)

the A. C. Nielsen Company first issued regular radio ratings based on its Audimeter, an electronic device installed in the home and connected to the broadcast receiver. Figure 9 pictures the latest model.

The records produced by the Audimeter show precisely when the television or radio receiver is tuned in and the channel or station to which it is tuned. In order to obtain the record of station tuning, it is essential to make connections with the circuits in the receiver. This does not interfere with reception, but the cost of building and servicing a sufficient number of Audimeters is considerable. There is compensation in the fact that this instrument provides what is probably the finest research procedure available to the advertising business.

The mechanical recording method furnishes information on specific sets and homes, indicating the complete tuning pattern of one or more receivers per home during the entire period selected for measurement. It shows whether and where the set was tuned prior to the particular program, whether the set was tuned in during the broadcast or changed from the program before it ended, and whether the set remained tuned in during commercial periods. This latter point is especially important to advertisers, since the Audimeter gave the first convincing evidence that few sets are actually tuned out during commercials within the program format. A number of factors contribute to the makeup of a program audience, and these are shown graphically in Fig. 10.

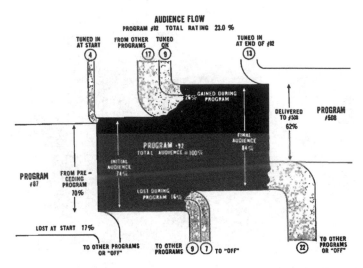

FIG. 10. Network audience flow. (*Courtesy of A. C. Nielsen Company.*)

According to the diagram, some of the sets tuned to the program at the start were already in operation, and some of these had been tuned to other stations. Other sets are originally turned on at the start of the program. During the broadcast, some sets are switched in from competing broadcasts, and some are turned on for the first time. Others, already tuned to the program, may be switched elsewhere or turned off. At the close of the program, some sets remain tuned to the station, some are switched elsewhere, and others are turned off. A study of this pattern will help in the understanding of definitions of ratings to be discussed next.

National Nielsen TV Ratings cover a period of two weeks and report each week separately. The total audience *rating* is the number and percentage of television homes tuned to each of the network programs for at least six minutes. A rating of 20.0 per cent, when there are 50 million television homes in the United States, would be projected to 10 million homes tuned to the program. This is the *total audience* of homes.

Since the Audimeter keeps a continuous record around the clock, it is possible to add up the total time spent on a program by the entire audience and then to compute the equivalent number of homes tuned in full time to the program. This is more commonly called the *average audience* of the program, and is the same as the average number of viewing homes tuned to the program minute by minute throughout the broadcast.

The *average audience* is always smaller than the *total audience,* since there are always some viewers who tune in for only part of a program. An exception might occur in the case of a five-minute program, with very high rates of "flow" in and out of the program by viewers. Computation of the *average audience,* in effect, weights each home in proportion to the time it is tuned to the program.

A third computation, extremely important to the sponsor in estimating the popularity of a program, is his *share of audience* of all simultaneous programs. In the above example, if 20 million of the total 50 million television homes have a set tuned in at the particular time period, then the *total audience* of 10 million homes tuned to the program becomes a 50 per cent share of audience. While the share-of-audience figure confuses the relative popularity of the program with its ability to get people to tune in who would otherwise have the set idle, it is useful in better interpreting the other ratings.

The continuous Audimeter record permits reporting of program audiences by 15-minute periods or any other arbitrary unit. A satisfactory minimum period of tuning for inclusion in the total rating can be accurately cut off; the Nielsen minimum for inclusion in the total rating is six minutes. This amount of time provides for a good chance of seeing a commercial and an even greater likelihood of knowing the sponsor's identity. Breakdown of tuning time into periods of actual commercial broadcasts, including spot commercials other than by sponsors, is one of the features of this mechanical method.

Because of the fine breakdowns of time made possible by Audimeter records, an answer has been found to one of the most tantalizing questions about television commercial reception. Does a large part of the audience turn off the set or change the tuning when commercial messages are broadcast? The A. C. Nielsen Company gives this answer: "Audimeter records have shown clearly, over a period of twelve years, that the number of families turning their sets off *or* shifting to another station at the time of the commercial announcement is *negligible;* in fact it is so very small that it cannot ordinarily be measured." [1]

While the indicated period began exclusively with radio measures in the United States, the American pattern did not change with the advent of television.

Problems in Mechanical Measurement

While mechanical recording of set tuning is generally convincing proof of program and commercial reception by a household, there are some questions and problems. The electronic record shows only where and when the set was tuned. It does not show how many were viewing or attending to the program, nor does it prove that anyone was near the receiver except to change the tuning. There are also occasional power failures or mechanical failures, and people are sometimes careless about either inserting a new cartridge in the Audimeter or putting the finished tape in the mail. Households may purchase additional receivers or otherwise make the record less than complete for the family unit. All of these problems have been studied; where they represent substantial considerations, attempts have been made to overcome them.

Briefly, other measuring methods must be used in conjunction with the Audimeter in order to estimate and describe the human audience for programs. The A. C. Nielsen Company supplements its national television ratings of homes tuned in with a matched sample of households near each Audimeter home, keeping diaries of program viewing. Neither cooperating household is aware of the other.

Human inertia can also be overcome a bit by rewarding Audimeter families with two 25-cent pieces which are automatically ejected from the mailable tape cartridge each time it is installed. Removal of the tape activates a loud buzzer which ensures that a new cartridge will be installed promptly. Information on new-set purchases and other household changes affecting the Audimeter operation can be reported or checked during the regular field servicing calls. These problems have not been so great as to interfere with practical use of the electronic method of measurement.

Hazards inherent in the mechanical measuring procedure have to be

[1] Arthur C. Nielsen, *Television Audience Research for Great Britain* (Chicago and Oxford: A. C. Nielseen Company, 1954), p. 116.

taken into account. One was suggested by the references to mailable tapes and servicing calls. It is highly important to keep these activities as infrequent and as unobtrusive as possible in order to minimize possible conditioning of viewing and listening behavior in metered homes. The small recording magazine of the Audimeter is usually removed at the end of two weeks and dropped into a self-addressed, stamped container ready for the mail. The replacement, which has arrived in the meantime, merely has to be pushed into place lightly with the fingers; this is the action which releases two quarters for compensation. Service calls are held down through the use of automatic equipment of fine workmanship; yet some calls are required for special service and for regular checking. It is believed that these reminders of the recording process have very little influence on audience activity, except perhaps for a few days after original installation.

Much more serious than audience conditioning is the problem of securing permission to establish a measuring household in the first place. Households are selected on a known-probability basis, and there is the usual problem of nonresponse expected in population surveys. There is also resistance to recruitment of a home for any regular commercial purpose and to installation of any instrument interconnected with the receiving set. Compensation and guaranteed payment for a share of possible repair service give some assurance, but the problem is not completely solved.

The alternative is not merely to add another random household, since certain easy-to-ascertain facts indicate differently. The size of the family unit in the unavailable household can ordinarily be learned—and this is one of the chief factors affecting television viewing. The usual substitution procedure is to seek out another family of equal size within a reasonable distance. Sampling is probably the biggest and most costly problem in the mechanical recording of a representative group of television households.

Instantaneous Mechanical Measurement

When mechanical records are obtained for a period of weeks and then have to be mailed to a central point for tabulation, valuable time is required. One solution is to connect all recording units by wire to a central point for continuous, quick tabulation.

The Instantaneous Audimeter of the A. C. Nielsen Company and the Arbitron of the American Research Bureau produce just such findings in limited urban areas, including New York City. Telephone facilities provide leased wires, independent of telephone service, and selected households are connected in suitable circuits. Since the wire-service cost is closely related to distance served, it is expensive to connect widely separated homes in rural areas.

When sample households can be selected in groups within small areas, as in crowded New York City, it is economical to connect some 25 television homes on a single wire circuit. Independent signals from all sets in a circuit can be received and tabulated automatically within a matter of seconds. A sponsor can sit at the central point and keep informed continuously of the sets tuning to his program, observing each change almost the instant it occurs. Reports from various cities, as in the former American Research Bureau Multi-city reports, can be coordinated and printed for air mail delivery within hours of a broadcast. When broadcasters and advertisers are willing to pay for such service on a national scale, technologists are ready to supply it. The centralized system is superior to independent meters in that failures are detected immediately and disturbance of the household and its receiving equipment is at a minimum.

MEASURING AUDIENCES BY DIARIES

A diary of broadcast reception is a record kept by the viewer or listener showing a complete listing or log of programs received. It should show the name of the program, the station or channel, the clock time and date of the broadcast, and the actual part of the broadcast time which was received. A diary keeper may maintain only his own record or keep the complete record for a household or group.

One of the first radio studies employing a diary was made by students of New York University in their own homes. The diary was used in conjunction with personal observation of set-tuning behavior by other members of the family. Since the observer was required to disqualify himself from normal tuning activity and since the sample was limited to homes having an available observer, the possibility of obtaining representative findings was ruled out; but the nature of the findings and the low operating cost aroused the interest of the Columbia Broadcasting System and led to extensive diary research.

The diary of a member of a broadcast audience is not intended to be filled in at bedtime or at the convenience of the diary keeper. If a diary is to have any likelihood of dependability as a record of attending programs, it should be filled in for each program while it is being received.

An accurate diary, unlike records of set tuning, can include information covering all persons in attendance. The original diary included full details

on who tuned in the program, behavior of the audience during the broadcast, and comments made about the program and about the commercials. A
diary can break down the program time into units as small as desired.
Diaries can also show audience flow in and out of particular programs or
stations (compare Fig. 10). Usually diaries are kept on carefully designed
record forms.

Problems Connected with the Diary

The attractive features of the diary method cannot be examined in proper
perspective without taking into account some possible limitations. The danger of omissions is especially great for radio, since radio may be heard in
and out of the room and with or without an enormous amount of competing activity. Background radio is especially likely to be forgotten in diary
keeping, as are the shorter or less popular broadcasts.

On the other hand, in the period of popular evening network radio
programs, there was a demonstrated tendency to exaggerate attendance to
leading shows. In other words, radio was not conducive to accurate diary
keeping by those who had agreed to cooperate.

So long as the number of television sets per household is small, the
prospects for accurate television diary records are much better than for
radio. Television is more confining to the viewer, both as to his location
and as to his indulgence in major competing activities. This also makes
television viewing a more important activity than radio listening ever was,
and the keeping of the diary may seem more significant.

These factors and the growing preoccupation of advertisers with useful
television data for individual markets have made the diary a major tool for
television research. Diary data can be gathered in many markets much too
small to justify the costs of mechanical measures of set tuning. Both the
A. C. Nielsen Company and the American Research Bureau supply single-
market television diary reports for hundreds of American cities.

The A. C. Nielsen Company has made considerable effort to ensure a
practical maximum in the keeping of accurate diary records. All diary homes
in the national sample supplementing the Audimeter and all households in
single-city samples of some 200 major markets are equipped with a signaling and time-counting device called the Recordimeter. This instrument is
easily plugged in with the television set and keeps an accurate count of the
number of hours of set operation. Signaling is both visual and auditory,
including a red light and a buzzer—one or both to remind the viewer every
half-hour to fill in the Audilog diary. With the aid of these prompting

signals and with the time record as a basis for validating the daily diary report, it is possible to ensure greater accuracy of the findings. Diary records which do not coincide with the indicated time of set tuning are discarded.

Even with these added safeguards, though, the diary does not replace the Audimeter as a basis for projecting national audiences by the A. C. Nielsen Company. Rather, it supplements the ratings of sets tuned in with a description of the human audience.

Two inherent features of any diary process are (1) the problem of obtaining agreement to keep a diary and later on additional records, and (2) the problem of avoiding the "conditioning" of viewing behavior as a result of too much consciousness of the whole operation.

While cooperation can be encouraged by the offer of substantial reward, the danger of conditioning is thereby increased. Many people who will gladly be interviewed will not agree to keeping a continuous record of viewing by themselves and the family. If they do agree to participate, many will turn in unsatisfactory records or none at all. The problem is that perhaps the people who keep the diary best may be the ones whose viewing is most likely to be affected by doing so. The increase in numbers of television receivers in each household will only serve to increase the problems of keeping adequate diaries.

Reporting and Quality of Diary Findings

Within its technical limitations, the diary provides an enormous amount of information. The time units are usually broken into fifteen-minute periods; except for the breakdown of smaller time segments, the diary contains all information furnished by a mechanical recorder and a great deal more. It shows total viewing audience and a breakdown of audiences for longer programs into fifteen-minute units.

It provides information for computing share of audience. It shows when the set is turned on and it shows audience flow from program to program and from station to station. More importantly, it provides information as to which members of the household make up the audience of any particular program. Audience flow is extremely important to the broadcasting station or network, and audience composition is of utmost importance to the advertiser and to the builder of a program.

The diary "falls down" when it records more in-home viewing than is indicated by the Recordimeter time check or when it shows viewing of sets that were not actually operating. During the heyday of radio, experiments with diaries under critical comparison with mechanical recorders in the same households led to the rejection of the diary for projecting radio audience totals. Experiments involving television have not been as damaging to the diary, but national projections based exclusively on the diary are not recommended.

An explanation of audience definitions is given later in the chapter (page 257).

MEASURING AUDIENCES BY COINCIDENTAL INTERVIEWS

Radio Hooperatings, based on coincidental telephone calls, began in 1934. Those ratings continued and were later complemented by Trendex coincidental ratings of television. Both operations depend upon telephone interviews with any household member capable of giving the required audience information.

The unique feature of this method is the fact that a complete rating is established on the basis of what program is being seen or heard at the instant of the call. It is not capable of measuring total audience or the audience flow from program to program. Instead, it provides a measure of the average or minute-by-minute audience and is based on human reporting but not subject to the failures of human recall. The principle underlying average measurement will be discussed next.

How Coincidental Calls Measure Average Audience

All population surveys require a sample of the universe being measured. The coincidental method requires also a sample of broadcast time. It is essential to keep the interviewing going continuously throughout the broadcast or at least to obtain an adequate sample at representative points in the audience pattern. The usual procedure is to attempt continuous sampling, making equal numbers of calls during nearly all of the minutes of the broadcast. A brief interlude is allowed for tuning the program in at the beginning and turning it off at the end. Since it requires about one minute to obtain and complete a television interview, there is justification for suspending calls for a minute at the end of each fifteen-minute period or other segment being reported.

Interpretation of the coincidental measurement of audience is based on the sampling principle. Any sample survey of a population presumes equal opportunity for each individual to be drawn into the sample. The coincidental sampling of time presumes that each viewing or listening home will have a chance of being "caught" attending a program in proportion to the total time that home gives to the program.

Those who view a fifteen-minute show all fifteen minutes are certain to count as viewers. These full-time viewing homes are counted as one viewing unit, and if every family viewed the program every minute, the rating would be 100. Or if all viewers watched complete programs, the rating would always equal the total viewing families. This is not the practical situation.

Suppose that during a fifteen-minute broadcast each of three different families viewed the program for five minutes. The chance that any one of these families would be called while viewing would only be 5 out of 15, which is 1 out of 3. The likelihood of finding a viewer by calling all three famiiles, each at a random point during the broadcast, would be three times one-third (1 out of 3) or 1. In other words, the chance that three families, each tuned in for five minutes, would be counted as a viewer is the same as the chance for a single family viewing all fifteen minutes, namely, 1.

In a similar way, two families, one viewing ten minutes and the other five, would most likely count as 1 when called by the random coincidental method. Any combination of families with a total viewing time of fifteen minutes would most likely produce only 1 point or unit in the final rating.

The coincidental rating is, then, based on total viewing time of all viewing homes or the equivalent of full-time viewing by some. But a measure of equivalent full-time viewing is the same as a minute-by-minute average of the audience attending an average minute during the show. This is what the industry calls the *average audience rating*.

While the coincidental method produces evidence of the total amount of viewing or listening *or any other measured activity,* it cannot assess the total audience. It seeks no report on behavior during earlier minutes of the broadcast or any assurance as to the likelihood of attending the remainder of the broadcast. Such information would be too crude. Even if a half-hour program is reported in 2 fifteen-minute segments, there is no way of knowing whether the audience of the second half includes people from the first fifteen minutes or a whole new audience.

The lack of information on individual families during a span of time makes it impossible to put together the pattern of audience flow throughout an evening or the pattern of loyalty to successive broadcasts of the same show. The coincidental method measures just one thing, namely, the *average audience* for the measured time unit.

The share of audience is also an average share of the average number of homes with sets operating. The coincidental method makes it possible to ask about the number of people in the household viewing or listening to the program. Average audiences can be expressed in terms of individuals as well as homes, and the same qualifications apply to the meaning of average audience and average share of average audience of all simultaneous shows.

Advantages of coincidental telephone measurement grow out of the fact that almost all homes have a listed telephone; the fact that someone in almost every home answers the telephone; the fact that very few refuse to give a short coincidental interview; and the fact that nonresponse to the telephone gives useful information.

To these facts are added the economy of telephone interviewing; the avoidance of memory loss by obtaining information of the moment; and the availability of responses for immediate tabulating and reporting. The useful information obtained when a call is not answered is that presumably no one is at home attending a broadcast. This makes it possible to include nonresponse homes as part of the base of the surveyed sample.

Limitations of the telephone coincidental method grow out of its inability to measure either total audience or audience flow and also out of doubts as to the dependability of personal reporting. It is well known that people are often almost apologetic when a coincidental call reaches them with the set turned off.

In addition, the abrupt kind of introduction necessary to keep the interview brief is likely to suggest status for viewing or listening. For example, to start with a statement that the call is from a television rating service is likely to enlist a desire to report some viewing. There appears some tendency for some people to report the set turned on when the facts are otherwise (compare page 31). This was demonstrated dramatically in a report in 1947 concerning radio listening by families of college students.[2]

An unpublished study of TV viewing in Syracuse, New York, included both telephone interviews and personal interviews, using the coincidental method.[3] Personal interviews followed the coincidental questions with an inspection of the TV set to check tuning and channel. The sets reported in use over the telephone during the popular evening hours exceeded those

[2] M. D. Kaplon, "The Observational Method in Radio Audience Measurement," *The American Psychologist*, Vol. 2 (September, 1947), p. 335.

[3] *A Study of TV Viewing in Syracuse, New York,* conducted by TPI Ratings, Inc., May, 1958, unpublished.

reported and checked by personal calls by about 15 per cent. While direct, definitive evidence of the general pattern of exaggerated claims of set tuning is not available, there must be an assumption of some exaggeration in coincidental telephone reports of broadcast reception.

A final, though not fatal, handicap of the telephone coincidental method is the fact that every reported time period requires a complete sample. The calls are short, making it possible to complete many calls per interviewer, but each fifteen-minute period or other reporting unit gains its entire base from calls made during that same segment of time. Samples for a year include millions of homes, and many households are called more than once the same year. This makes the coincidental method cost more than the recall method and more than the simplest kind of operation.

However, after more than a quarter of a century of industry support, it is clear that the virtues of the telephone coincidental method outweigh the disadvantage of high sampling expense.

Program Popularity Ratings

Of all the rating methods, the telephone coincidental technique is probably best adapted to quick comparisons of program popularity. The people who create network shows have a special interest in obtaining quick ratings of their shows in competition with other network programs. The immediate question concerns how many people—in areas where signal strength and competition are relatively equal—choose one program in preference to one or more others simultaneously available. There are only a limited number of cities which have adequate signal strength from all leading networks and which have the same combination of programs available on those networks at the same time.

The telephone coincidental method has several advantageous features for making the kinds of popularity comparisons just described. Telephone penetration of homes is high in urban areas served by all networks. The coincidental method can be economically applied on a small scale to measure the popularity of a single broadcast. The data can be tabulated and analyzed quickly. And the coincidental method is considered to be one of the more accurate measures.

Electronic measurement, especially the instantaneous type, would be excellent, but it is expensive to equip a large number of cities for this purpose. Diaries require time for processing, they are a rougher method of measuring, and they are better adapted for measurement of all programs over a period. Even the recall method, which measures a span of several hours at a time, is more crude and is not as well adapted to short periods of measurement.

Popularity ratings of competing network programs have been likened to comparisons of the drawing power of as many theaters at a crossroads— all with free admission. Since the relative drawing power of the shows varies in different areas or communities, it is desirable to check over a wide area. The telephone coincidental method can be easily brought into action by alerting interviewers in all desired cities for the period of broadcast. Since the data are all coincidental with the broadcast, there need be no delay for callbacks or late reports. Assembly of reports by wire services makes possible complete tabulations within a matter of hours. Trendex (on a custom basis) and Hooperatings are currently available for coincidental telephone reports on television and radio, respectively, including sponsor identification, in many of the network cities.

SUMMARY OF CONCEPTS

A summary of concepts and implied definitions from the earlier part of this chapter will aid in arriving at conclusions. Following are the chief broadcasting ratings now employed in the industry:

Total individual audience is the number of individuals attending to some minimal part of a particular program.

Total audience of households is the number of households with sets tuned to the program or with a family member attending to some minimal part of a particular program.

Total audience rating is usually expressed as the per cent of sample (sample of individuals, or sample of television or radio homes, as indicated) attending to some minimal part of a particular program.

Average audience ratings provide the above information on the basis of average minute-by-minute audiences in contrast with *total* audiences.

Sets in use usually refers to the percentage or number of households with a receiver tuned in to any and all programs at a particular designated broadcasting period.

Share of audience is a way of expressing the *rating* (based on all television- or radio-equipped homes) as a percentage of those homes or households which have a set turned on, regardless of which program it is receiving. In other words, "share of audience" expresses a rating as a percentage of the total *sets in use*.

IMPLICATIONS

Early in the development of television network broadcasting, the Advertising Research Foundation set up a committee to recommend standards of measurement for the industry.[4] The committee included leading research experts from advertisers, advertising agencies, and the broadcasting business. It did not include research organizations, although the rating services cooperated through discussion and by revealing details of their operations not otherwise known. On the basis of this expanded information and through a review of concepts involved, the committee agreed upon a report recommending certain practices and standards to the advertising business.

The discussion of the committee report will be devoted to the implications of three of their major recommendations. They are as follows:

1. Exposure to a broadcast should be measured in terms of set tuning.
2. The unit of measurement should be the household.
3. The measurement should report the average instantaneous audience.

Let it be emphasized that, if precise information were available on alternatives to these three recommendations at the same cost, the present authors would disagree with all three recommendations. Ideally and as a concept, it is felt that some psychological unit of viewing or listening is superior to the mechanical fact of set tuning; it is felt that individuals are considerably more important to advertisers than the household units which they comprise; and it is felt that the total audience having some minimal program contact is of more advertising significance to an exclusive program sponsor than is the confusing concept of an average audience. The average audience probably is more useful to participating advertisers.

Accordingly, the three points will be discussed strictly as concepts and without reference to the practicability of their measurement.

It hardly seems necessary to argue that the act of viewing a program or listening to it is more significant to an advertiser than the availability of a tuned-in set. All advertising communication and influence depends upon sensory attitudes of people. Psychologists have succeeded in providing definitions sufficiently precise to be used for determining whether or not a broadcast is being attended to, with or without competing activities.

[4] *Recommended Standards for Radio and Television Program Audience Size Measurements* (New York: Advertising Research Foundation Inc., 1954), insert following p. 25.

The advantage of considering individuals rather than households is that individuals have great market significance; futhermore, information on individuals can always be recombined into household units. Most purchases are planned and made by individuals solely for their own consumption. Even in the family unit, one individual is often the unofficial purchasing agent for the group. Certainly there is a great advantage in being able to study advertising opportunities with individuals, regardless of whether one person or a family unit is to be the ultimate customer.

The average instantaneous (or minute-by-minute) audience, like the household unit, necessarily conceals valuable information from the advertiser. An average rating does not tell how many individuals or how many households are involved. Like the household, it represents a conglomeration of individuals, exposed in varying degrees, without revealing how many there are altogether. Some programs by their nature require almost complete reception in order to have entertainment or informational value; serious drama is an example. Other programs, such as variety shows, can be picked up in part or in whole with complete satisfaction. The most important thing for the advertiser is that people hear one or more advertising messages and identify his sponsorship. The total number, with proper sub-classifications, is the most useful kind of rating for appraising advertising opportunity.

Need for Goals

The contrast of opinions between those of the present authors and the group speaking for the industry is aimed at the setting of goals for ultimate evaluation of broadcast advertising. The authors are first concerned with these goals and the reasons supporting the views they have expressed. The most practical immediate course may be somewhat different, depending on what measures are available, their adaptability and flexibility for use by advertisers, and their costs. There is also the consideration of how well the rating organizations conduct their surveys and report them to the industry. The latter consideration is one which can be interpreted only on the basis of knowledge of current practices.

The Three Techniques

Each of the three chief measuring techniques discussed is better adapted to one kind of measurement than another. The mechanical method, with all of its precision, measures *set tuning*, as recommended by the industry committee. Individual ratings and audience composition must be obtained from supplementary sources. Both diaries and telephone interviews take advantage of the opportunity to measure viewing or listening, although they can also report *sets in use*.

The mechanical method is also ideally adapted for measuring *household* units, especially where only one receiver is available or is dominant in the home. Again, this meets the committee recommendation, although diaries and telephone interviews can also produce household information. Over all, there can be no doubt that the mechanical method is superior for *household* measurement of *set tuning* and is, therefore, best suited to the committee specifications up to this point.

Because the electronic records of set tuning are continuous down to a matter of seconds, they can be transcribed into both *average* and *total household set tuning*. On this point, both the present authors and the committee can be satisfied with the mechanical method.

For practical reasons, the *diary method* has been restricted to measurement of audience totals, although quarter-hour breakdowns are possible. The *coincidental method* meets the committee recommendation by producing an *average instantaneous audience* measurement. It cannot, by any coincidental check, produce a total audience rating. While some might argue that a telephone coincidental measure—all things considered—is as accurate as any practical mechanical measuring device, the current sample is not sufficient to provide projectable ratings even for telephone homes.

In Summary

In summary, the Audimeter or mechanical method meets the three committee recommendations and directly satisfies only one of those proposed by the authors. The diary method meets the committee recommendation on *household* measurement and can report *set tuning,* but "falls down" on measuring *average audience*. The telephone coincidental method measures *average audience* and can report *set tuning by households*.

However, the two latter methods can hardly compete with the mechanical recorder for ascertaining *set tuning* with precision. The only method which fully meets the committee recommendations is the mechanical recorder or Audimeter, even though set tuning does not prove the presence of viewers or listeners.

The present authors do not arrive at such a simple solution, since *no single method measures total individual viewing or listening with sufficient accuracy*. Granted that the mechanical method is accurate for measuring set tuning, the conversion of set tuning by means of diary information to estimate individual human audiences is not ideal. The diary method, taken by itself, falls short for reasons discussed earlier. The telephone coincidental method is ruled out for obtaining total audience information. So long as the present measuring methods remain, the authors agree with the implications of the committee favoring use of the mechanical method. They also believe that the best available method for projecting national totals of individual viewers or listeners is to supplement the mechanical method with the best possible diary procedure.

The net of this comparison of views is that the authors would add the diary data to Audimeter information, which alone appears to meet the basic standards of the Advertising Research Foundation committee. Since the committee also recommended that supplementary information be obtained on individuals in the audience, it appears that diary data are an essential addition to mechanical measurement.

Only on the matter of psychological definition of viewing or listening ing is there a practical difference in recommendations. The committee felt that an adequate psychological definition of viewing or listening which would be capable of application to measurement is too remote for present consideration. The authors believe that adequate definitions already exist.

Gains in psychological knowledge may lead to viewing and listening definitions which are more acceptable to research leaders in the advertising industry. Improvements in research technology are likely to bring psychological measurement of viewing and listening closer to practical realization.

So long as television viewing tends to concentrate around a single set in the household, the recommendations of the advertising industry are admirably met by the Audimeter of the A. C. Nielsen Company. Nevertheless, it is desirable that methods be improved for converting Audimeter records into viewing and listening by individual people in order better to serve the needs of advertisers. If present psychological definitions are inadequate, then the burden is on research technicians to improve them. If those definitions are already useful and practical, then it is up to research technicians to develop more precise ways of interpreting the already precise electronic Audimeter data.

twelve

Exposure of
Advertisements

EXPOSURE AND PERCEPTION

EXPOSURE TO COMMERCIALS

EXPOSURE TO MAGAZINE ADVERTISEMENTS

EXPOSURE TO OUTDOOR AND

   TRANSPORTATION ADVERTISING

IMPLICATIONS

The previous chapters have dealt with audiences of issues of printed media and audiences of broadcast programs. In the present chapter we turn to a consideration of a different kind of problem, *exposure of advertisements.*

Nearly every advertiser prefers, where possible, to study his own advertising opportunities in media in terms of actual exposure of his messages to media traffic. An advertiser is one step nearer to success when his message is *exposed* to an audience, rather than just carried physically by a media vehicle to its own larger audience.

EXPOSURE AND PERCEPTION

A medium can take exclusive credit only for bringing traffic to where advertisements will be exposed. What follows exposure is a dual function of media and of copy. (Once more, as stated at the beginning of Chapter Nine, it needs to be emphasized that the word "copy" is used throughout this book to refer to all features of an advertisement, either print or broadcast, that distinguish it from all others.)

As to the dual function of media and of copy, Alfred Politz holds that the media buyer should be more concerned with knowing the *exposure* of his advertisement (the media function) than the *perception* or readership of his advertisement (the copy function).[1]

Certainly it is important to understand the differences between advertising exposure (*can* see or hear the message) and advertising perception (*does* see or hear the message).[2] This has been well put by James Playsted Wood:

> Exposure is not synonymous with perception. It is a cliché of humor that one was exposed to this or that but that no contagion ensued. . . . Exposure does mean that the opportunity for perception takes place. It establishes one *sine qua non* of experience, contiguity. Unless the object is there to be seen, felt, heard, smelled, tasted, or otherwise recognized, it cannot be experienced. A magazine takes an advertiser's message to the point of perception. It brings reader and advertisement into physical proximity. The advertisement is brought within range of the reader's sense and his mind. There it must compete with everything else in his immediate environment for the reader's attention.[3]

In other words, a specific advertising medium cannot be held accountable for the entire communication process for an advertisement; but the medium can and should be held responsible for exposure of the message—within the framework of a good editorial environment—to the people the advertiser wants to reach.[4]

It should be recognized, though, that there are other views as to the significance of exposure as compared with the significance of perception. This is shown in the work of the Audience Concepts Committee of the Advertising Research Foundation, which for intermedia comparisons took the position that perception is the most logical measure of advertising,

[1] Alfred Politz, "What Is Essential to Know from Magazine Media Research?" *Media/scope*, Vol. 3 (April, 1959), pp. 3–8.

[2] Alfred Politz, "Media Performance vs. Copy Performance," *Media/scope*, Vol. 4 (November, 1960), pp. 61–63.

[3] James Playsted Wood, *Advertising and the Soul's Belly: Repetition and Memory in Advertising* (Athens, Ga.: University of Georgia Press, 1961), p. 1.

[4] *Exposure of Advertising*, an experimental study conducted for *Life* by The Audits & Surveys Company, Inc. (New York: Time, Inc., 1959), p. 2.

although not the ultimate measure.[5] The committee also considered measures of exposure, whether vehicle exposure or advertising exposure, as invalid for intermedia comparisons.

In any case, it is important for the advertiser to know how surely a media vehicle will expose his messages to the people in its own audience, how many times each message will be exposed to each member of the media audience, and how variable the exposure opportunities may be in different locations in the structure of the same vehicle.

Exposure has somewhat different meanings in connection with different media and different cost units. In television and in magazines where the individual advertiser is prominent in the medium (as with a sponsored network program or a full-page advertisement), the fact of exposure is very important, and there is a strong likelihood of perception. Outdoor posters and transportation advertisements also have a good opportunity of converting exposure into perception (see pages 278 to 282).

But newspaper advertisers, normally using small space in competition with many others on a large page, usually have a less commanding position than do advertisers using television commercials or full pages in magazines. For this reason and because of problems of defining and measuring exposure in newspapers, this largest of all media "dollarwise" will not be examined in this chapter.

EXPOSURE TO COMMERCIALS

Sponsors of television and radio broadcasts have their maximum opportunity for effective exposure when the property is exclusive and when stations are not overly exploited by other advertisers during station breaks.

The early years of television were marked by considerable advertiser control of programs and a minimum of unrelated interruptions during or adjacent to the scheduled time. Under these conditions, the sponsor was free to schedule commercial announcements at suitable times, often with some relation to the specific content of the program. As television grew and as the competition for time increased, the stations were able to assume more control of programs and to insert unrelated commercials at station breaks. Ultimately, the breaking down of exclusive sponsorships and the sale of participating or spot commercial time have combined to reduce the

[5] *Toward Better Media Comparisons,* a Report of the Audience Concepts Committee of the Advertising Research Foundation, Inc. (New York: Advertising Research Foundation, Inc., 1961), p. 29.

relative opportunity of any one advertiser. At the same time, growth of total network audiences has helped the total-exposure opportunity of each advertiser to remain highly attractive.

Fairfax M. Cone of Foote, Cone & Belding has pointed out that in recent years practically all television advertising, in a sense, has become spot television.[6] Whereas there used to be one sponsor only for a TV program, the sponsor eventually became an alternate sponsor or even shared the program with more than one other sponsor. Next, "with his advertising distributed among three or four different products over two weeks instead of concentrated on one each week, he was soon to become no sponsor at all. He would be merely another advertiser on a purely spot basis. This he has become." [7]

Also, television-advertising opportunities are closely related to set tuning. The Nielsen Audimeter (see Chapter Eleven) gives positive evidence of whether a set is turned on and remains tuned to a particular station at the time of commercial announcements. It has been repeatedly demonstrated that the vast majority of sets tuned to a program retain that tuning during *middle* commercials, or other announcements within the main body of the broadcast. If a set is turned on to view a particular program, those who are viewing the program may miss all or part of the opening commercial; likewise, people who are turning off sets may not wait for the closing commercial. If people are changing stations between programs, the commercials of particular advertisers may gain some and lose others. Advertisers have learned to cope with the hazards when a show opens or closes, and often move the commercial in or provide some incentive to keep tuned.

Set tuning would indicate that substantially all the households tuned to a program have some opportunity for the exposure of internal program commercials. The *average* audience of homes tuned in would be a better guide than the *total* audience for the purpose of estimating exposure of a commercial. Data on exposures to individuals are less available and less convincing, though, making the advertiser less sure of the number of individuals to whom a commercial is exposed. Information from diaries is the chief guide, and the usual diary unit of fifteen minutes makes it possible to estimate advertising exposure during different segments of an evening half-hour or longer show.

[6] Fairfax M. Cone, "TV Magazine Concept Is Here . . . ," *Advertising Age*, Vol. 32 (December 11, 1961), pp. 73–76.

[7] Page 74 of citation in footnote 6.

The actual availability and behavior of members of a television audience of homes or individuals during commercial announcements is obviously less than set tuning. The commercial of a sponsor is ordinarily a program interruption, and people who do not resist the commercial by changing the set tuning may use this opportunity to exit briefly or to participate in activities which reduce commercial contact. Conversing with others, looking away from the television screen, or attention to other matters may lessen the reception of an advertising message.

In fact, the claim was made at one time by the water commissioner of Toledo that he could measure the degree of attention to television by the amount of fluctuation he found in the water pressure for the city. Apparently the theory was that in a city with only one television station, lack of attention to what was on the TV screen was highly correlated with the use of plumbing facilities. The method was dubbed "Program Popularity through Pumpage and Pressure."

Of course, the person who remains in the room with the television set may converse actively and at the same time be watching and listening with care to see when the program resumes. Another individual, who may read or look elsewhere during a commercial, may also listen carefully for a cue to the resumption of the show. Very few viewers make any physical change of the tuning during the main body of the program just for the purpose of avoiding commercials entirely, and those who merely try to turn off their minds during commercials may absorb a great deal of what the advertiser is trying to convey. The producers of television advertisements take into account the various possibilities of reduced cooperation. Usually there is something for those who only see, something for those who only hear, and a great deal for those who think they are ignoring the message of the sponsor. Available evidence indicates that a middle commercial is exposed with some effect to more than 80 per cent of the average program audience.

Any estimate of audiences exposed to spot television commercials during station breaks is not likely to be very precise. It has been a common practice to estimate such exposure by taking an average of the average audiences of the two programs before and after a station break. But it is clear that such an estimate is on the high side, since this is the time when people are tuning in and out or are turning sets on and off.

To determine what happens at this period, the New York *News* conducted a survey of the New York City market immediately after station breaks for a large number of prime time evening shows.[8] The survey covered three network stations and four independent stations. It was found that more than one-fourth of the viewers of the preceding and of the succeeding programs had their television receivers turned off during the entire station break. Another group of the respondents who viewed preceding or succeeding shows reported some kind of serious diversion from the station-break contents, even though the set remained turned on. The results indicated that little more than one-half of the "average" audience of individuals had exposure to station-break commercials comparable to the exposure during the internal commercials of a program.

EXPOSURE TO MAGAZINE ADVERTISEMENTS

Publication advertisers are intensely interested in the possibility that some advertising locations offer better opportunities than others. Studies of editorial traffic in both newspapers and magazines have been used to estimate traffic for past advertisements. The problem has been of particular concern to advertisers in magazines, since customarily they pay the same rate for nearly all locations and, in most instances, have no choice as to location of their advertisements. Since the more significant studies of page exposure have been done on magazines, the present discussion will deal with that medium.

It is customary to request certain locations in the issue, even though nearly all leading magazines have very few designated locations for sale. Nor do publishers admit of any lessening of exposure in some parts of the magazine, since the price of each location is usually the same. There have been many decades of skirmishing to gain advertising advantages—usually with few concessions on the part of leading publishers to meet advertising demands.

Studies of editorial traffic through magazines support the practice of charging equally for most advertising locations. Reading audiences—the traffic for advertising exposure—have shown amazing evidence of thorough traffic through editorial features. Unfortunately, though, surveys in recent years of reading and noting of advertisements have indicated a declining level of traffic throughout magazines. The chief distorting factor, seldom

[8] *Profile of the Millions,* 3d edition, (New York: *New York News,* 1962), special section, "At Home Viewing of Evening Television, Including Station Breaks, by Adults in the New York Metropolitan Area," especially p. 2.

fully overcome in commercial surveys, is the growing boredom of respondents as interviewers show them the advertisements in an issue they have already read. This long record of spurious evidence of a rapid dropping off of advertisement noting, especially in a thick, prosperous magazine, has helped to perpetuate an incorrect assumption about issue reading. On an average, the drop in noting claims is equally great, regardless of whether the interview starts on the first page or at some later selected point.

Some Fundamental Concepts

Before discussing some of the significant studies on exposures to magazines and their advertising pages, it may be helpful to describe some fundamental concepts. The following explanation and examples of *issue audience, issue exposures, ad-page audience,* and *ad-page exposures* are based on material supplied by Seymour Banks of the Leo Burnett Company and discussions with him.

Consider a hypothetical example of a group of five people who are interviewed about their readership of one particular issue of a magazine which contains one page carrying advertising material (see Table 7).

TABLE 7. Hypothetical Example of Magazine Reading

People	Exposed to the issue (issue audience)	No. of days exposed to the issue (issue exposures)	Exposed to ad-page X (ad-page audience)	No. of days exposed to ad-page X (ad-page exposures)
A	Yes	1	Yes	1
B	Yes	2	No	0
C	Yes	3	Yes	2
D	No	0	No	0
E	No	0	No	0
Totals	3	6	2	3

The audience of the magazine consists of three people—A, B, and C—who read the issue. They are people who, having been taken through a copy of the magazine and encouraged to talk about their interest in various subjects, answered "Yes" to the following question (after being cautioned that they might have seen similar items elsewhere): "Now that we've been through the whole issue, are you sure whether or not you happened to look into this particular issue before?" [9] This is the *issue audience.*

[9] *Ad Page Exposure in 4 Magazines* (Philadelphia, Pa.: *The Saturday Evening Post,* 1960); *Advertising Exposure, Audiences, Issues, and Advertising Pages,* Vol. 1 (New York: *Reader's Digest,* 1960).

A looked at the issue during one day, B looked at it on two different days, and C looked at it on three different days. The sum of these numbers of days is the total number of issue exposures; in this case, there were six issue exposures. The true number of issue exposures might well exceed six, since all that has been counted is the number of days in which a person was exposed to the issue. Thus, this measurement might properly be named *issue-reading days* rather than issue exposures.

The next two sets of data deal with exposure to the advertising page in this issue. Exposure to the ad page means opening a pair of pages fully so that both pages are exposed if either is exposed. Two people, A and C, went through the issue in such a way that they completely opened two facing pages, one of which was the page carrying advertising. Therefore, the ad-page audience was two.

A opened the issue to the ad page during the day in which he looked into the issue. C exposed himself to the ad page on two of the three days on which he exposed himself to the issue. Therefore, the total number of ad-page exposures was three.

Just as with issue exposures, the ad-page exposures should properly be called *ad-page-exposure days*. These data record the number of days upon which a respondent exposed himself to a particular advertising page.

To sum up: Four types of measurement data for possible use in evaluating magazine readership behavior are *issue audience, issue exposures* (really, issue-reading days), *ad-page audience,* and *ad-page exposures* (really, ad-page-exposure days).

These concepts are especially important to an understanding of the study *Ad Page Exposure in 4 Magazines,* conducted by Alfred Politz Media Studies (compare page 215). Issue audience means the number of people who are willing to count themselves as being sure that they had looked into a particular issue of a magazine before. Issue exposures (issue-reading days) represent the total number of days upon which the people who were exposed to the issue read it. Ad-page audience represents the number of people who opened an ad page fully so that they could, if they wished, see an advertiser's message. Therefore, ad-page exposures (ad-page-exposure days) are the number of occasions on which each person was exposed to the ad page, to the extent that these occasions took place on different days.

Looking at these terms in another way: Data on issue audience and on ad-page audience refer to *people* who perform a certain action, and data on issue exposures and on ad-page exposures refer to *person-day* counts.

Exposure Studies of Magazine Advertising Pages

Numerous methods have been tried—with only partial success—in the attempt to furnish objective evidence on the actual exposure of magazine pages carrying advertisements. Examination of fingerprints and the sensitizing of small areas of each page to light have been two approaches to the question of page traffic. Fingerprints were an especially promising clue, since they offered hope of determining traffic by individual readers; and the objective method of direct observation of advertising-page exposure has proved feasible with the theater playbill, but only because the time and location of reading are known and convenient for research.

Glue-sealed Issues

Despite early studies based on fingerprints and direct observation, it remained for experiments with glue-sealed pages to accomplish the first important breakthrough.[10] *The Saturday Evening Post* first published a study based on this method; it was carried out by Alfred Politz Research, and paved the way for substantial research of magazine advertising page exposure.

The Saturday Evening Post reported the sealing of facing pages by means of a small spot of glue which was hardly noticeable to the reader. The glue seal was affixed approximately one-third of the distance from the spine to the outside edge of the page, centered midway between top and bottom. Opening of the pair of pages sufficiently to break the seal, two-thirds of the way in from the free edge, ensured considerable exposure of the two-page spread. Later applications included the simplified process of applying a strip of glue on the outside edge of the top of the magazine, one-third of the way between the binding and the outer edge.

The glue requirements were as follows: (1) The glue must adhere until the page is opened; (2) once the page is opened, the glue must not readhere; and (3) the glue must interfere as little as possible with the opening of pages—it must not rip the page or discourage or prevent opening.

Measuring magazine-advertising exposure in households is possible through the use of glue-sealed issues. The method offers much of the objectivity of mechanical measurement of broadcast reception. Substitution of sealed copies in the regular subscription mailing makes it possible to

[10] *The Readers of The Saturday Evening Post* (Philadelphia, Pa.: Curtis Publishing Company, 1958).

draw the sample from a subscriber list. Some leading magazines have a sufficient percentage of subscription circulation to justify this sampling method. Later, preferably before there is much likelihood of issues being passed along to other homes, the copies may be picked up and checked for evidence of page opening.

In 1959, *Look* magazine first reported such a survey, covering a sample of *Look* subscriber households in the United States.[11] The total sample was 500 *Look* subscriber households, distributed on a known-probability basis in 50 areas of the United States. Two issues, each with a sample of 250 homes, provided interviewer work loads of five homes per issue in each selected area. The sealed copies had a spot of glue on each page, about one-third of the distance from the spine of the issue to the outer edge. The seal was imperceptible to the reader, and when the seal was broken, it would not readhere.

It was anticipated that some glue seals would break merely from handling and mailing. A special test, involving copies mailed out to interviewers and back to the central office, produced breakage of 12 per cent of the page pairs. But the breakage occurred in a random pattern, making it possible to compute a correction for final score on each page.

The uncorrected pair-page scores for 343 copies of *Look* reclaimed within one to fifteen days after arrival at subscriber households are shown in Table 8 at 10-page intervals. When the average correction factor,

TABLE 8. Pair-page Scores for 343 Copies of **Look**

Pair page	Percentage of households opening issue	
	March 17	March 31
0–1	99.2	95.8
10–11	97.5	92.1
20–21	94.2	94.2
30–31	95.4	94.6
40–41	93.8	95.8
50–51	98.3	95.4
60–61	97.1	95.0
70–71	95.8	90.0
80–81	92.9	95.0
90–91	91.3	94.6
100–101	91.3	—
110–111	89.6	—
Average for all pair pages ..	93.7	93.9

[11] "A Study of Advertising Penetration in *Look* Households" (New York: *Look,* 1959).

The questioning not only absolves the respondent in advance for any errors he may make, but it also uses the word "might" which implies "probably not." Emphasis on a "split-second opening" minimizes the importance of the act and reduces blame for either errors or dishonesty in making excessive exposure claims. Yet only the definite "no" responses are dropped in tabulating the page-exposure claims.

Positive support for the subjective interviewing procedure lies in comparative findings using glue-sealed issues with the same respondents in preliminary tests. The pressure for admissions of exposure was increased until a point was reached where subjective admissions were equal to glue breakage, on an average. The measured exposure of specific pair pages was not always the same for both methods, but the errors of verbal exaggeration were offset, on the average, by omissions of claimed exposure of pages which had the seal broken. The interviewing method regarding total pages exposed would be justified only on the basis of coincidence, were it not that experimental work with four magazines showed similar validity in application to different types of publications. Apparently the method elicits some minimal level of discrimination which makes it sensitive to different publications. In many respects, the subjective questioning violates the basic principles of interview design.

The *Reader's Digest–Saturday Evening Post* survey of four magazines employed three different measures: the average issue audience of each publication, the average number of reading days for each publication, and the average number of total page exposures. A summary of results is given in Table 9.

TABLE 9. *Summary of* **Reader's Digest–Post** *Findings*

Publication	Average-issue audience of individuals	Issue-exposure days per reader	Average-advertising-page-exposure days	Advertising-page-exposure days per issue reader
Reader's Digest	35,131,000	5.0	60,947,000	1.7
The Saturday Evening Post..	23,547,000	1.9	30,861,000	1.3
Life	31,519,000	1.4	30,110,000	1.0
Look	27,495,000	1.6	30,702,000	1.1
Four publications combined *	67,802,000	4.5	152,620,000	2.3

* Because of duplication or overlap, each of the figures relating to the four publications combined is smaller than the arithmetical total for the four magazines.

At the time of the survey, the most conspicuous fact was the nearly identical number of total advertising-page-exposure days for three vigorously competing magazines. As was expected, the monthly publication was picked up and read on more different days than the publications having more frequent issues. The right-hand column in Table 9 indicates that all four publications gave the advertiser an average chance of exposure on at least one day to every issue reader. There was considerable variation by publication. One limitation of the method is that it did not measure the total number of individuals exposed to the average pair page, nor was it possible to break down the exposed people according to frequency of exposure. These facts are also of interest to advertisers.

An Experiment on the Value of Multiple Exposures

Regardless of the exact pattern of accumulation of multiple exposures, it is helpful for advertisers to know how repetition of exposures increases advertising effect. If a medium provides for more than one exposure of an advertising page, for example, is there any increased value to the advertiser? If so, how much for each successive repetition?

If each exposure has the same value—regardless of the number to whom the advertisement is exposed—then it appears that three of the above magazines have almost precisely equal values. If the first exposure is worth more than later repetitions, then the magazine exposing the advertisement to the largest audience would have most value in the above example.

The Post sought to compare the value of a second day of advertisement exposure in a study made in a single market.[14] Twelve carefully chosen real full-page advertisements representing somewhat familiar brands of different products were bound in new copies of *The Saturday Evening Post.* Only four or eight advertisements were bound in any particular copy, according to the requirements of the design. Three parallel samples of 50 people were randomly selected from households drawn on a known-probability basis from subscribers in the survey county. Instead of having the subscription copy arrive by mail, an interviewer delivered the copy, which contained four additional advertisements inconspicuously added to the issue and sealed together with a tiny spot of glue. The respondent was asked to agree to open all pages of the magazine on the first day, read what he cared to, and then to place the copy in an envelope and seal it.

Two days later, the interviewer returned to the same respondents, picked up the envelope containing the copy, and handed the respondent a second copy of the same issue. The second copy, unknown to the respondent, con-

[14] "The Rochester Study" (Philadelphia, Pa.: *The Saturday Evening Post,* 1960).

tained all the advertisements in the first copy, plus a group of four not previously exposed to him. Again the respondent was asked to agree to open all pages, read what he cared to, and then place the copy in an envelope and seal it. The interviewer returned about 3½ days later and asked each person a uniform set of questions about the 12 test-advertisement brands. If later examination of the test copies showed that a respondent had not broken the seals on the test advertisements, his report was not tabulated.

An experimental design, known as a Latin square, was used to control the pattern of exposure frequency and to provide maximum significance for scores obtained with only 150 respondents. The placement of the 12 test advertisements for each of the three sample groups and for the two test days is shown in Table 10.

TABLE 10. Experimental Design for Twelve Test Advertisements

Advertisements in the copy read on first day	Sample I (50 people)	Sample II (50 people)	Sample III (50 people)
Four in group A	Absent	Absent	Present
Four in group B	Absent	Present	Absent
Four in group C	Present	Absent	Absent
Advertisements in the copy read on second day			
Four in group A	Absent	Present	Present
Four in group B	Present	Present	Absent
Four in group C	Present	Absent	Present

Examination of the table will reveal that a different set of four advertisements was absent from both copies read by each of the three sample groups. A second group of four advertisements—different for each sample —was exposed only once. The remaining third group of four advertisements—again different for each sample—was exposed both days.

This permitted each group of four ads (1) to serve as part of the experimental control for one sample, (2) to be exposed only once to another sample, or (3) to be exposed twice to the third sample. As a result, the total control scores represented an average for all 12 advertisements, as did the scores for both the single and the double exposure.

The evaluating questions, which were related to each advertised product brand, were asked on the third call, as follows:

With respect to brand familiarity

1. Thinking about (Product), what brands of (Name of product) come to your mind first?

2. After these, what other brands come to your mind next?

With reference to familiarity of claims

1. Regardless of whether or not you believe them, which of these claims about (Name of product) have you noticed? (Show card.)

2. (For each claim noticed) What particular brand or brands of (Name of product) are claiming . . . ?

With regard to belief in claim

1. What do you think is good about (Brand and product)?

The overall total results showed almost *double* the value of two exposures over one exposure on both brand familiarity and claim awareness. Two exposures increased belief in the advertising claims by *triple* the amount gained with a single exposure.

In the case of established brands, two exposures were even more effective. Charles E. Swanson of the Curtis Publishing Company summarizes: "The advertising for the established brands proved almost three times as effective in increasing brand familiarity, more than twice as effective in producing familiarity with the advertisers' claims, almost twice as effective in creating belief in these claims, and four times as effective in creating a willingness to buy the brand." [15]

There were two shortcomings of the experimental test: the forced nature of the advertising exposure, and the fact that all single impressions were made on the second forced inspection of the entire issue. The forcing of exposure may have introduced some bias favoring either the single exposure or the double exposure. All the double exposures included an exposure in both first and second copies. The fact that single-exposure measurements were all confined to the second tour of the magazine, as shown in the design, may also have created a bias for or against single exposures. However, correction of this feature of the study would have been difficult and would have greatly increased the fieldwork.

The Meaning of Advertising Exposure

What advertising-page exposure means here, from a physical standpoint, is that the advertising area was probably exposed within normal reading distance of the eyes of members of the issue audience. Psychologically, exposure under these conditions should mean much more. Magazine readers are not normally compelled to open pages in which they are not interested. It seems likely that even the act of thumbing magazine pages is motivated

[15] From letter from Charles E. Swanson, June 22, 1962.

either by a desire to explore or by a desire to complete some unfinished activity. The latter might be the continuing columns of an editorial feature.

Whatever the circumstance and the motivation, the normal reader is seeking reward, and the least response he can make to any page is to reject it. Rejection obviously implies some minimal perception of features not sought or the absence of what is sought. In a certain context, color might indicate the presence of advertisements when the reader is searching for editorial matter. Variation from text format might indicate that a page or spread does not contain continuing reading columns of a story or article begun earlier. The reader or thumber who makes choices—even when they are based on such simple cues or guides—must at least skim something and give the advertiser some opportunity to deter him. It is very difficult to rationalize page exposure as something apart from probable perception of page content. Exposure means genuine advertising opportunity.

Survey evidence on the perception of pages exposed briefly, as in page thumbing, has been obtained by New York University students. The setting for the interview is a catch-as-catch-can situation in which the observer sees someone open and close a magazine pair page quickly. Among family and intimate friends it is possible to interrupt immediately, locate the last exposed point, and get control of the issue to prevent reference by the reader to the issue. The reader is then asked immediately to describe any remembered clues from the pair of pages just closed. Exploration with this method has shown considerable evidence of recall of something specific after such a short interval. Generally, there is some recollection of color or the presence of a picture; very often the respondent accurately reports the presence of an advertisement or a cartoon. No representative data, obtained under such natural reading conditions, are yet available.

EXPOSURE TO OUTDOOR AND TRANSPORTATION ADVERTISING

The measurement of advertising opportunities through the use of outdoor posters has traditionally been based on *audience* exposure, that is, traffic counts. More precisely, it has been a measure of the total number of potential exposures during any day up to the thirty days of the media contract.

Poster panels are placed at points and in positions calculated to offer maximum human traffic. The same individual may pass a number of panels of the same advertisement on his daily routine trips on twenty or more days in the same month. When the total trips of all passers of a showing are combined, the total exposures in an area probably exceed those of any other regular medium.

The Traffic Audit Bureau has long provided reports on estimated numbers of people and numbers of passenger vehicles passing within range of a poster showing. The fact that posters are advertisements makes it desirable to consider their exposure in this context of advertising exposure rather than as media audiences. The fact that people must come to outdoor advertisements (rather than the other way around) makes measurement of this medium much different from measurement of broadcasting and publications, which bring advertisements to people. Traffic Audit Bureau reports can provide evidence that people pass within range of a poster, but cannot demonstrate a relationship between outdoor-advertising exposure and the primary purpose of those who are passing. Television audiences view commercials while viewing programs. Magazine audiences read advertisements while reading editorial features. Pedestrians and automobile passengers, on the other hand, may see poster advertisements while they are out sightseeing, or the advertising exposure may simply be incidental to the process of getting somewhere.

Estimates made by the Traffic Audit Bureau have been based on the traffic past particular posters during hours selected for actual counts. Not all of the people passing in a direction favorable to viewing are counted, since it is believed that the mode of travel has a bearing on advertisement viewing. Pedestrians and people in passenger cars are discounted 50 per cent to allow for nonviewing; bus passengers are discounted 75 per cent, since not all are equally exposed to the panels. Even with these conservative procedures, the total audience estimates for outdoor showings are enormous and leave advertisers doubtful as to exactly how many and what kinds of people are actually exposed.

However, the Outdoor Advertising Association of America has reported a tested procedure for converting traffic audits into estimates of local vehicles or households.[16] Observation of traffic for auditing purposes shows that automobiles account for approximately 90 per cent. The number of vehicles averages about 61 per cent of the number of people reported in an audit. By counting and estimating the percentage of local cars (indicated by license plates which may identify the county), it is possible to arrive at an approximation of the number of daily panel exposures to people in local vehicles.

[16] *The Wilbur Smith Study of Outdoor Advertising* (New York: Outdoor Advertising Association of America, Inc., 1959).

Data gathered in 13 markets by recording and tracing automobile license plates enabled the association to determine the percentage and frequency of all local cars passing one or more panels in a 100 showing. (A 100 showing is the number of properly located poster panels required to establish complete coverage of major travel routes in any area or county.) The results indicated that in a market where 70 per cent of the traffic going past posters was local, over 40 per cent of all cars registered in the county passed at least one panel daily. Around 88 per cent of all local cars passed a panel in a week, and 93 per cent of all cars passed some time during the posted month.

Attempts have been made to estimate exposure of bus cards and car cards in urban markets by counting total traffic in the vehicles. It is difficult to make such counts on the basis of fares paid or by observing passengers; it is impossible to measure total unduplicated audiences on this basis. Surveys made in households to estimate exposure of outdoor posters or car cards can measure the total local traffic, but miss the transients, who may also be important to national advertisers. While patterns of travel—minutely examined in some studies—help to estimate total unduplicated populations exposed to outdoor posters and car cards, the relationships between traffic and actual advertising exposure are not clear. Measures of traffic in motion are even more difficult to interpret, and most checks of moving traffic are seriously lacking in precision.

Photographic recording of traffic exposed to advertising, both vehicles and pedestrian, has been successfully demonstrated by Alfred Politz Research.[17] The unique procedure was first applied to outdoor advertisements. Cameras facing the highway were concealed in the measured displays on the assumption that if posters are exposed, then people are exposed to posters. Daylight film was adapted to making records of daytime traffic; infrared lighting and camera filters were required in order to photograph the traffic past illuminated showings at night.

Since it is neither necessary nor practical to keep a continuous photographic record of traffic at all times, the method relies upon the sampling of time as well as outdoor locations. Successive photographs which cover a few seconds at properly selected intervals are sufficient for estimating total traffic. Camera specifications will depend upon the need for accurate counts of car passengers and identification of license plates. (The latter are not required on the front of the car in all states.)

[17] George Mihaly, "Camera Facilitates New Media Measure," *Industrial Photography,* Vol. 4 (November–December, 1954), pp. 18–20.

Under the sponsorship of the National Association of Transportation Advertising, Alfred Politz Research made an especially successful adaptation of the photographic technique to measure audiences exposed to traveling displays carried on the outside of buses.[18] Specially designed cameras were equipped with timing mechanisms and installed in buses in window locations just above the displays. Two combined cameras were sufficient to cover an angle of 120 degrees, as indicated in Fig. 11, photographing

CAMERA EQUIPMENT AND PLACEMENT

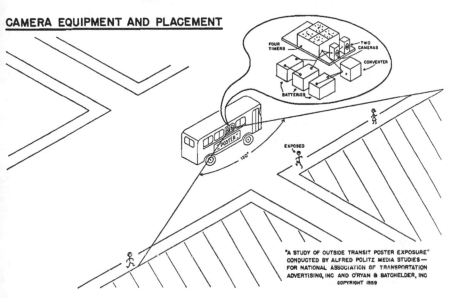

FIG. 11. Photographic method of recording of people exposed to outside transit posters. (*Courtesy of Alfred Politz Research, Inc.*)

pedestrians and car passengers who were exposed and who presumably could see the displays. Only persons clearly photographed and with both eyes visible from the bus were counted—on the assumption that they were most likely to see the advertisement.

The sampling of time in the study (made in Philadelphia in June) was representative of the day from 6:30 A.M. to 8:30 P.M. Every ten minutes the cameras were set to record 11 photographs each, taking one picture per second over a ten-second interval. All days of the month were covered, and the sample of routes was representative of the entire system.

The photographs for each ten-second interval were examined as a group,

[18] "A Study of Outside Transit Poster Exposure" (New York: National Association of Transportation Advertising, 1959).

and the count was limited to individuals *entering* the scene during the interval. Anyone making more than one separate appearance during the interval was counted but once. The study demonstrated that there were 16,330,000 pedestrian exposures and 1,380,000 automobile-passenger exposures to a full showing of 150 posters in a month, or a total of 17,710,-000 exposures. The population of the area served by the buses was about three million, but neither the number of transients nor the total number of unduplicated exposures can be computed by this method.

IMPLICATIONS

It is important for anyone concerned with the impact of advertising to understand the difference between *advertising exposure* (the media function) as contrasted with *advertising perception* (the copy function).

It is also useful to distinguish what is meant by *issue audience, issue exposure* (issue-reading days), *ad-page audience,* and *ad-page exposure* (ad-page-exposure days).

In any case, there are certain implications with respect to broadcast and magazine-advertising exposure and to outdoor and transportation-advertising exposure.

Broadcast and Magazine-advertising Exposure

Advertising exposure on network broadcasts and in magazines includes most of the audiences of both types of media vehicles. Because broadcasting suspends competing features for the full commercial period, it almost ensures some perception or communication of advertising ideas by nearly all of the average program audience. Sponsored television shows exploit the program time also, either by using background signs or, more generally, by benefiting from sponsor identification. A measure of exposure to broadcast commercials, based on mechanical records of set operation, provides household data. Information on individuals is less precise, but can be estimated from fifteen-minute audience records obtained in diary form.

Magazine-advertising exposure, while it results from an active process of page turning, can be exceedingly brief. However, magazine exploration is voluntary, and advertisements which occupy one or two pages are logically assured of at least some minimal inspection and perception before the area is rejected for further reading. It can be assumed that exposure of large advertisements in magazines usually imparts enough clues to the issue reader to enable the advertiser to compete for his favorable attention.

Since some magazines expose the average advertising pair page to nine out of ten reading households and four out of five individual readers, the potential advertising opportunity is not much less than the total issue audience.

Both broadcasting and publications, whose primary function is the communication of information and entertainment, provide advertising opportunities not far short of the audience of each vehicle. Planning of media schedules can be based on exposed audiences when such data are widely available on numbers exposed by accumulated and combined use of vehicles.

As discussed above, methods of measurement are not adapted for estimating either accumulated or combined exposures of magazine-issue audiences. Until such data are available, schedules based on the audiences of vehicles are satisfactory approximations, provided some discount is allowed for the difference between program or issue audiences and the smaller advertising-exposed audiences.

Extension of planning to include radio and newspapers must also be considered, although documented evidence is neither as available nor as essential for these media. They are used chiefly to serve regional markets and to supplement national advertising by intensifying coverage where needed.

Outdoor and Transportation Advertising Exposure

Exposure opportunities are only one of the factors considered by advertisers in evaluating outdoor posters or displays connected with public forms of conveyance. These mass media operate most effectively in more densely populated areas and seldom can be combined as primary media for national campaigns.

They are also unique in that they require a special type of display, which is best adapted to pictorial and slogan copy and with emphasis on identification. Because of the simplicity of copy, outdoor and car-card advertisements can usually be perceived easily and with minimal exposure time.

thirteen

Audiences of Advertisements

What is an advertising audience? Is measurement of an advertising audience possible?

An audience includes only people who perceive something. But such a definition would mean little to an advertiser if most people perceived only a splash of color or some black lines. It has already been shown (in the previous chapter) that page exposure practically guarantees some minimal perception. A more useful definition of advertising perception for purposes of media evaluation is based on the perception of an advertisement *as an entity*. Such a definition does not require identification of brand or company, but does require at least an awareness that there is an advertisement.

The method of measurement, unlike the measurement of exposure, cannot be an entirely objective process. Perception is subjective and cannot be observed from without. In order to measure perception, it is first necessary to let it occur. There must then be a waiting period for some kind of behavior to indicate that perception has taken place.

If an interviewer could be right on hand or near a telephone, as is possible with television, he might ask a person exposed to a commercial to report what he has noticed or perceived. When magazines or newspapers are considered, immediate checking is more difficult. However, there is generally a delay during which time some noted or perceived impressions are going to be weakened or forgotten. The measurement of advertisement noting, therefore, is based on an assumption that something is *perceived* and is *remembered* until there is an opportunity to apply measurement. The problem was examined in Chapter Three on recognition tests and in Chapter Four on recall tests.

Because of differences inherent in major media, the amount of data available on projectable overall advertising audiences is very limited. Magazines have long had reports available on advertising audiences, but these data are generally not projectable. Television advertisers and writers of commercials have attached little importance to measures of mere noting; and research of actual advertising audiences has not been encouraged very much. However, two different research organizations—Trendex and Audits and Surveys—provide data applicable to this process. Despite the general unavailability of basic advertising-audience information in major media, many research leaders have favored such comparisons for arriving at meaningful evaluations of media vehicles.

THREE PRINCIPLES

With respect to audiences of advertisements, we start with three basic principles: [1]

1. There is no one medium (or type of media) best for everything—all media have their place, dependent upon circumstances.

2. Media recommendations should be developed only after decisions as to both creative and marketing strategy.

3. The more that is known about audiences of advertisements, the better the media recommendations will be.

[1] Based on discussions with Seymour Banks of the Leo Burnett Company, Inc.

The fact that people have noted an advertisement or are aware of it is highly important to the company it represents. The media vehicle which encourages the greatest number of the right kinds of people to notice a particular advertisement at the lowest cost may be the best one to buy. But the fact that the appeal of the advertisement and of the product or service may have much to do with the size of the advertising audience—or the proportion of the audience recalling exposure—makes media evaluation on that basis difficult.

Nevertheless—regardless of the potential audience which a medium might provide—nothing encourages an advertiser quite so much as an actual audience which he or someone else has reached in that medium. Advertising audiences—unlike potential audiences—are *delivered audiences*.

ADVANTAGES OF ADVERTISING AUDIENCES IN EVALUATING MEDIA

The fact that advertising audiences are realistic evidence of advertising accomplishments in a media vehicle is axiomatic. Measures of program and issue audiences are *always* larger than advertising audiences and are *never* fully achieved at the advertisement-noting level. Not so big as media-vehicle audiences, but *always* larger than actual advertising audiences, are the numbers of exposed households or individuals.

It seems certain that some media and some vehicles do a better job than others in getting the people to whom advertising is exposed to look, to examine, or to listen. If one of two vehicles, having equal audiences or exposures, provides better motivation or a behavior pattern more favorable to the noting of advertisements, then it does a better advertising service. More importantly, stimulating the actual noting of advertisements helps to start the advertising process, a function which is not inherent in either media audiences or exposure opportunities.

Another realistic consideration which favors advertising-audience measurement in evaluating media is the expectation that space and time units of different prices will perform differently. If noting or perceiving advertisements is a step in producing results, then it is logical that the more expensive unit should get more attention, communicate more fully, or both, or with an emotional quality of greater value to the advertiser.

Magazine *exposure* is essentially the same for a two-page double spread, a single page, and any major fraction of a page. By all logic and according to limited available evidence, *magazine-advertising audiences* range in size roughly in proportion to the size or color and cost of the space unit. Advertising audiences mean real performance of media units, and variations in performance levels can guide the purchase of space and time units.

The measurement of media performance on a basis related to costs of media units cannot be stressed enough in view of unceasing misuses of the cost-per-thousand index.[2] On the basis of magazine circulation, it is logical to state that it costs a specified amount to print and circulate a known number of copies of a particular space unit. On the basis of set tuning, it is also logical to state that a network delivers to the measured number of households at a known cost a minute of program time containing a commercial. But when a survey counts people and uses a measurement not related to media unit costs, there is little logic in relating some arbitrary space or time unit to cost-per-thousand in the audience.

It means little to say that one magazine excels another because it has more average-issue readers per dollar spent in a black-and-white full page or any other cost unit. The same applies to comparisons of page exposure, which are not sensitive to units of advertising. But actual advertising audiences achieved by copy in specified cost units are a function of cost, are meaningful, and are comparable between media vehicles. This is a logical and proper basis for cost-per-thousand comparisons.

Advertising audiences have an additional feature of practical importance in media choices. Copy tests based on audiences attracted in magazines have always been extremely sensitive to product appeal. The audiences of some media are more interested in particular products than others, or the nature of the medium creates a setting more favorable to consideration of certain products in that environment. Advertising-audience measurement should provide a highly profitable guide to the selection of those media best adapted to presenting particular products.

This same selectivity, so universally reported in the noting of particular advertisements, shows the extent to which copy content determines the audience size. Two facing full-page magazine advertisements can have relative differences of 2 to 1 or more in reported noting levels. Obviously, the media vehicle provides approximately identical exposure opportunities to facing full pages. Both pages have an opportunity to achieve at least the larger of the two ratings. However, a different media audience might change—or possibly reverse—the pattern of noting for the same two facing advertisements. The advertising-audience measurement is then, in part, a

[2] Darrell B. Lucas, "The Cost-per-thousand Dilemma," *Media/scope,* Vol. 1 (March–April, 1957), pp. 29–32.

qualitative evaluation of media vehicles, a guide for product adaptation, a measure of responses to different cost units, and always a measure of actual advertising accomplishment in the particular vehicle.

MEASUREMENT OF ADVERTISING AUDIENCES

Since the noting or perceiving of specific advertisements cannot be observed at the time by others, measurement of advertising audiences must occur after the fact. Evidence is usually sought in the form of some kind of behavior, and product purchase might be ideal audience proof if sales could be traced. The playback of advertising content (see Chapter Four) is also evidence of advertisement noting, but it is seldom of such proportions as to reflect the total media accomplishment.

A much less objective method, widely considered to be the basic measure of advertisement noting, is simple reporting or *recognizing* of advertisements, as discussed in Chapter Three. This general method, which has been applied extensively to magazine advertisements and on a smaller scale to broadcast commercials, produces much the largest scores of any measuring device. Recognition ratings, at their maximum, sometimes indicate that two-thirds to three-fourths of all exposed readers, viewers, or listeners have noted a particular advertising message. Average scores ordinarily run much lower and vary a great deal.

Reports of advertisement noting are based to some extent upon actual noting of specific messages, followed by accurate recognition at the time of interview. The pattern of most national advertising campaigns is such that recognition of individual advertisements in association with one measured medium is almost beyond the limits of measurement. Furthermore, since people vary both in their capacities and in their motivation for accurate reporting, there will be varying distortions according to copy and according to media audiences. Any measurement which penalizes a media vehicle for lower memory levels or higher "honesty" of its audience—as compared with the audiences of competing vehicles—cannot provide reliable comparative facts.

Magazine-advertising Audiences

For a generation, magazine-advertising audiences have been reported on the basis of recognition, lacking controls and lacking definable samples. Early evidence showed startling differences between publications and usually favored the less prosperous publications which were of little interest to most advertisers. Part of the explanation was found by examining the advertisements, which revealed the fact that only the companies which advertise almost everywhere are likely to appear in the weaker publications. These same advertisements usually obtain high ratings because they are familiar and probably also because they are effective. More prosperous magazines, which contain unique advertisements, those with specialized appeal, and those of occasional advertisers, naturally obtain lower average ratings and thus appear at a disadvantage.

There was another reason why well-patronized magazines obtained low average scores, while rejected magazines enjoyed higher and higher ratings until they ceased publication. The interviewing method put a heavy burden on respondents, and thicker magazines prolonged the interview into an experience of increasing boredom or fatigue. As a result, average scores for an issue would drop; even the scores for the same advertisements would be lower than in less fortunate competing magazines. If, in addition to this interview disadvantage, the more prosperous magazine also had more conservative or discriminating readers, the relative distortion of actual advertising audiences could have been substantial.

Transportation Advertising Audiences

The National Association of Transportation Advertising was the first media group to make a serious effort to measure *projectable* advertising audiences. Surveys in member cities were begun in 1944 and continued until after the reporting of a 13-study summary published in 1950.[3] This series of studies measured audiences of car cards in member cities; it also provided a basis for figuring unit audience costs by projecting the sample findings to total audiences of people fifteen years of age and older. Advertisers could take average audiences of all measured cards, or maximum performances of cards with wide audience appeal, and actually compute the cost per thousand individuals "impressed" one or more times by copy in this medium. No other medium was in a position to furnish comparable information.

Samples for the transportation-advertising studies are chosen on the basis of known probability in the market served by the transport system. The lower age limit of fifteen years is an arbitrary choice. One individual is interviewed in a household. Twelve advertisements which were never previously used in the community are measured, using a controlled-recognition

[3] *13-study Summary of the Continuing Study of Transportation Advertising* (New York: Advertising Research Foundation, Inc., 1950).

procedure (compare Chapter Three). This requires two complete samples to measure audience claims—one before advertisements are carded in the vehicles and the other immediately after the cards are removed at the end of the thirty-day showing.

There is no mixing and binding of advertisements with editorial matter, as in a publication. Car cards are seen more in isolation, and position is equalized by rotating the card locations in different vehicles. Since the cards are not bound and since they are of a size suitable for interview display, the original advertisements may be assembled in kits of convenient thickness. There is no need for the respondent to identify them with a specific issue. Since the controlled method measures only noting and since copy is short on car cards, the method practically measures the audience of the complete advertisement.

One of the requirements of controlled measurement is that the general familiarity of advertisements shown in both the preexamination and the postexamination kits be about the same. This is accomplished by inserting 12 familiar previous advertisements along with the exclusive new test advertisements in the preexamination interview kits, all in random order. This reduces the likelihood that a respondent will conclude that he has not seen any of the copy being shown to him and so give uniformly "No" answers. Since the 12 test advertisements will be in the vehicles and will be familiar by the time of the postexamination, the *filler* cards in the second set of kits are 12 entirely new advertisements, which have never been used in the community. This again ensures that a respondent will have little chance of giving "blanket answers" on the assumption that he has seen all or none of the advertisements.

Measures of individual advertising audiences, as well as their averages, should be significant, since each advertiser has the benefit of average position through rotation in each of the interviewer's kits. Since car cards also have equal advantages of location in the vehicles as a result of rotated positions, there is no position problem in evaluating regular cards. There are some premium locations available, and car cards vary in length, usually in units of 7 inches. These differences, involving cost as well, should show up in car-card-audience measurement. Limited data confirm the sensitivity of car-card audiences to these cost factors.

The projection of car-card audiences to all adults fifteen years of age and older involves several steps of computation. Population data include all individuals, whereas car-card audiences are measured on the basis of people riding the vehicles during the thirty-day showing. Computation of the per cent of riders noting a particular card begins by using the preexamination claims to correct for inflation of the postexamination claims. This involves not only the subtraction of the former from the latter, but also the application of a further formula step (see page 64) to estimate actual noting by unreliable respondents. The formula percentage is then multiplied by the percentage of population riding the vehicles before the resulting figure is applied to the total adult population. Some examples are shown in Table 11.

TABLE 11. Illustrated Computations of Car-card Audiences

Product adver- tised	Post ex- amina- tion score (in per cent)	Preex- amina- tion score (in per cent)	For- mula score (in per cent)	Per cent rid- ing	Per cent of popu- lation noting	Adults in total market	Total audience
A	40	8	35	78	27	440,000	119,000
B	39	10	32	78	25	440,000	109,000
C	65	39	43	78	33	440,000	145,000
D	49	16	40	55	22	1,310,000	290,000
E	56	27	40	72	29	80,000	23,000

Advertisements A, B, and C in Table 11, all measured in the same city, were a 28-inch card, a 21-inch card, and a card in a premium position. The differences in resulting audiences happened to coincide with unit costs, although the data were inadequate for stable comparisons. The remaining two advertisements were measured in two different cities; one city had only 55 per cent monthly riders of the carded vehicles, and the other had a relatively small total population. In every case, costs should have some general relationship to audiences reached, although the larger cities should offer some advantage in dollar performance. In the transportation advertising medium, the general average audience per dollar runs around 300 unduplicated adult individuals.[4]

Published studies of advertising-audience costs in other media have added little to a few early experiments with outdoor, magazine, and newspaper advertising. Since demonstrating an audience of people noting posters in one market, the outdoor industry has returned its emphasis to traffic exposed. The more successful magazines may have been deterred by the fact that thicker magazines lose some in the noting or remembering or claiming

[4] Page 31 of citation in footnote 2.

recognition of individual advertisements. There is also a reluctance to enter the business of measuring individual advertisements for the purpose of determining average audience costs. The resulting demands by advertisers for their own scores and explanations of the many variations could "submerge" publication research operations.

Newspapers would have the same problems as magazine publishers, only perhaps with more complications. Broadcasters have been content to permit measures of cost per thousand homes per commercial minute, although audiences of specific commercial units could be measured.

Only the ultimate demands of advertisers themselves are likely to lead to general information on accurately measured, projectable advertising audiences for each media vehicle.

PROBLEMS IN MEASURING ADVERTISING AUDIENCES

There are a number of problems in the measurement of advertising audiences of the various media.

While the transportation advertising industry has met no major problems in audience measurement, two difficulties exist.

One problem is the requirement of new, exclusive test advertisements which may not always be representative. Another problem is the instability of scores on highly confused copy and the occasional negative scores that result. The latter phenomenon measures something which is logically impossible, yet which can be avoided only by using distinctive copy for test purposes.

Outdoor advertising should have no greater problems than the transportation medium, except for the problem of displaying advertisements in the interview. Miniature reproductions can be used, or slides may be projected to simulate distant viewing of posters outdoors.

Controlled measures of magazine advertisements require removal of copy from the issue context and usually limit the total number of advertisements which can be covered in an interview. Controlled measures of television commercials require a procedure for reproducing both the visual and the auditory elements for interview purposes. For technical reasons, reproduction of adjacent parts of the program is not recommended, but would ensure maximum recognition of commercials. The problems are not insurmountable, but add to both complexity and costs of research.

There is little incentive for television network sponsors to evaluate the entire medium on the basis of cost per thousand in the advertising audience, since their own programs are a very small part of the medium. Networks, on the other hand, have an opportunity to serve advertisers better by providing a measure of actual audiences of available spots and participations on a cost-per-thousand basis. Likewise, magazines have an opportunity to evaluate their own advertising audiences, especially in relation to particular products and regarding their more selective audiences. The measures in both media could be obtained as averages without actual estimates for individual insertions.

The average cost per thousand for each medium and category could also legitimately rest on the performance of preselected copy which is chosen for its likelihood of attracting the attention of maximum numbers.

The measurement of magazine-advertising audiences can be sharpened and simplified if advertisers prepare exclusive test copy, even in the case where campaigns are running. The features which would make individual advertisements indentifiable need not be so unusual as to destroy campaign value. It would be essential to use approved methods for identifying issue readers and to use controls on advertisement recognition. Interviewing kits could be standardized with a uniform number of items for all publications and categories. If only averages by publication or by category were used, it would not be necessary to compute performances of individual advertisements separately. It would not be necessary to obtain preexamination and postexamination scores on the same copy, but only to examine average scores on carefully selected prepublished and postpublished copy. This eliminates the needs for two separate surveys on each advertisement, with resulting economy. The selections and computations would be made separately, of course, for each product category and for each media cost unit.

Measurement for television spots and participations would not involve the complicated considerations of program effect on sponsor sales or on the commercials themselves. Like the magazine measures, television-audience measures would be sharpened if based on exclusive copy and restricted to advertisements preselected for maximum performance. There would be a problem of presenting large numbers of commercials in a single interview, and it might be desirable to reproduce only those most likely to establish a basis for recognition.

The chief point is that media vehicles are entitled to sell to advertisers on the basis of their best performances, since anything below the best is a result of limitations of copy appeal or vividness. Breakdowns for television spots and participations on the basis of product categories and of media unit costs would be highly desirable.

The above proposals are not expected to lead to data eliminating many national media vehicles from competition, nor is it to be expected that all would come out with equal costs per thousand in the advertising audience. Advertisements that are noted in one medium or vehicle may have a considerably greater selling opportunity than when noted in another. The presentation of a particular kind of copy in one medium might be far superior to presentation of that same copy in a different medium. The particular advertising audience available through one medium might be more desirable than another audience, even at a higher unit cost.

There are a great many factors which might still sway a media decision after cost comparisons of advertising audiences have been obtained. When advertisers have such data, they can make such decisions more intelligently, and the media should benefit because each vehicle will be assigned the advertising tasks which it does best.

One important factor, not yet discussed in this chapter, is the need for media planning in combination and in continuous schedules. Chapter Sixteen deals with audience accumulation and combinations and applies to the use of advertising audience data. However, there are some unique considerations which need to be discussed here.

PROBLEMS IN MEASURING COMBINED ADVERTISING AUDIENCES

The problems in measuring combined advertising audiences, especially in print media, center around the fact that there is so little that is unique about a message in different media vehicles. Whereas all magazine publications are different, it often happens that identical advertising copy appears in many different magazines. The result is that measurement methods based on the ability of readers to discriminate between magazine issues may be totally inadequate for separating several impressions of the same advertisement. The use of controls on the recognition method does not solve this research problem, and the alternative of eliminating controls has little to recommend it.

A clearer perspective of the problem can be gained by reviewing the meaning of noting or *perceiving*. This subjective process, which can be stimulated by identical advertisements in different vehicles, can be measured only on the basis of subsequent behavior. If the behavior is a specific claim of recognizing an advertisement, it is evident that a second impression, made in a second vehicle, may not differ from the first. If the advertising copy is identical in two publications, there is no direct way of establishing which impression is being reported. Only some feature unique to a particular insertion would provide direct evidence of the source of the impression.

Magazines and sponsored broadcasts, which are unique for each advertising insertion, provide an opportunity for indirect evidence on impressions of the same advertisement. The issue or program context, especially in juxtaposition with the advertising message, may be used to establish *exposure* and thus lend support to reported advertising impressions. Experimentation with magazine advertisements—involving substitution of either the advertisement or the editorial context—has shown context to be a highly unreliable aid to accurate recognition. Substituted prepublished copy may be expected to obtain about the same degree of "recognition" as the original advertisement located in that particular space.

Another avenue of approach—not to be ruled out entirely—is the use of extensive questioning about the time and context of perception for a particular advertising impression. Respondents may be reminded that they could have seen an advertisement elsewhere and told that the purpose of the interview is to find out just when or where the advertisement was noted. The respondent may be able to affirm that a particular impression was not the first, that it occurred earlier in another vehicle, and that the later impression took place on a specified date while he was reading a story on the facing page. He might also report that he spoke to another member of his family at the time regarding some feature in the copy. But such subjective reporting, even if it were assumed to be highly dependable, would limit the number of items covered per interview. This, in turn, would make measurements of advertising audiences in combinations of vehicles cumbersome and expensive.

Measurement of *accumulation* of advertising audiences, where campaign advertisements are scheduled in successive insertions in the same vehicle, is more feasible than measuring *combinations* of audiences of an identical advertisement. All the limitations of the regular recognition method (see Chapter Three) must be taken into account, especially where campaign copy is relatively uniform. This procedure has been applied only to a limited extent, and one of the applications has been to the repetition of identical copy in succeeding issues of a publication. This kind of experiment has usually indicated about equal success for each of two or more repeat insertions.

The discussion of measuring problems has little or no bearing on the wisdom of scheduling the same advertisement in many vehicles, or even repeatedly in the same vehicle. Advertisers have been extremely reluctant to reschedule the same copy for fear of poor results and possible audience boredom. Yet both common sense and some research (see Chapter Nine, pages 214 and 215) imply that there has been too much compulsion to change copy too often.

EXPECTED PATTERN OF ADVERTISING-AUDIENCE COMBINATIONS

What can be expected as knowledge of combined advertising audiences is advanced? An advertising message is seldom noted or clearly perceived by substantially everyone in the audience of its media vehicle. The measured advertising audience in magazines is often only 50, 25, or sometimes a smaller per cent of the issue audience. This bears an important relationship to the pattern of advertising-audience increase as publications or issues are added to a schedule.

The most obvious fact is that the absolute difference between combined advertising audiences and combined issue audiences should tend to increase until penetration approaches a saturation point.

If advertising audiences are smaller than the audiences of published or broadcast vehicles, there is at least a presumption that duplication in combined vehicles will be even smaller. If an advertisement has only one-fourth of the audience in each of two vehicles used, then it would be expected to overlap by only one-sixteenth (one-fourth $\times$ one-fourth), even if the vehicles precisely duplicated each other's audiences.

Since this is not to be expected and since vehicles acquire substantial unduplicated audiences, the duplication of the above advertising audience would be very small. This same analysis applies to successive issues of the same magazine, which may acquire as many as one-third new readers. All of the audience of a second advertisement, noted by one-fourth of the issue audience, *could* come from the "untouched" new readers of the second issue. This is unlikely.

It has been pointed out that issue- or broadcast-audience turnover tends to follow a chance pattern in successive units of the same vehicle. Household exposure to page locations in some magazines (as described in the preceding chapter) follows an almost completely chance pattern. Apart from a small proportion of devoted and thorough readers of a publication, there is a substantial majority in the issue audience who pick up copies largely on a random basis and who turn pages even more at random. This evidence of probable and actual exposure of advertisements should not be carried over to the perception process. Attention, or the directing of the process of perception, is highly selective. Advertisements are noted because of selective factors to a large degree, and the choice of what to notice within the total exposure range is anything but random.

Apart from "rough" data obtained by the regular recognition method, little is known about the duplicated and unduplicated audiences of the same or campaign advertisements in combinations of vehicles or in sequence in the same vehicle. There is no reason to assume that all of the people exposed to the copy of one advertiser will perceive or notice it each time. Even though the overlap of exposures often includes a large part of the duplicated audiences of vehicles, it cannot be expected that advertising audiences will overlap as much; in fact, it was shown above that they may overlap relatively little.

When the same person is exposed to two campaign advertisements in successive issues of a magazine, the fact that his selective processes favored the first one may predispose him to notice the second one also. When the same advertisement appears concurrently in different vehicles, the effect of exposure on repeat perception of the same copy is difficult to estimate. Much would depend on the degree of interest aroused by noting of the first impression of the advertisement or possible incompleteness of its communication.

Discovery of the true facts about perception of the same advertisement on repeat exposures of the same insertion, or of a reinsertion in the same vehicle, or of a combined schedule of insertions in different vehicles must await improved research methods.

The fact of *exposure* is something which can be objectively measured and which can occur any number of times without raising new problems of definition. The fact of *perception* or *awareness,* which is not accessible for objective measurement, is complicated by each renewal and increasingly dependent upon subjective reporting. When an advertisement has already been perceived once, just what is perceived on a second occasion, and how can repeated impressions be measured and added up? Adding each new exposure is an uncomplicated process, but defining and adding up each new unit of perception defies simplification.

IMPLICATIONS

The facts and discussion in this chapter and the preceding one are intended to show what kinds of progress can be made in each stage of the concepts described in Chapter Nine.

Physical units of media vehicles have little meaning in evaluating advertising opportunities. Measurement of opportunities in terms of people begins with the audiences of vehicles, and these are comparable even though defined in different ways. Much is known about the audiences of vehicles, both singly and in various schedules or combinations (see Chapter Sixteen).

If methods and applications had progressed as far in the measurement of advertising exposure in vehicles and combinations, the advertiser could come one full stage closer to evaluating vehicles and schedules. There is no special problem of defining exposure opportunities, but measurement is costly and cumbersome if applied to individuals exposed through extensive media schedules.

Technically, no available method is acceptable for measuring total numbers of individuals exposed through publication media. Information on *total numbers of exposures,* however, can be used to refine judgments regarding the choices of particular vehicles in a national schedule.

Actual measures of advertising audiences, which would enable advertisers to make still more meaningful evaluations of media schedules, are largely confined to a few vehicles. There is no technical obstacle to estimating average advertising audiences by product class and by media cost units for any single vehicle. When such data are available, they will be more significant than exposure data in guiding independent choices of vehicles.

Problems of definition and measurement, however, continue to complicate the measurement of advertising-audience combinations and duplication for typical national advertising schedules.

Communication of ideas and stimulation of attitudes, for which advertising is designed, have also been measured on a small scale in relation to media. Problems of definition and quantification have delayed any substantial research in this direction, and the research aspects are not sufficiently advanced for reporting here. This area represents the final stage of copy and media effect short of actual sales and profits.

It is assumed that media vehicles differ in their adaptability and efficiency at this stage. A vehicle which may maximize noting or awareness of specific advertisements may fall far short in enabling full and vivid communication. By contrast, a television commercial might be relatively costly up to a point of first perception or awareness, but could combine exposure time, controlled sequence, color, visualization, motion, and the human voice to communicate with exceptional impact. Media measurement at any previous stage has no opportunity to evaluate these aspects of media's influence on successful advertising.

Available techniques and their current applications reveal only a part of the facts essential for combining the most effective media schedules. Until exposure information for advertising audiences has been developed through application of improved techniques, the recommended practical approach is through analysis of the audience combinations of vehicles (see Chapter Sixteen).

Audiences of television network broadcasts and of average issues of leading magazines are available both singly and in combination as a basis for national media planning. Units of people or households in each vehicle cannot be assumed to have equal value. Exposure data and advertising-audience measures can be used to assign weights to each human unit in the audiences of vehicles. Such a basic approach, designed from data on audiences of vehicles and adjusted for expected exposure or actual perception of advertising units, offers the most scientific basis for building efficient media schedules.

fourteen

Kinds of People
in Media Audiences

CLASSES AND MARKETS

SIGNIFICANCE OF SEX AND AGE TO ADVERTISERS

UNIFORM FAMILY CHARACTERISTICS

IMPLICATIONS

The effectiveness of any advertising medium depends on reaching the right kinds and the maximum number of people in a favorable frame of mind.

The other chapters on measurement of advertising media concentrate on measurement of numbers of people, with very little stress on what kinds of people make up the audience of a vehicle or of a combined media schedule; but fortunately, most quantitative media measures provide for ready breakdowns of audiences into classes or groups.

This chapter will discuss meaningful class groupings as they relate to media; the following chapter will consider the attitudes or frame of mind of audiences of particular media.

CLASSES AND MARKETS

There are a number of class groupings of intense interest to advertisers. Some classes are more likely than others to buy and consume particular products, and these are the people to be cultivated most. If there are non-consumers who are influential in buying, these are to be cultivated, too.

Indirect as well as direct contact through advertisements should be considered in buying advertising media.[1] Part of the function of media is to reach those classes of audiences who will most effectively extend advertising influence through their own leadership and word-of-mouth communication of advertised ideas.

The more obvious market groupings are based on heavy users, light users, and nonusers of a product. There are also "markets," according to differences in age, sex, life cycle, economic level, occupation, education, and geographic location. Purchasing patterns and media relationships are also often sharply divided according to these factors. Population density and family size are related both to needs and to buying patterns.

Specifically, women are the consumers of certain products, they are the buying agents for other products which they do not consume, and they influence many other purchases. Young people in their teens not only spend lots of dollars, but they also influence many expenditures by their elders. Poor people try first to satisfy their *needs,* but the great majority of Americans spend more on discretionary *wants* than on basic requirements. Members of certain professions may surpass others in buying power, but they also have different wants and preferences. People of higher educational attainments may live differently and spend differently from those who leave academic surroundings earlier. The mere fact of living in one locality predisposes people to like certain things and to shop in a pattern common to that locality.

Yet almost every observation about differences in buying must be quickly revised in our dynamic society. Women were not always the shoppers, nor did they consume the same things in generations past. Young people could not buy heavily in the days before easy credit, nor did their elders have as much money as now. Discretionary spending was once a privilege of the rich, but a federally protected economy has ensured even the average family of sufficient income to spend a good deal on discretionary choices. The leveling off of occupational differences in income and the moderate differences related to education tend to equalize buying potential. Regional differences and differences between urban and rural areas are constantly being eroded by rapid travel and communication. Integration of ethnic and nationality groups may neutralize former traditional distinctions. All in all, the sharp differences in buying, based on the class distinctions mentioned earlier, are constantly shrinking or undergoing changes.

[1] R. D. Buteux, "On the Indirect Extension of Advertised Ideas," unpublished doctoral dissertation, New York University, 1957.

There are also psychological considerations, not so easily defined or identified, which determine buying behavior. Among these are intelligence, specific interests, and such personality traits as cautiousness or venturesomeness. Such distinctions as ethnic and national origins are still factors, but they are of secondary importance to most national advertisers.

As differences in class behavior, based on objective distinctions, keep changing and losing their significance, the patterns of buying related to psychological classes tend to become more important. As discretionary spending grows, the relationship of purchases to interest patterns becomes more significant. A growing share of these interests relates to leisure activities, and a growing share of expendable income goes to foster these interests.

Basic differences in psychological capacity, associated with the concept of intelligence, have come to play some roles in market behavior; indeed, the more that psychologists learn about intelligence and its measurement, the smaller and the less stable class differences appear to be. One obvious personality trait which inescapably relates to advertising is the disposition of a consumer to venture into new living patterns and to buy new things. National advertisers have a growing need to identify people in psychological patterns and to cater to their characteristics.

Audience Research

One early influence in reducing advertising emphasis on objective class distinctions was the audience research of major national media. Many magazines supposed to be read by men were found to have equal female audiences. Women's magazines, which were designed for the homemaker and career woman, were read by an equal percentage of teen-age girls. Picture magazines, which were supposed to appeal to youngsters and the uneducated, were found to cover all classes in much the same proportion as predominantly text magazines.

Early radio ratings provided little evidence on class breaks, but by the time television had full networks and projectable ratings, detective stories and western drama no longer separated the urban from the rural homes or the uneducated from the educated. One of the greatest single discoveries through measurement of media audiences (especially magazines) has been *the similarity of audience distributions of different media vehicles among seemingly diverse classes of people.*

An oft-repeated statement over the years has been that going to an outdoor movie is like sitting in a "passion pit" of teen-agers and super-teen-agers. Yet an objective study of the audiences of drive-in theaters showed that this idea is considerably off base.[2] "It was found that the drive-in audience was noticeably different from the general population. They generally had better jobs, higher income, more education, more children, more home ownership, more cars, more major appliances, and more conveniences. . . . Of those more than 15 years old who attended drive-ins, 66 per cent were married." [3]

Despite the dynamic nature of population changes and interactions, advertisers have a strong incentive to study and to understand all definable classes as related to advertising influence and to purchase patterns. There is better opportunity if advertising is designed for and directed toward the most responsive markets. If some media give more economical access to the best market groups, it is important to find those media and to learn how best to schedule them.

It does not matter how much population classes are defined, but how to identify them, how to talk their language, and how best to reach them through available media does matter. A first step is to examine the classes already identified, to study their distribution in media audiences, to appraise their market importance, and to look for psychological characteristics which may be a key to their future role.

SIGNIFICANCE OF SEX AND AGE TO ADVERTISERS

Family units are alike in that they tend to have a common income and geographic location and an approximate educational level. Families are startlingly different, however, in that they tend to be made up of extremes in two respects important to advertisers, namely, *sex* and *age*.

When a television network advertiser has a family type of program, he must adapt commercials for males and females and for young and old. When he uses a general magazine, he loses some of the very young and the uneducated, but again he must appeal to both sexes and to a wide range of ages. The weekday program sponsor and the women's service magazine advertiser may have a simpler problem, for they can assume that sex and audience purpose are more alike.

What are the differences between men and women in their buying patterns, and how can advertising best meet the situation?

[2] Steuart Henderson Britt, "What Is the Nature of the Drive-in Theatre Audience?" *Media/scope,* Vol. 4 (June, 1960), pp. 100–104.
[3] Page 102 of citation in footnote 2.

Sex Differences in Media Coverage and in Buying

It is instructive, first, to examine the male and female audience composition of national advertising media. Magazine audiences, as reported by the Nielsen Media Service, 1960, include the information given in Table 12.

TABLE 12. Magazine Audiences 18 Years and Older
(Nielsen Media Service, 1960; copyright, A. C. Nielsen Company, reprinted with permission)

Magazine	Male	Female
Life	14,372,000	13,972,000
The Saturday Evening Post	9,671,000	10,215,000
Reader's Digest	14,696,000	15,733,000
Better Homes and Gardens	3,944,000	10,802,000
Ladies' Home Journal	1,675,000	11,506,000
McCall's	1,837,000	11,095,000

The nearly equal division of audiences of publications not oriented to women's activities is a demonstration of the similarity of general reading interests of men and women. An examination of what men and women read in these magazines would show some marked contrasts, but at least one of the publications (*The Post*) was once assumed to be basically a man's magazine. The two women's service magazines show an expected preponderance of women in the audience; the fact that men make up more than 10 per cent of the total audience is of interest, but does not suggest an economical way to exploit them through advertising. The male and female advertising opportunities in all publications are reflected largely by their audience make-up.

Audience breakdowns of network television programs, or of groups of similar programs, are not difficult to understand, since there is a specific type of interest appeal. Table 13 shows the percentages of adult men and

TABLE 13. Percentages of Men and Women Making up Television Network Program Audiences (Midwinter 1960–1961) [4]

Type of program	Men	Women
Suspense-mystery drama	34	44
Situation comedy	27	40
Westerns	32	38
Variety	34	48
General drama	32	49
Quiz-audience participation	33	49

[4] *The Television Audience* (Chicago: A. C. Nielsen Company, 1961), p. 30.

adult women in the audiences of each of the leading types of network television programs in midwinter of the year 1960–1961. The total adult share of audience is indicated by the totals for men and women. While women exceed the men in all of the audience averages, the most conspicuous fact is the similarity of proportions for different types of programs. Women even dominate the audiences of westerns, although the margin is slightly less than for other program types.

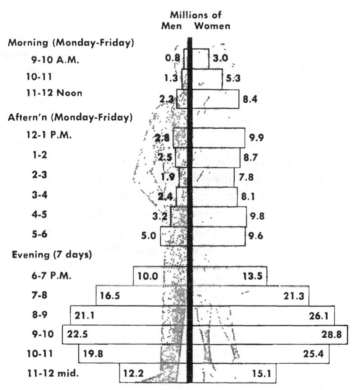

Millions of
Men   Women

Morning (Monday-Friday)		
9-10 A.M.	0.8	3.0
10-11	1.3	5.3
11-12 Noon	2.3	8.4
Aftern'n (Monday-Friday)		
12-1 P.M.	2.8	9.9
1-2	2.5	8.7
2-3	1.9	7.8
3-4	2.4	8.1
4-5	3.2	9.8
5-6	5.0	9.6
Evening (7 days)		
6-7 P.M.	10.0	13.5
7-8	16.5	21.3
8-9	21.1	26.1
9-10	22.5	28.8
10-11	19.8	25.4
11-12 mid.	12.2	15.1

FIG. 12. Male and female viewing of television. (*Courtesy of A. C. Nielsen Company.*)

The fact that there are some men in the television audience at all times of the day has led to an exaggerated impression by some of "sex equality" in TV viewing. Actually, the tendency of women to dominate television audiences, both day and evening, is reflected by data on male and female viewing, as shown in Fig. 12.[5] The facts indicate that women viewers

[5] "The True Picture of Who Views When and How Much." *The Nielsen Newscast,* Vol. 8 (Chicago: A. C. Nielsen Company, October, 1959), p. 3.

exceed men in the United States by almost four to one during the morning, by three to one in the afternoon, and by 25 to 35 per cent during the evening. Women are generally better "consumers" of major media than are men; and television continues to be a female-dominated medium for the most part.

The importance of women in the consumer market took a dramatic upturn during the first half of the twentieth century. Women gained recognition for their shopping skills, they had more money to spend, they gained possession of two-thirds of the savings accounts and one-half of the stocks, more of them had their own incomes, and all of them were given mobility mostly through private automobiles.[6] Early research showed that women were the best advertising audiences in general media. Copywriters adapted their appeals to the one they came to recognize both as the family buying agent and as a very substantial consumer in her own right.

During the period of greater female ascendancy, most men surrendered willingly anything which resembled a chore or which offered release from budget worries. Women, with more time to shop and to think about the family, took major responsibilities for their own needs, the children's needs, the low-cost household items, and even for some things used exclusively by their men. One survey reported that women bought four out of five white business shirts for men and made the choice of styling and brand.

When men let the trend reach the point of sharing earning responsibilities with their wives, there was some area of readjustment. One of these areas is the increased presence of men shoppers in supermarkets, which is facilitated in part by extended store hours for evening access. With the patterns of male and female buying in such a state of flux and with disposable income ever growing, no clear statement of differences in buying would hold for long. It seems probable, however, that women's increasing role as wage earners in most families will continue to be accompanied by a major role as buyers.

Psychologically, there seems no chance that men and women will surrender all of the differences which circumstance and social evolution have established. Intelligence tests have shown that males and females mature at about the same average level, and there is little test evidence that they differ greatly with regard to basic emotions. But social standards have permitted women more public display of emotions and have encouraged advertising copywriters to make emotional appeals more openly to women.

[6] Steuart Henderson Britt, *The Spenders* (New York: McGraw-Hill Book Company, Inc., 1960), p. 238.

Even in the areas of spectator sports and some participation sports—once reserved for men—there has been growing interest and participation by women.

Despite these leveling influences, men remain physically stronger and retain superior records in sports requiring ruggedness and strength. Women, on the other hand, play a different role in courtship, run most households, have the babies, and keep the family operations going. Some, but obviously not all, of these differences may decrease or disappear.

The great sex difference which is significant to the advertiser consists of the interest patterns which develop around each behavior pattern. Girls have interests which boys look upon with disdain. Young housewives have interests in home decoration which cause financial stress on unsympathetic husbands. Mothers concentrate on a great many areas of personal and family interest which the male breadwinner neglects. Grandma tries to stave off the signs of age when her spouse loses interest in her appearance. But then, social change has taught many older men to be fastidious and to go along with their wives in a campaign to think and act young. As retirement approaches, the couple who have been growing apart may find an increasing identity of interests. Later, living together the whole day, they may find almost no area of incompatible interests. All of these patterns are dynamic; advertising must discover them, identify them, adapt to them, and keep up with them, for the sexes will always be different as well as alike.

Age Differences in Media Coverage and in Buying

The pattern of age changes was suggested in tracing the changing relationships of men and women. The family has the task of reconciling interests at different age levels and between male and female interest patterns.

A shortening work week, a traditionally short school week, and increasing expenditures and activities in family recreation projects have combined to intensify the need for integrated interest patterns. Consumer advertising media make most of their contacts in the home, and there is much overlapping of contact over almost the complete age spectrum. Television especially entertains tots and aged people through different programs and sometimes with the same program. Magazines furnish audiences to advertisers from about ten years and up. Table 14 shows the age distribution of female readers reported by *McCall's Magazine* in 1960.[7]

[7] Adapted from *McCall's Female Audience* (New York: *McCall's Magazine*, 1960), p. 15.

McCall's is a magazine which grew from primary emphasis on style to a women's publication designed to reflect many interests of the family. While it has appealed to the unmarried career woman as well as the more domestically oriented woman, there would be reason to assume a degree of maturity for all readers. Table 14 shows that teen-agers—some of whom are married—provide 18.5 per cent of the total audience of *McCall's Magazine*. At the same time, the penetration of the publication among female teen-agers is 18 per cent of all teen-agers in the population (this is different from the 18.5 per cent mentioned in the previous sentence).

TABLE 14. *Female Readers of McCall's Magazine by Age Groups*

Age (in years)	Total readers	Per cent of total audience	Per cent of age group in audience
10–19	2,419,000	18.5	18.0
20–29	2,182,000	16.7	19.7
30–39	2,789,000	21.3	21.5
40–54	3,315,000	25.4	20.4
Over 54	2,369,000	18.1	14.4
Total	13,074,000	100.0	

Examination of both percentage columns in Table 14 shows a striking similarity in the number of readers and percentage reading at each age level up to fifty-five years. To the advertiser, this means practically an equal market of available readers at a wide range of age levels. From the editor's standpoint, there is ample evidence that *McCall's* begins serving women's interests at a very early age and keeps attracting about the same percentage of women in the population at most age levels. The only definite drop is in the two oldest groupings, when the struggles of leading a household and competing with other women are tapering off.

The percentages of magazine penetration in Table 15 show a considerable degree of uniformity at all age levels.[8] The serious business of *Time* and *Better Homes and Gardens* may account for a slight lag below fifteen years of age. The editorial style of *Reader's Digest* may account for its sustained interest in the oldest group. Male and female combined penetration does not clearly reflect the success of the women's magazines, but the teen-age appeal of *McCall's* shows through.

An examination of editorial features read at different age levels no doubt would reveal greater variation than is true for overall issues. Never-

[8] *The Audiences of Nine Magazines* (New York: *Look*, 1958), p. 16.

theless, the advertiser can only conclude that leading magazines offer him almost equal opportunity of reaching all buying age levels. Also, since all columns in Table 15 add to well over 100 per cent, it is obvious that there is an enormous overlap of reading interests.

TABLE 15. *Magazine Penetration According to Age Levels* 1958
(In per cent of each age group reading each magazine)

Publication	10–14	15–19	20–29	30–39	40–54	Over 54
Life	21.5	29.2	29.0	25.0	26.7	19.6
Look	21.2	28.9	25.1	22.4	22.2	14.9
The Saturday Evening Post	17.1	21.3	21.5	16.9	15.7	13.6
Time	6.4	9.2	10.4	8.2	9.1	4.5
Better Homes and Gardens	4.6	12.3	10.6	15.5	16.3	10.4
Good Housekeeping	8.4	9.5	10.1	10.5	10.8	7.7
Ladies' Home Journal	6.8	9.6	12.3	12.0	10.6	9.3
McCall's	10.0	14.1	12.1	10.0	9.0	7.2
Reader's Digest	18.7	31.8	25.0	29.9	29.1	25.8

Table 16 shows how different age levels attend to evening network television programs of various types. The fact that much of the evening viewing is a compromise choice of the entire family tends to conceal the effects of free choice. Shows of the same type vary somewhat in the age levels to which they appeal, and this is not evident in the averages presented. Despite these equalizing influences, the ratings reflect a definite pattern of program selection according to age of the viewer. Most of these programs were sponsored and undoubtedly were chosen by advertisers to appeal to markets of greatest interest to them.

TABLE 16. *Average Nielsen Total-audience Composition for Evening Network Television Programs According to Age Levels* (Mid winter 1960–1961) [9]

Type of program	Per cent of total audience		
	Children	Teen-agers	Adults
Suspense-mystery drama	11	11	78
Situation comedy	22	11	67
Westerns	19	11	70
Variety	10	8	82
General drama	11	8	81
Quiz-audience participation	10	8	82

[9] Citation in footnote 4.

Despite their reputation, teen-agers are the most consistent group in their participation in all types of program viewing. Situation comedy and Westerns are the types of evening network programs in which preteeners are most prominent among the viewers. Otherwise, their participation is uniform for the other types of programs.

Television has such a unique appeal to the very young—and this is not without advertising significance—that the audiences of specific programs at different ages are of wide interest. Batten, Barton, Durstine, and Osborn advertising agency used its national consumer panel to obtain estimates of television viewing by children in 1955.[10]

The panel of 3,397 families having children up to eighteen years of age included a total of 7,524 children. Percentage ratings, based on avid or frequent viewers of 10 programs and ranging from strictly children's programs to those with more universal appeal, are shown by age levels in Table 17.

TABLE 17. *Percentage of Children of Different Age Levels Reported as Frequent Television Viewers* (1955)
(In per cent)

Program	Per cent of age group				
	Under 6	6–8	9–11	12–14	15–18
Big Top	33	31	23	20	8
Captain Midnight	14	27	27	20	8
Ding Dong School	44	8	3	2	1
Howdy Doody	42	38	24	12	4
Mickey Mouse Club	55	66	60	38	12
Disneyland	65	80	79	65	39
Lassie	50	64	63	47	26
Rin-Tin-Tin	54	69	74	57	23
Robin Hood	35	51	55	44	22
Zoo Parade	18	22	22	16	9

The ratings of avid viewers in 1955, based on two-thirds of the households having a television receiver, are national network estimates for all 10 programs. The selectivity of most of the programs at various age levels is probably not exaggerated. Nearly all of the television households had but one receiver, which means that program choices were sometimes compromises, especially for the older children. Most of the programs in the

10 *What Do Children Watch?* (New York: Batten, Barton, Durstine and Osborn, Inc., May, 1956).

lower part of Table 17 could be considered to have general family appeal, although there is an apparent liberation from television dependence at about age fifteen. Much viewing by grade-school children is routine, merely filling certain hours in their long day. Regardless of motivation for viewing, the enormous exposure to children is a vast advertising opportunity which is not overlooked.

The interaction of the family both in program viewing and in product purchases must be considered in interpreting available evidence. The fact that those who view a program are not always the selectors was evidenced in a factor analysis of 600 Eastern metropolitan television diaries by the American Research Bureau for the Leo Burnett advertising agency.[11] While program content appeared to be a strong determining factor in male viewing, the study succeeded in accounting for only about one-third of the total pattern of adult male viewing. The influence of females and of those at different age levels apparently led to male viewing of programs below first choice. Another impressive factor was the influence of block programing by networks as they endeavored to frustrate competing networks. Block programing is apparently successful in holding the audiences of a network. Program viewing by adult males is not the same as if the man could choose freely from the week's listing without regard to time, network scheduling, and preferences of more persuasive members of the same household.

Both the changes in what is bought and in the ability to buy it have important bearings on market potentials at different age levels. Earning power in business and the professions has a cumulative tendency which often enables the older household head to spend beyond his desires, despite taxes. Both the tax structure and easy consumer credit have encouraged more buying at younger age levels; otherwise, many people would not buy as much as they do now.

Houses without down payments enable the young couple to "own their own home," to improve it, and to buy furnishings with more of an expectation of stability than they had in the past. Easy financing of private automobiles and travel enable people to buy and to enjoy while they are still young enough to enjoy. This increasing trend makes markets much more responsive at lower age levels than ever before.

The tendency toward merging of interests of different age levels can only go so far. The very young are very active, and their desires are almost unlimited. Although there are limits to what they can buy, there is no limit

[11] Seymour Banks of the Leo Burnett Company, Inc.

to their persistence in asking their parents to buy for them. The great potential of youth is not confined to their present buying, but extends to their coming maturity and growing market significance. If advertisers have been slow to make major commitments to reach the *youth market,* mass media have brought the reach of general advertising increasingly to younger levels. The growing appeal of general magazines to teen-agers and the even greater subteen appeal of television have brought advertising heavily into the very young age groups.

Market patterns through maturity and into retirement age levels are affected by basic forces which may be permanent. Starting a home requires major money outlays; and raising of children is accompanied by expenses which may, in a sense, grow faster than bodies. School and an ever-extending period of college training call for big sums of money, as do all the group activities and needs of a young and vigorous family. Even the encouragement of delayed spending for the purposes of saving and investment makes a market for advertisers during the same years when buying is greatest. Retirement usually comes at an age when buying to satisfy sensory pleasures is reduced and when there is some restraint, as modest budgets are matched against possible later needs. Older people eat less, they go fewer places, and clothing lasts longer than when they were at a more active age. Buying for their own use is definitely on the ebb.

Psychological patterns may change even more than behavior patterns with age, although basic mental capacity changes little after adulthood is reached. Intelligence-test scores for the average person level off around the age of twenty, and capacities may decrease before fifty, although decline appears to be highly individualistic. In contrast with the relative stability of intelligence, interest patterns are constantly changing and lacking in consistency. Increased leisure time and increased discretionary spending power for satisfying whims make *interests* the best single guide to advertising strategy.

Magazine editors are keenly conscious of variations in interests at different age levels, although these interests often reflect a combination of characteristics. Fiction, the chief ingredient of consumer magazines, appeals mostly to young people. Romantic fiction, which appeals to girls and young women, appeals also to the unmarried, the less educated, and the lower economic levels. Often these characteristics tend to combine, since the unmarried young girl may not have completed her education and is not yet the controller of finances for a family. Romantic fiction brings fulfillment of interests not yet realized and an escape from the restrictions imposed by limited income and surroundings. Marriage, the arrival of a family, and possibly improved economic status produce striking changes of interests.

Style and beauty emphasis are high with women when they are young; and these interests are cultivated to a much later age than was once the case. Interest in food preparation and home decoration reaches a peak during earlier married years. Interest in current events, in broad social and economic questions, and in such diversions as gardening—these tend to come in later years.

The changing pattern of these interests, which so closely coincides with the requirements and activities at certain age levels, strongly suggests that interests are largely an outgrowth of circumstances. Insofar as men participate in the same patterns and insofar as they happen to be subject to similar social standards, it may well be that their interests would develop the same way. There are, of course, individualized interest patterns, but they may have little bearing on the cultivation of mass markets.

Qualitative age considerations should not be considered entirely a function of behavior patterns. Young people are more eager, active, and attracted by opportunities to try out the new. They are cautious and conforming, yet at the same time venturesome and daring. As they mature to their full powers and achieve some major successes such as occupational advancements, they have reason for optimism and may abandon some of the earlier restraints of caution and conformity. Advancing age definitely slows down some activities, reduces interest in sensory satisfactions, and brings about a reduction of optimism, especially if health or finances are limited—but almost no interest pattern is completely dependent upon age. Nevertheless, these general trends are consistent enough to hold in relation to total audiences of most mass media.

UNIFORM FAMILY CHARACTERISTICS

Families tend to be homogeneous with regard to where they live, their "race" and religion, their economic level, social status, and educational aims. Since national advertising media depend mostly upon contacts in the home, it is advantageous to have so many common dimensions within the family unit.

The most selective major national medium—magazines—has long been selective with regard to economic and educational levels. Magazines are becoming increasingly adaptable to geographic locations through regional advertising arrangements. Most national advertising adapts broadly to "racial" and religious differences, although these factors continue to establish class distinctions. Yet legal restraints on ethnic and religious discrimination cannot coerce the abandonment of the characteristics themselves or completely wipe out their marketing significance.

Economic Levels

The family characteristic most obviously important to advertisers is that of economic level. Buying power, brand preferences, and behavior patterns are all related to family finances. So is social status, although money is only a partial clue to one's standing in society.

Buying power is not necessarily identical with spending tendencies, nor does buying increase uniformly in all product categories as income increases. Food, for example, takes a decreasing share of the budget after a certain level of income is reached. It is in the areas of discretionary spending that increased income has greatest effect, but the contrasts have declined as mass discretionary spending has grown. Media which require some expenditure on the part of consumers, are only slightly dependent upon income levels for buying, but are much more dependent upon economic level for consuming.

The distribution of reader penetration for selected magazines in the United States at a time when the median household income was under $5,000 is shown in Table 18.[12] The magazines show a clear pattern of

TABLE 18. Readers of Nine Magazines by Average Annual Household Income (1958) *

Magazine	$2,000 or less (pop. 18.15 million)	$2,000 –2,999 (pop. 18.2 million)	$3,000 –3,999 (pop. 17.15 million)	$4,000 –4,999 (pop. 27.2 million)	$5,000 –6,999 (pop. 27.8 million)	$7,000 –or more (pop. 20.6 million)
Life	13.2	18.8	22.3	27.2	27.9	35.5
Look	14.4	15.1	18.7	23.1	26.3	27.8
The Saturday Evening Post.	9.9	14.4	13.9	13.8	20.4	27.9
Time	3.9	3.6	6.3	7.6	9.3	14.7
Better Homes and Gardens.	4.6	9.1	9.1	12.1	15.5	20.9
Good Housekeeping	5.7	9.1	7.2	10.3	10.7	12.9
Ladies' Home Journal.....	6.0	6.9	7.4	10.7	10.8	18.6
McCall's	4.5	8.4	8.7	8.8	11.8	15.6
Reader's Digest	15.6	19.0	21.0	26.2	32.6	43.0

* Calculations based on readers ten years of age and over.

[12] Page 47 of citation in footnote 8.

increased penetration among that portion (one-sixth) of the population ten years of age or older living in households where annual income exceeded $7,000. Most of the nine magazines show a sharp drop in reader penetration below the $2,000 income level. The individual differences among magazines were important at the time, but are likely to vary over a period of years.

Of greater significance is the size and consistency of increase in penetration going up the economic scale. This is quite different from the age pattern, which shows relatively uniform penetration over a wide range of ages. Magazines clearly bring their heaviest advertising impact to income levels best able to buy.

Television evening network programing differs notably from magazines in its almost uniform pattern of viewing by economic levels, as shown in Table 19.[13] Upper and lower economic levels are almost identical in the

TABLE 19. Income and Evening TV Viewing

Family income level	Average no. of hours of set usage *
Upper	21.2
Middle	22.6
Lower	21.1

* Calculations based on hours from 6 P.M. to midnight, seven days a week.

number of evening hours during which the family has a television set turned on. Since there are only forty-two evening hours in the week after 6 P.M., it appears that families at all economic levels use the television set about one-half of the total evening time. The 3-hour daily average of both high-income and low-income families stands in sharp contrast to the comparatively light penetration of leading magazines at the lower end of the income spectrum. This might be interpreted as meaning that television serves the entire market better for advertisers than do magazines. However, the better markets are obviously the higher-income families. Thus the two media complement each other by enabling the advertiser to reach all economic levels, and in so doing to gain heavier impact as desired on the more prosperous homes.

Television differs from magazines in that once a receiver is purchased, all of the programs on the air are equally accessible. Magazine access is limited somewhat by the fact that the buyer pays a substantial part of the cost of producing each issue. Some people cannot buy all of the magazines

[13] Page 40 of citation in footnote 4.

they might want, and this is reflected by the tendency for used magazines to be passed along to others in many lower-income families.

The fact that television activity holds to such a uniform level over a broad income range does not mean there are no differences in program choices. Programs, like magazines, appeal differently to people in different classes, including economic classes. The specific program, like the individual magazine, "selects" people according to their interests. Since the interests of any group (including income groups) are not permanent, the advertiser, the editor, and the program builder must keep constantly alert to the current interests of any group they may want to reach.

There is little need to pause for analysis of the relationship between economic levels and response to advertising. All income groups need food, clothing, and shelter—and usually an automobile. The percentage of families whose budgets are exhausted by these purchases grows smaller as the proportion of disposable income increases. The upper-income groups can and do spend such a large proportion of income for nonessentials that advertising can concentrate on other than basic satisfactions. Products and their prices can be considered almost entirely on the basis of psychological satisfactions. Obviously people will learn to buy at almost any expenditure level that incomes will permit, particularly when there is some kind of "built-in" long-range security for nearly all.

Aside from differences in buying attitudes, the upper-income groups have some fundamental psychological differences. Children from more affluent families tend to perform significantly higher on intelligence tests than those from more modest backgrounds. Just how much of the advantage in ability comes from true selectivity and how much is an outgrowth of training and opportunity is still not clearly known. Testing procedures are too crude to tell the advertiser much, except possibly that wealthier markets are a little more intelligent and discriminating. Except for the extreme top levels and the very low levels, there is no need to stress the adaptation of copy and of media to each economic group.

As with other market classes, the chief economic distinctions—other than money—are the varying *interest patterns*. Even here, the well-known tendency to keep up with the Joneses is a leveling force opening all interest areas to most people. Almost every activity common to people of wealth has a fringe of "ordinary people" who may sacrifice many things so as to participate. Memberships in exclusive clubs, attendance at prestige social gatherings, possession of a fine painting or musical instrument, polo playing, or whatever may represent one all-out effort on the part of lower-income people to satisfy an expensive taste—or to ape such a taste. Nowhere is the adaptability of tastes more striking than in the case of a family which lives in a low-rent run-down apartment which is furnished with the finest in television matched by a Cadillac for that Florida vacation trip. These exceptions prove the accessibility of interest patterns across class lines. Nevertheless, money is not the rigid determiner of market classes that it once was.

Educational and Cultural Levels

Distinctions of permanent importance to advertisers because of their direct relationship to specific interests are educational and cultural levels. Insofar as they are also allied with economic and social status, education and culture may appear to have exaggerated influence on living and buying. As they relate to preferred media patterns, education and culture may determine the avenue of advertising approach. The penetration of leading magazines according to adult levels of education (see Table 20) reflects a clear bias favoring higher academic attainments.[14]

TABLE 20. *Adult Magazine Readers, According to Educational Level* (1958) *
(In per cent of penetration according to highest grade attended)

Magazine	Grade school (pop. 35.95 million)	High school (pop. 47.05 million)	College or beyond (pop. 20.75 million)
Life	15.4	26.0	38.2
Look	14.1	23.5	26.2
The Saturday Evening Post	8.4	16.5	30.4
Time	2.2	6.6	20.5
Better Homes and Gardens	7.8	14.0	21.4
Good Housekeeping	5.4	11.0	14.2
Ladies' Home Journal	6.0	11.8	17.4
McCall's	3.9	11.1	14.6
Reader's Digest	13.4	29.2	48.1

* Figures based on adults twenty years of age and over.

Several points stand out in the penetration of magazine reading, as shown in Table 20. The penetration of all magazines of importance to major advertisers depends a great deal on educational level. The heavy pictorial content of *Life* and *Look* magazines, which might seem designed for un-

14 Pages 18–19 of citation in footnote 8.

educated readers, shows a marked increase in penetration at the college level. Despite the fact that picture magazines are successfully edited to penetrate so well at higher educational levels, this is the class analysis which most clearly shows the selectivity of text magazines. Penetration of the text magazines is three or four times as heavy at the college level as it is at the grade-school level. The national trend toward higher education should ultimately bring magazines to a greater share of the total market.

Network television penetrates to lower educational levels than do the leading magazines. There is also a difference in types of programs with regard to the percentage of viewers with various periods of formal education. Table 21 shows the composition of the audiences of leading types of evening network programs with respect to the education of all male and female heads of households in the audiences.[15]

TABLE 21. Total Heads-of-Households Audience of Leading Types of Television Network Programs, According to Years of Formal Education (In per cent)

Type of program	Under 9	9–10	11–12	13–14	15 and over
Suspense-mystery drama	15	12	41	14	18
Situation comedy	20	14	40	10	16
Westerns	19	15	42	10	14
Variety	17	12	39	10	22
General drama	14	11	37	12	26
Quiz-audience participation..	21	15	33	11	20

Situation comedy and Westerns do a little better relatively speaking than the other types of programs among households where educational attainments are lower. General drama and variety are favored a little more strongly than other types of programs among the better educated. The absolute levels of popularity are not indicated, since the scores represent distributions of all heads of households in the audiences according to levels of education.

Households whose heads are at high educational levels are also high-level consumers of most products and services. "Even when income is held constant, the person who has attended college tends to outspend the lesser-educated for all goods and services. Another remarkable factor about the

15 Scores computed by combining audience composition percentages from 56 evening network television programs, as reported in *The United States Television Audience* (New York: American Research Bureau, Inc., October, 1961).

better-educated households is their *leadership status*—here are the experimenters and innovators. They respond strongly to the new. . . ." [16]

There are, then, three points of emphasis regarding the relationship of education to markets. *People with more education are heavier consumers generally. People with more education set the pace for others, especially by buying and trying new products. The percentage of education is on the increase and presages even bigger future markets.*

Psychological capacities and interests are closely related to educational attainments. Formal education is a selective process and, while it may aid performance in intelligence tests, tends to select fundamentally better candidates at each new level. Even in specialized schools, education is becoming increasingly recognized as a means to a way of living instead of merely a means to earning a living. Despite the growing proportion of the population completing high school and college, the marks of an educated person are evident in his cultural and leisure activities. Not the least of the marks of the more educated is the tendency to entertain more and to participate as a social individual. *Education probably has more influence on interest patterns than any other single factor discussed in this chapter.*

Social Class

Another important distinction from a media standpoint has to do with social class; but whether it can be effectively separated from such objective elements as income, education, and occupation remains to be seen. The distinguished contributions of A. B. Hollingshead of Yale University are acknowledged in advertising.[17] Hollingshead convincingly defines five social groups which have a very considerable income overlap. However, he has proposed identification on the basis of a weighted index, combining education and occupation of head of household. This approach leaves some doubt as to whether social class should be considered separately, even though both media habits and buying patterns are clearly related to social status. A three-factor index—of age, education, and occupation—would probably be a better predictor.

Instances are reported where product consumption is closely associated with social status. Two product brands of equal price were found to have wide differences in distribution within the same social groups. The groups which bought three-fourths of all purchases of one brand bought only

---

[16] Page 96 of citation in footnote 6.

[17] Thomas Kemm, "Defining Markets: Who Belongs to Which Social Class, and What Are His Wants?" *Printers' Ink,* Vol. 264 (August 29, 1958), pp. 60–62.

one-half of the total purchases of its competitor. Different social groups had different brand images of the same products and bought them for different reasons. Two newspapers in the same community had widely different audiences by social levels. One was claimed as read by more than one-half of the topmost 3 per cent of the socially elite, whereas the competitor was claimed as read by only 1 per cent of the same upper class.

Comparison of newspaper reading and other reading habits at different social levels remains to be more firmly determined, even if the Hollingshead education-occupation index is used. Pierre Martineau prefers a more subjective basis for social-class distinction, and holds that newspaper advertisements should be adapted to specific social classes.[18] He has concluded from Chicago *Tribune* surveys that no single style of advertising can be effective with all social classes. This would indicate that newspaper advertisements should be prepared to appeal to specific class groups and that neither products nor advertisements should attempt to embrace widely differing social groups.

Both the national advertiser and his agency are cautioned to "get in step" with the proper markets according to sociological definitions. Magazines with more specialized appeals to social classes would appear to be recommended over mass magazines appealing to extensive markets. There need be no question as to the existence of social groups with varied outlooks, but much needs to be learned before revolutionary changes in advertising approaches can be safely recommended.

Geography and Population Density

Geography and population density also continue to be important advertising and marketing considerations—they do not disappear with improved communication and transportation. Mobility of the population, which has greatly increased, does not erase these differences as much as might be expected.

Apparently, individuals and families do a great deal of adapting as they move about. Even the magazine subscription, which can easily be moved with the family, does not seem to be reflected in audience figures based on locality and population density. Table 22 shows geographic break-

[18] Pierre D. Martineau, "Social Class and Its Very Close Relationship to Buying Behavior," in Martin L. Bell (editor), *Proceedings of the Winter Conference of the American Marketing Association, 1960* (Chicago-American Marketing Association, 1961), pp. 185–192.

downs of magazine reading, and Table 23 shows a similar breakdown according to density of population areas.[19]

TABLE 22. *Percentage of Magazine Readers in Four Geographic Areas* (1958)

Magazine	Northeast (pop. 32.85 million)	North Central (pop. 39.6 million)	South (pop. 38.55 million)	West (pop. 18.1 million)
Life	29.8	24.1	22.3	23.2
Look	22.4	25.0	17.4	21.6
The Saturday Evening Post	15.8	19.1	13.4	22.3
Time	8.0	8.0	6.0	11.0
Better Homes and Gardens	12.3	15.2	10.0	11.2
Good Housekeeping	9.4	10.3	9.2	8.9
Ladies' Home Journal	10.1	11.2	9.6	10.6
McCall's	6.5	12.2	9.7	11.0
Reader's Digest	25.3	29.5	24.2	31.1

TABLE 23. *Magazine Readers in Urban and Rural Areas* (1958)
(In per cent)

Magazine	Metropolitan areas (pop. 75.75 million)	Nonmetropolitan areas with cities and towns	
		2,500– 49,999 (pop. 18.7 million)	Under 2,500 (pop. 34.65 million)
Life	27.6	26.4	18.1
Look	22.4	26.1	17.5
The Saturday Evening Post	17.0	19.0	16.0
Time	9.2	7.0	5.4
Better Homes and Gardens	12.6	14.1	10.9
Good Housekeeping	9.1	13.3	8.5
Ladies' Home Journal	10.4	12.5	9.1
McCall's	10.0	11.1	8.8
Reader's Digest	28.1	30.4	22.9

Except for some individual differences in magazines, the penetration of the South is lighter than that of other areas. The differences are not great and may grow even smaller, but still they are significant.

The differences according to population density are more conspicuous,

[19] Pages 26–27 of citation in footnote 8.

especially when rural areas are contrasted with all others. Areas with no town over 2,500 population contain one-fourth of the population among whom penetration of leading magazines definitely falls off. They are served more adequately by publications of their own choosing; but even so, the people probably read fewer magazines than do people in metropolitan areas.

Both locality and population density are related to income and product purchases. In general, families in the North and families in metropolitan areas have greater incomes than do those in the South or in rural areas. Climate is not the only determining factor on product purchases according to locality, although the influence of other factors is diminishing. Television, the automobile, and family shifts from one locality to another—all reduce psychological differences. Some differences persist, of course, such as the fact that people in rural areas produce more of what they consume and may have less need to buy certain food products.

Farm Groups

Farmers are a special consumer group not only in that they satisfy some of their own needs, but also because they buy production equipment and do more of their buying as family units. Lower cash income and the fact that many items are bought partly for production purposes may lead to lower-cost choices on certain items.

The automobile, for example, or its tires may be purchased to aid the farming operation. The same kind of pride which may motivate the more monied urban buyer must be mixed with considerations of investment, profit, and use. Farming is becoming an increasingly industrialized operation, and the old distinctions of a predominantly agricultural society have decreased considerably. The farmer himself often engages in other kinds of business and is becoming more and more difficult to identify as such. While market differences may continue for a time, the advertiser is coming to consider farming more as an industry than as a way of life.

Regional Groups

Psychological abilities and interests undoubtedly relate to localities and population density, but abilities are no longer a serious consideration. Interests, on the other hand, may be varied as well as temporary.

Just at a time when differences in local interests became of less market importance, leading magazine publishers began to specialize in regional editions. While the regional service is largely designed to accommodate advertisers, there is also a growing trend to fit editorial matter more to geographical interest patterns. It seems unlikely that such adaptation to local preferences will accentuate or even sustain current differences.

Ethnic Groups

Ethnic class distinctions are of interest to advertisers for many reasons, despite governmental efforts to protect and assimilate minority groups. So long as there are economic differences, differences in interest patterns, differences in choices and rates of consuming products, there will be adaptation by advertisers.

The most obvious difference in the United States, since immigration has been minimized, is the contrast of white and nonwhite populations. Negroes are a growing proportion of the population, representing approximately one-eighth of the total, and they are very important to the national advertiser. More than any other nonwhite group, they are served by different media and also are "consumers" of the leading magazines. Table 24 shows the penetration of leading American magazines among white and nonwhite populations.[20]

TABLE 24. Magazine Readers by White and Nonwhite Origin (1958)
(In per cent)

Magazine	White (pop. 116.2 million)	Nonwhite (pop. 12.9 million)
Life	25.5	18.7
Look	22.3	15.4
The Saturday Evening Post	18.2	5.9
Time	8.2	4.8
Better Homes and Gardens.............	13.0	6.7
Good Housekeeping	9.8	7.4
Ladies' Home Journal	10.9	5.8
McCall's	10.3	5.9
Reader's Digest	28.2	16.8

The nonwhite group, which is predominantly made up of Negroes, has considerably less penetration by leading magazines than the white group. However, this gap is filled in part by selective media adapted to language needs or, in the case of Negroes, to their own preferences and needs. There are broadcasting stations which serve different language groups and some stations which are intended to serve the Negro market. It is even more difficult in the case of broadcasting than with publications to determine how exclusively their audiences are made up of Negroes.

[20] Page 29 of citation in footnote 8.

Different ethnic groups may conform in varying degrees with native whites as markets for products, but differ in their influence upon the whole market. A study of four ethnic groups in the New York City marketing area succeeded in establishing a few basic facts.[21] People of immediate Italian ancestry, for example, have brought new food habits to the United States; the Italians have been rapidly absorbed into the population, and so have many of their favorite foods. The Jewish population has also established food habits of its own, but some of these are associated with religious ritual and are not absorbed readily into the typical American menu.

Puerto Ricans and Negroes both have food customs which may be associated with a low economic background and which do not appeal widely to the general population. Puerto Ricans and Negroes—both of whom are generally native born—differ greatly in their absorption into the population. The Puerto Rican comes to an English speaking area with a foreign language, but he and his children melt away into the population almost as fast as they learn to speak English. The Negro, who already has crossed the language barrier, has retained his identity for generations, and it remains to be seen whether his integration into the white community will significantly lead to loss of identity as a Negro.

Advertisers have long catered to nationality and language groups in local markets, but little national advertising is geared to any ethnic group. As the largest single English-speaking minority group, the Negro has ready access to the same media as the majority of the population. He has moved up rapidly on the wage-earning scale since World War II and often can spend at the same rate as his white counterpart in the same community. Any reduction of bias and of restrictions as to his living habits should quickly enable him to show his true abilities and patterns of interests, but any attempt to assess these before free movement and equality of opportunity are fully achieved would be premature.

IMPLICATIONS

Advertising media of one kind or another reach all classes of people in the United States, although the lower educational levels are "light" consumers of magazines.

The most evident fact about market classes—still significantly different

21 M. Alexander, "The Significance of Ethnic Groups in Marketing New-type Packaged Foods in Greater New York," unpublished Ph.D. dissertation, New York University, 1959.

in many respects—is that current social and economic trends are reducing those differences. Growing incomes and easy credit have been accompanied by a philosophy favoring more spending. That trend was dramatically emphasized when, during a very mild recession in the 1950s, President Eisenhower urged people to buy certain high-priced items faster rather than try to get along with the old models. The best economic citizens are no longer just those whose credit is extended least.

While there is a strong social movement to establish *both equality and conformity* at all class levels, there is no reason to assume that class distinctions will disappear from the market. Rather, the change is a switch from emphasis on capacities to emphasis on *interests* and *preferences*—and interests and preferences can change very rapidly.

To establish a correlation between a classification variable (such as social class or ethnic group) and a consumption variable is pure description. It serves as an indefinite predictor for the short term and a dubious predictor for the long term. Given the clustering of responses along a classification of so-called independent variables (high income, high education, high social class, etc.), there is still no way of knowing from the clustering of these variables why the phenomenon exists. Is it due to different perceptual systems or life styles or social roles played or what? The grouping of such variables makes suspect those decisions and rationales posited on a single, univariate scale. Thus social class may be a better predictor of some events simply because it is a combination of marketing-proved ingredients—not because it uncovers some mystique.

Meanwhile, the consumer has become king; the advertiser must keep him in mind while he designs new products as well as when he prepares his advertising copy.

Media research will continue to seek out differences of penetration in various class groups. There is no special research problem in making class measurements of the reach of media. There will always be an emphasis upon *who,* as well as *how many,* are reached by particular media vehicles. Such knowledge is invaluable to advertisers in determining how best to make their media investments.

fifteen

Attitudes of
Media Audiences

WHAT ARE THE QUALITATIVE CONSIDERATIONS?

MEASUREMENT OF AUDIENCE ATTITUDES

ATTITUDES TOWARD TYPES OF MEDIA AND THEIR
    ADVERTISEMENTS

IMPLICATIONS

Major media make possible the quantities of audiences and exposures which are so essential to the success of major advertising expenditures. But media, as well as copy, stimulate attitudes and motivations which affect buying responses. A media vehicle which reaches a maximum in building favorable associations of attitude may be able to offset a considerable advantage of competing vehicles with bigger advertising audiences per dollar. This is axiomatic in advertising.

When media-audience measurement was new, there were many buyers who resisted and resented quantitative data. They had been accustomed to forming judgments of *both* quality and quantity, and the audience measures stressed factual quantities almost entirely. There was also some disbelief, prompted partly by the large size of measured magazine audiences and partly by divergences of facts from intuitive opinions.

It required a score of years for projected audience measures to gain

326

general acceptance and even longer to be broadly applied in media buying. This is not intended to devalue the qualitative factors, but rather to suggest that judgments of quality be realistically applied in the light of known differentials in quantitative performance by various media vehicles.

When a media buyer prefers one media vehicle to another because of assumed advantages in attitudes, associations, climate, or environment, it is not realistic to disregard entirely the number of people reached. The quality of response to a particular medium may be such as to offset 10, 20, or perhaps 30 per cent disadvantage in numbers. Whether any major vehicle can survive a 2-to-1 disadvantage in numbers reached solely on the basis of better audience attitudes is quite a different question.

What are these matters of quality and attitude and climate which are so important to some media buyers? Are they attitudes which relate solely to the medium, or do they carry over partly or fully to advertisements in the particular vehicle? How much influence do they have on response to advertising—apart from the impact of the sales message itself? Do some vehicles have vastly greater qualitative impact on their advertisements than others?

These questions and the techniques for qualitative measurement are the subject of this chapter. Because of lack of pioneering research in these areas, the answers are far from complete.

WHAT ARE THE QUALITATIVE CONSIDERATIONS?

It is assumed that all media vehicles have some unmeasured effects on response to their advertising which space and time buyers should take into account. This qualitative area is not concerned with who the audience prospects are—this was the subject of discussion in the previous chapter.

It is assumed that people approach each media vehicle in an appropriate frame of mind and that they have an image of the vehicle and an attitude toward it and toward its advertisements. The important thing to the advertiser is the audience attitude toward his particular message, but media effects are seldom so specific. The advertiser and his message must also be responsible for any unique effects obtained by his advertising copy.

It is fallacious to talk about a definable audience of a certain publication or a certain radio station as if there were not many instances of *overlapping* with all sorts of other audiences of other specific media. This has been well put by Ernest Dichter:

We talk glibly about the *Time* reader, the *Esquire* reader, the *Saturday Evening Post* reader. I would like to believe that these exist, but, actually, there is no such animal. . . . We are exposed to newspapers, magazines, radio, and TV, and most of us are exposed to half a dozen TV shows, we may listen to several radio programs, read at least two newspapers and as many magazines.

It is meaningless, in our cultural climate, to talk about a *Saturday Evening Post* reader; at best we can talk about a magazine "favorer," or "non-favorer," and explore his feelings and his reasons for favoring or not favoring a particular medium.[1]

Since our emphasis is chiefly on attitudes, it may simplify the discussion to identify three specific attitude areas as the primary qualitative elements: (1) the attitudes of the audience *toward the medium or media vehicle,* either as a whole or by specific segments; (2) the attitudes of the audience *toward advertisements in general in this particular medium or vehicle;* and (3) the attitudes *toward specific advertising messages in the medium or vehicle.*

Both the general media classes and specific vehicles are mentioned above because it is assumed that general as well as specific attitudes exist in each case. It may also be assumed that all these attitudes contribute to the others. If one has a favorite magazine, he seems likely to give the advertisements some advantage in that particular vehicle and may even assume some favorable classification for relatively unknown companies or brands which he learns about through its advertisements.

"Environment" and "climate" are terms which suggest that all elements in a media vehicle, including advertisements, contribute to the qualitative surroundings. This includes the product classifications represented, as well as the prestige of neighboring advertisers, since a lone advertisement in an unexpected product class has an element of novelty or surprise.

Another consideration, the *media image,* has broader implications, but again contributes to the attitudes with which people approach a medium. One magazine or television program may be approached because its image includes heavy emphasis on entertainment; another media vehicle may fall chiefly into a utility image, to be consulted for help or information.

All of these qualitative considerations include attitudes of expectancy or involvement which are established by media vehicles or their advertisements. These provide most of the motivation for approaching a media vehicle and may finally extend to audience motivation favorable to a particular advertiser.

[1] Ernest Dichter, "10 New Concepts in Media Research," *Media/scope,* Vol. 3 (July, 1959), pp. 44–47, at p. 45.

MEASUREMENT OF AUDIENCE ATTITUDES

There is a paradox in measuring qualitative aspects of media since the term "quality" often is used somewhat loosely to designate what is not measured or measurable.

As soon as a feature of media can be accurately measured, especially in relation to total advertising effectiveness, it is no longer considered qualitative. Audiences can be measured with useful accuracy, and doubling an audience of the same quality is expected to produce about double the advertising effect. There is no comparable dimension for doubling the favorableness of audience attitudes, nor is there literally any objective measure of attitudes. This means that there is, as yet, no clear concept of dimensions of attitudes, nor is there any practical measuring procedure having widespread acceptance.

Because of problems in forming a concept as well as inadequacies of measurement, existing qualitative media research constitutes a highly controversial area. Lack of approved procedures and absence of objective check data have attracted original and unrealistic research pioneers as well as demagogues and charlatans. An examination of available studies and reports will confirm the difficulties, but will not classify the research operators.

Early Qualitative Measures of Media

Conventional attitude questions were used in some of the early qualitative studies and for many reasons produced confusing results. When applied to a population sample, questions about a magazine lack meaning since only the attitudes of readers are of value to advertisers. Questions about attitudes toward advertisements in a particular vehicle have little meaning since the advertising copy and the advertiser chiefly determine specific attitudes. The point is so obvious that respondents will preface their own responses with substantially that statement. Comparative studies, sponsored by one medium, have produced meaningless attitude data by confining the survey to their own subscribers. In a number of instances, the questions and their sequence have been so prejudicial as to *ensure* the advantage of the sponsor.

A variation from generalized questions is an indirect technique in which people are asked about their *belief* of claims in specific magazine advertisements when they are presented within the covers of *different* publications. This method should be confined to readers of the tested publications, as suggested above. In fact, the only proper basis for comparing the effects of two publications on belief in their advertisements is with the common audiences who read *both* publications. They are the people who are competent to judge and who evidently have something in common with both publications.

Preliminary fieldwork, using a common audience, has failed to reveal significant differences. The people who read two or more publications carrying the same advertisement apparently begin with a favorable bias for each medium; any differential is too slight to demonstrate that one publication has more advertising believability than another among common readers of the publications if they are general magazines. There might be different results from a comparison of attitudes of people who read two quite different kinds of specialized publications, for example, *Popular Mechanics* and *Playboy*.

The method of rating believability of advertisements in magazine covers is called an *indirect approach,* since the questions are centered on the advertisements and not the publication. Evidence obtained in this way about media influence is not open to the same criticisms as direct attitude questions which are not a dependable method of measurement. Around the World War II period, *McCall's Magazine* sponsored a series of qualitative studies which employed an indirect technique to advantage. Questions were asked on the following three key points, but they were sufficiently separated in the interview to conceal their purpose from most respondents:

Women were asked to list their top four interests in magazines.
An inventory was made of current magazine issues in the home.
Later, the same women were asked to state with what degree of interest they looked forward to receiving the next issue of each of the magazines in the home.

While the directors of the *McCall's* surveys did not claim to have measured the interest appeals of individual magazines, there is reason to believe they succeeded in doing so. If a woman listed *style* as her topmost interest, if she had the current *McCall's,* and if she reported a high degree of anticipation of forthcoming issues, there would be considerable presumption that *McCall's* satisfied her style interest rather well.

Neither of the indirect techniques just described is subject to ready interpretation and projection. Testing the believability of advertisements in magazine covers and confining the evidence to the small common audience of readers makes it difficult to generalize or project to all readers or all people. Meanwhile, there is reason to think that the method is not sensitive enough to reveal important differences within even a limited sample.

The three-step method of evaluating women's interests in magazines cannot reflect the combined intensity and extensity of publication performance. The usual questionable interpretation is confined to intensity of reader interest in a particular category. As a result, a magazine with a small number of devoted followers has an advantage over a less appealing publication with any number of followers.

Clinical Techniques in Advertising Research

There were also early applications of clinical or psychological methods to the qualitative evaluation of media. The clinical methods were especially designed to reveal attitudes and motivations. They include unstructured interviewing and projective tests (compare Chapter Six); the latter carry the hope of discovering attitudes without making the respondent aware of his revelations. This should counter the accusation that direct questions on attitudes toward media produce prejudiced replies.

Clinical methods also have some limitations for projectable results because they are usually difficult to apply to representative population samples; the responses are not adaptable for simple tabulations, but require interpretation; and there is no widely accepted system for interpreting verbatim responses.

Better Homes and Gardens was the first prominent magazine to publish the findings of a study employing projective techniques. Word associations and sentence completions were used. The phrase, "When I read *Better Homes and Gardens* . . ." could evoke a statement about features or articles or, in one instance, "I always read the advertisements." A few similar responses were obtained, but such a nondirective approach did not produce enough favorable advertising references to be tallied and converted to an impressive percentage. The research firm examined all of the responses, and one of the chief conclusions was to the effect that the readers had a genuine interest in improving their homes!

The same research firm conducted a more elaborate study of women in relation to advertising for *Good Housekeeping* in 1954.[2] The study had the subtitle "A Motivation Study of the Attitudes of Women toward Eight Magazines." It was later stated that the study reported attitudes rather than motivations. Unstructured interviews and projective techniques were ap-

[2] *Women and Advertising* (New York: *Good Housekeeping*, 1954).

plied with housewives selected at convenience in seven cities. It was called a random sample, since "no one person or group was knowingly included or excluded."

Major conclusions begin with the statement that women's service magazines are more *useful* than *Life* or *The Saturday Evening Post* to women who read both a women's magazine and one of the weekly magazines. This noncontroversial conclusion about usefulness was followed by three numbered conclusions:

1. Women recognize the service magazines studied as being designed for their needs and interests, and their attitudes specifically reflect this.

2. As a result, learning of women-directed material is more easily accomplished through the service magazines than through the weeklies studied.

3. A housewife's reactions to advertisements appropriate to the service magazines' editorial content are significantly more positive when the advertisement is in a service magazine than when it is in either *The Post* or *Life*. And action is therefore more likely to occur.

Conclusion No. 2, it may be seen, is a deduction from No. 1, and No. 3 ends with a deduction. In other words, the conclusions from the research were controversial and competitive.

While sentence completions, cartoon completions, and other cartoon techniques were used extensively, there were a number of direct attitude questions. Some of the more skillful aspects of the study were partially offset by the controversial sequence of direct questions. After determining that a woman was a reader of a service magazine and also a reader of one of the weekly magazines, the following questioning sequence was used:

Question 4 was a discussion of the favorable aspects of the women's service magazine read by the respondent.

Question 5 asked the respondent to name her favorite magazine.

Questions 6 and 7 were concerned with the good features and the *bad* features of the weekly magazine read by the respondent.

Question 8 asked the respondent which magazine she could most easily do without.

This sequence would seem to favor naming the women's service magazine as the favorite and nominating the weekly magazine for the discard. The interviewer did not necessarily follow the exact question sequence, but the whole atmosphere of the interview was concerned with women in relation to service magazines.

Citing of the above deviations from conservative research practice in an otherwise interesting and original study would not be in order were it not that these points represent fundamental elements of research controversy. The conventional research approach aims at getting accurate answers either directly or indirectly from a carefully constructed interview. The clinical and social psychologists are more inclined to study responses from almost any kind of unstructured or projective interviews in search of patterns and insights. The clinical analyst—in the absence of any accepted system of interpretation—is willing to devise his own system or simply form a hypothesis. If the basis of his hypothesis seems sufficiently supported by the responses from most of his sample, he often seems willing to generalize to whole markets or populations. More conventional investigators have less confidence in intuition.

In 1955, *Puck—The Comic Weekly,* resolved to apply the best skills of the clinical and social scientists in as conventional a research approach as possible.[3] The basic purpose was to find out *why* people read the Sunday comics and the kinds of satisfactions which they seek. Working in collaboration with the Advertising Research Foundation, the organization employed objective systematically controlled sampling methods. The survey was confined to people twelve years of age and older in the Chicago metropolitan area.

The multistage interviews began with a formal questionnaire used to stratify and select a subsample for case study. The first interview gathered certain behavioral and status information. Response was obtained from 72 per cent of the prescribed sample of 700, and some replacements were selected for the remainder of the sample.

Case studies followed with 120 people chosen from the original respondents in the *Puck* survey. The cases were grouped to represent both sexes; high, moderate, and low exposure to major media; varying levels of interest in reading comics; and a significant number of Negroes.

Each individual was interviewed from two to five times intensively and in unstructured fashion. It was the purpose of the field workers and the central office analysts to test the urgency of various impulses and trends which displayed themselves in the interview situation. However, it became evident at an early stage that the prevalence or generality of either personality characteristics or social dynamics relating to comics could not be established for the whole population. Instead, the report is essentially a listing of verbatim responses for use by creative people in communicating ideas in the *comic* medium.

[3] *The Sunday Comics: a Socio-psychological Study with Attendant Advertising Implications* (New York: *Puck—The Comic Weekly,* January, 1956).

Any initial hopes of generalizing about a population in the above survey were restrained by inherent elements rather than weaknesses in design or execution. Large sampling of a population for intensive case study is not always practical because of costs, but the *Puck* study had the advantage of being capable of reproduction by others. A second obstacle to generalized conclusions is the requirement of interpreting rather than tabulating the results. While a reproduction of the survey might obtain equivalent verbatim comments from respondents, any interpretation would either employ a system or be entirely subjective. There is no system.

The *Puck* survey accomplished about all that could be conservatively done through unstructured case studies and served a useful purpose for copywriters. It did not measure the dimensions of a medium.

Media Image Profiles

Attitudes and opinions with reference to individual media vehicles may be revealed in media image profiles. They are arrived at by different techniques associated with the social sciences, such as scaling, and can be developed even from completely structured interviews. They may include any number of terms, such as "dynamic," "timely," "entertaining," and "provocative." Usually the number of distinct, relevant *dimensions* for any one media vehicle is limited to 20 or 30.

The media image profiles of 11 consumer magazines, as determined by the Bolger Company in the years 1960–1961, included 32 terms or dimensions.[4] The method used to select a word or words was unique and largely objective. Every word among some 52,000 in Roget's *International Thesaurus* was studied and selected if it could reasonably be used to describe a particular publication. The words were then divided into 109 synonym groups, using Webster's *Book of Synonyms* and later reduced to 32 through a judgmental process. This reduced the hazard of bias which occurs when descriptive terms are deliberately chosen to make a particular medium look good. The 32 words were reported as not being weighted in favor of any particular publication.

The 32 trait words and their definitions were printed on Univac tabulating cards, and a deck was given to each respondent who was a reader of the particular publication. The respondent sorted the cards according

4 *Media Image Profiles, Consumer Magazines, 1960–61: a Nationwide Study of the Sales Climate Created Editorially by Eleven Magazines as Described by Their Own Readers* (Chicago: The Bolger Company, 1960). Also see John F. Bolger, Jr., "How to Evaluate Your Company Image," *Journal of Marketing,* Vol. 24 (October, 1959) pp. 7–10.

to how well he thought they described the publication as "Definitely," "Yes," "Probably," "Probably Not," "No," and "Definitely Not." Weights of 1.5, 1.0, .5, —.5, —1.0, and —1.5, respectively, were assigned to the answers. When applied on a percentage basis, this permitted a range of

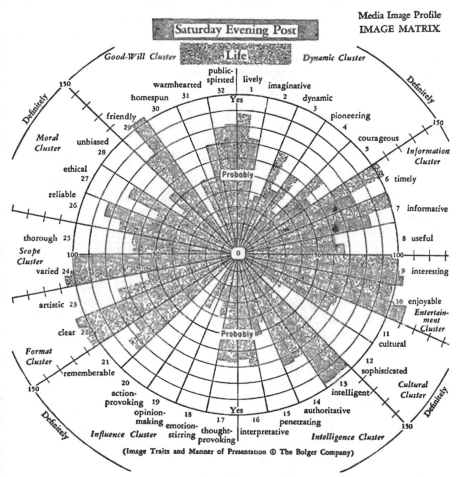

FIG. 13. Profiles of *Life* and *The Saturday Evening Post*. (*Courtesy of The Bolger Company.*)

scores from 150 to —150; but since primary readers are seldom completely negative on a publication, there were no appreciable negative responses.

The sample was chosen from 36 randomly selected counties in the United States. One hundred starting locations were selected from the telephone directory of the largest town or city in each of the 36 counties. Interviewers continued clockwise around the block from each starting address. Qualified readers of each magazine were interviewed as they were found. A qualified reader had to (1) be a male or female head of household, (2) claim to "read or look through at least every other issue or so" of the magazine, (3) claim to have done this for at least a year or more, and (4) show the interviewer one of the last three issues of the magazine.

Comparisons between competing magazines show vividly how differently they were held in the minds of their readers. Figure 13 shows the profiles of *Life* and *The Saturday Evening Post* as reported by 500 readers of each. This indicates that *Life* was considered more lively, dynamic, pioneering, courageous, timely, and informative. *The Post* held its own through most of the remaining points and was considered to be more reliable, ethical, unbiased, friendly, homespun, and warmhearted. Neither magazine was considered at all action-provoking, nor is it likely that the editors intend much overt response. Both publications were rated as moderately useful, a quality which may have been remote in the concept of those responsible for editorial aims.

Although the Bolger technique has been described in some detail, it should be realized that there are certain questions concerning this system which need to be answered. What is the relative saliency of the scales or items that were chosen for use? What criteria really are important or not important in measuring media image profiles? Certainly an improvement on the method would be to do some preliminary interviewing with magazine readers and find out from them what factors are important to them in various magazines.

Semantic Differential

Most comparative studies of media profiles or of profile changes apply the semantic-differential technique (compare Chapter Five), and the study reported above involves this technique.

An interesting report comparing images of radio, television, and newspapers covered the urban and suburban areas of Richmond, Virginia.[5] All available adults and teenagers in a random selection of 447 households drawn from carrier route lists were interviewed in November, 1958, concerning the local newspapers, using the scaling device shown in Fig. 14. The following January, approximately one-half as many households next door were interviewed in a similar way concerning radio and television.

[5] *The Climate of Persuasion; a Study of the Public Image of Advertising Media* (Richmond, Va.: The Richmond Newspapers, Inc., 1959).

YOUR FRANK APPRAISAL OF   The Richmond News Leader   ( )
Richmond Times-Dispatch   ( ) .

Think of this newspaper as though it were a person, a regular visitor to your home. Listed below are words to describe your feelings about the newspaper. By placing an X anywhere along each line, you indicate your feelings in each case. We want your honest, sincere opinion - so please be frank.

	0	1	2	3	4	5	6	7	8	9	10	
Aloof												Friendly
Untruthful												Truthful
Careless												Careful
Prejudiced												Unprejudiced
Immoral												Moral
Unintelligent												Intelligent
Dreary												Cheerful
Fearful												Courageous
Distant												Neighborly
Deceitful												Trustworthy
Superficial												Thorough
Intolerant												Tolerant
Irreligious												Religious
Poorly educated												Well educated
Unattractive												Attractive
Weak												Determined
Cold												Sympathetic
Dishonest												Honest
Inaccurate												Accurate
Unfair												Fair
Unscrupulous												Scrupulous
Poor judgment												Good judgment
Dull												Interesting
Easily influenced												Independent

FIG. 14. Scaling device. (*Courtesy of The Richmond Newspapers, Inc.*)

The results of the Richmond study (see Fig. 15) have been used to imply that the Richmond newspapers have a marked advantage in their personality image. The implications are that television conveys a degree of warmth, but that newspapers are far more intelligent, credible, moral, courageous, and reliable. The newspapers sponsoring the study concluded that the results were reasonable, although they could not properly be projected beyond the Richmond area, and even though there are questions about the methodology. They also concluded that "the public image of an advertising medium should be as relevant and meaningful to the advertiser as the personality of a salesman is to the sales manager. . . ." [6]

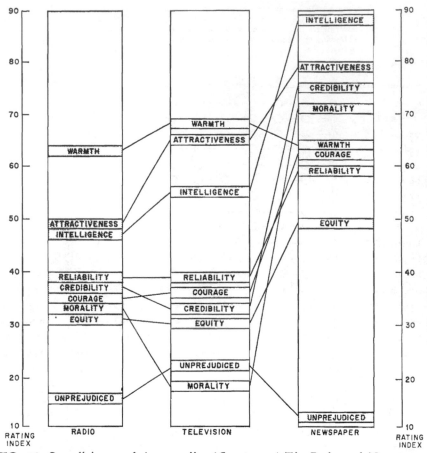

FIG. 15. Overall image of three media. (*Courtesy of The Richmond Newspapers, Inc.*)

Another example of the use of the semantic-differential technique involved individual media vehicles and also whole classes of media.[7] The findings in this study did not correlate well with the confidence of national advertisers in media, as reflected by their dollar expenditures. It would seem that ideal media vehicles should be highly "interesting," "in-

[6] Page 3 of citation in footnote 5.

[7] "Scripps-Howard Study Probes Inter-media Image," summarized in *Media/scope*, Vol. 4 (December, 1960), p. 58.

formative," "reliable," and "action-provoking," with the hope that these characteristics will carry through to the advertising. Whether the media profile ratings are representative and accurate and whether favorable media characteristics carry through to the advertising are not known. A carefully established profile may aid an advertiser in making his media selections, but profiles are complicated, and seldom is the choice clearly evident from the total pattern.

The objectives of scaling and of the semantic-differential technique (see Chapter Five) may sometimes be achieved by an adaptation known as the Q-sort.[8] *Good Housekeeping* used this procedure as part of a study comparing attitudes of women toward service magazines and general magazines.[9] A list of 40 statements of attitudes toward magazines was prepared on the basis of preliminary interviews. For example, one woman said, "I like X magazine because it's very practical." The 40 statements were put on separate cards (thoroughly shuffled), and housewives were asked to sort them for magazines they read, from most true to least true, on an 8-point scale.

The card sortings for different publications can be correlated, and they can also be correlated with a sorting for an assumed "ideal" magazine. In addition, it may be useful to correlate the ratings of the same magazine by different readers. For purposes of making combined interpretations, the average rank of a magazine on each item may be determined for the sample and compared with averages for other publications.

Another approach would appear much more satisfactory than complex subjective evaluations. However, attitudes are subjective experiences, and objective methods cannot measure them directly.

Few media are readily adapted to an objective approach for qualitative evaluation, but *Better Homes and Gardens* reported such a study in 1956.[10] The findings relate exclusively to one publication, and the technique appears best fitted to home-service magazines. The chief objective evidence, supplied to show the attitudes of readers and their involvement with the publication, included six types of reported actions: [11]

1. Writing for something

---

[8] William Stephenson, *The Study of Behavior: Q-Technique and Its Methodology* (Chicago: University of Chicago Press, 1953).

[9] Pages 66, 69 of citation in footnote 2.

[10] *A Twelve Months' Study of Better Homes and Gardens Readers*, (*Better Homes and Gardens*, 1956).

[11] Page 145 of citation in footnote 10.

2. Making a purchase
3. Shopping
4. Discussing or recommending something
5. Trying or using an idea
6. Clipping something from an article or advertisement

Saving and referring to back issues are also objective evidence of involvement with the magazine.

Interviews were made with a known-probability sample of individuals ten years of age and older in the United States. While the average issue audience of *Better Homes and Gardens* was found to be 15,500,000, there were nearly three times as many (44,150,000) who read one or more of twelve monthly issues.[12] Issue readers were determined by the indirect editorial-interest technique described in Chapter Ten.

The techniques of the study are noteworthy because the *action* of reading was measured by asking primarily about subjective interests or *attitudes;* yet *the measurement of attitudes was premised on objective evidence of actions.* Both techniques assume that respondents will reveal one type of information more accurately through an indirect approach apparently aimed at another type of information. There is strong psychological support for this view.

Among the six listed actions, one of the most objectively measurable is filing clippings which the interviewer was required to inspect in the home. Keeping issues four to twelve months old was also checked by actual inventory. Since there were only slightly more than 4 million copies to serve an average-issue audience of 15.5 million people, it is clear that there would be restraints on both clipping and issue saving. Yet one out of seven (14.7 per cent) readers clipped something from the articles or advertisements, and nearly one-half (44.7 per cent) took one or more of the six listed actions.[13] It was estimated that 9.9 million *Better Homes and Gardens* readers live in households saving issues four to twelve months old. These facts are substantial evidence of reader involvement with *Better Homes and Gardens,* and it seems doubtful that any other major national advertising vehicle could produce so much objective physical evidence.

An unusual contribution of this survey was the introduction of a breakdown of readers on a three-level scale of *venturesomeness.* Respondents were confronted with a list of seven possible new low-priced products that were not yet on the market and asked if they would probably purchase each

[12] Page 11 of citation in footnote 10.
[13] Page 58 of citation in footnote 10.

immediately or wait and see. A maximum of seven points could be earned by indicating early purchase of all seven items. The entire sample was then divided into three equal groups: venturesome, moderate, and cautious. In another section of the interview concerned with reporting actual purchases of new and novel costly items, it was found that those classified as cautious always ranked lower in possession of new types of products. This demonstrated that the rough attitude scale correlated with buying behavior in a logical fashion.

ATTITUDES TOWARD TYPES OF MEDIA AND THEIR ADVERTISEMENTS

There are several logical steps before an attitude toward some particular type of medium can have meaning to a particular advertiser. Does the generalized attitude toward a media type carry over to individual vehicles within that type? Does the generalized attitude toward advertisements in that media type or in that specific vehicle carry over to a particular advertising message? Does this attitudinal influence, if any, contribute to a more favorable response to the advertiser than if he had used some other vehicle? An answer to this last question would require a means of evaluating advertising response beyond the limitations of techniques discussed earlier in this book. As William M. Weilbacher of Dancer-Fitzgerald-Sample, Inc., has said, "It is doubtful . . . that this kind of comparison can be made *between* media, at least given the current state of the copy research art." [14]

A great deal of the research and discussion in this area has centered on publications, rather than broadcasting and other media. There is a very important reason for this concentration.

Whereas publications are recognized as entities with individual "personalities," broadcasters are little known apart from their programs. The public is aware of and has identification with programs, but usually viewers and listeners have little knowledge of the views of stations and networks, except for the negative assurance that the views of a commentator "are not necessarily those of this station." Networks and stations are privileged to editorialize and express their views, but have taken little advantage of that opportunity. Instead, they have been content to allow the programs to dominate in the public mind, and perhaps wisely so.

General attitudes of the public toward publications and toward broadcasting are naturally favorable since both are major media of communica-

---

[14] W. M. Weilbacher, "The Qualitative Values of Advertising Media," *Journal of Advertising Research*, Vol. 1 (December, 1960), pp. 12–17, at p. 16.

tion. Also, the great majority of people have a favorable attitude toward advertising in general, despite the objections from an articulate minority. A nationwide survey conducted in 1959 indicated that advertising was held in high esteem by an overwhelming majority of the American people—75 per cent of all adults eighteen years and older said they liked advertising.[15] There were 15 per cent who indicated a general dislike, and 10 per cent were noncommittal. The question was asked directly and not in a media context, although it may be assumed that publication and broadcast advertising are never considered completely apart from their media background.

Surveys of liking for advertising and belief in it usually show *newspapers* in a clear position of advantage, followed by magazines and television. Radio and outdoor advertising are lowest of the major media in the public estimate of their advertising level.

Newspapers and magazines undoubtedly benefit from their own established integrity and identity in the minds of readers. Newspapers benefit more because of the interest of readers in local store advertising and in the want ads. This reader tendency to "shop the advertisements" is not consciously concerned with most national copy, but the national advertiser probably benefits from the total context. Television and radio are both intangible and momentary, and neither is recognized as an entity to be trusted or opposed. Outdoor advertisements suffer from the offenses of those advertisers, mostly local, who deface the landscape. But these general remarks do not adequately evaluate audience attitudes toward the major media and their advertisements. Each has characteristics which are special and which may best fit it to the needs of a particular advertiser.

Magazines

Magazines are the largest advertising medium exclusively concerned with nonlocal advertising. Basically, magazines are a medium of entertainment and education. They are picked up in leisure hours and, depending upon the imaginative powers of editors and the readers, transcend the usual limitations of space and time. The readers are enabled to project themselves further into a real world, or into a world of fantasy. For many, the magazine is an escape from unpleasant realities as well as a positive source of pleasure.

Interest incentives in magazines keep changing, as editors and publishers well know. One of the best guides to current interests is the promotional

[15] *Public Attitudes toward Advertising* (New York: *Redbook*, 1959), p. 16.

material used by leading magazines. Fiction, which may well remain the long-time leader in magazines in general, is often subordinated to current events, biographies, and commentaries written by prominent personalities. Informative articles must always be written in entertaining style, and material about personalities must enable the reader to identify himself with the subject or author.

Women are the chief readers of popular magazines, and their interests can change rapidly. Evidence of these changes can be found in the contents of women's service magazines. While fiction may prove to be the long-time leading interest of women in magazines, economics and world events are fluctuating interests. Shortly after World War II, *McCall's Magazine* reported the following subjectively rated list of women's interests in magazines: fiction, food, style and beauty, home decoration, current events, pictures, advertising, social and economic, home management, gardening, and child care.[16]

Since that time there has been cold war, men have conquered space, work weeks have been shortened, incomes have multiplied, and television has become the greatest diversion of most families. These and many other factors have an impact on interests.

Magazine editors play an important role other than finding and choosing interesting subject matter to please their readers. The editor does much to give a magazine its personality and to guarantee its integrity. When a new editor first takes on his assignment, he may in his editorial columns tell readers his views on important subjects, his editorial aims for the magazine, and his desire to create or convert a following of readers. Perhaps his magazine is expected to take a stand on various public issues, so he may feel compelled to try to transform the views of his readers, even though he realizes what an extremely difficult task this is.

A magazine is in a sense a personality, with views and with a purpose. In that sense, an editor is cast in the role of a public leader. But he is also the producer of a product for sale; in that sense he operates like the manufacturers of other products sold to consumer markets. The integrity of the editors is evident in their efforts to protect the reader-consumer. Advertising space is the chief source of publication revenue, but editors insist on keeping full control so as to prevent possible advertising exploitation of readers.

While almost 60 per cent of the space in leading magazines is occupied

---

[16] Darrell Blaine Lucas and Steuart Henderson Britt, *Advertising Psychology and Research* (New York: McGraw-Hill Book Company, Inc., 1950), p. 652.

by advertising, the approximately 40 per cent of editorial space is carefully insulated from any tie-in with specific advertisements. Most of this separation of the two magazine functions is accomplished through an almost complete lack of communication between editors and the sellers of advertising space. Editors give out no information about contents of issues in time to schedule related advertisements. When an adevrtisement benefits from juxtaposition with reinforcing editorial matter, it is usually pure coincidence. The integrity of the editors of magazines is one of their sources of strength.

Magazine advertisements are admittedly not a primary incentive for reading of most issues, although advertisements were among women's top 10 magazine interests, as indicated above. This was reported at a time of extreme product shortage following a major war and is unlikely to remain so high. Instead, magazine advertisements have a sideline role as editorial reader traffic passes by, and every opportunity must be used to attract attention to the advertisements. Strong attention incentives are employed, including large space and effective color. Advertisements can interrupt the reader, but they can hold his attention only if they win him over; otherwise, he can quickly pass on to the next feature.

Magazine-advertising displays, like the editorial matter, often include appeals to the imagination and to the emotions, lifting horizons and awakening new desires or intensifying existing wants. There is this difference. The advertisements offer the reader a means of realizing these desires not in a world of fancy, but through the purchase of something that is for sale at a price. Often the actual degree of satisfaction is overemphasized; and emotional appeals to others in the audience may make the message look silly to those for whom it is not intended. In all cases, new desires require new outlays of money, and people are not likely to applaud new expenses. It is not surprising that magazines rank a little lower than newspapers in general approval of their advertisements.

Those who promote magazines are well aware of the fact that magazines stimulate wants for new products, whereas newspapers more commonly emphasize the specific price and place for satisfying recognized wants. A slogan states, "The newspaper tells, but the magazine sells." Actually, the more obvious comparison is not between national advertisements in both media, but between national advertisements in magazines and retail advertisements in newspapers. Because of the informational nature of local copy and because of display limitations in newspapers, the national newspaper advertisement tends to be more factual and informative than the typical magazine appeal. Newspaper copy often carries dealer identity and other evidences of local orientation.

Both the editors and the publishers of magazines and of newspapers are highly independent and individualistic. The one great difference centers on national competition, whereas newspaper editors and publishers have only their local counterparts to worry about. They may even imitate newspapers in other parts of the country and strive to emulate their performance.

Editors and publishers of magazines are in the interesting position of having to look upon *all* counterparts in the industry as competitors. Most magazine publishers participate in trade associations that serve their industry; but little is done jointly which might possibly demonstrate the superiority of one over the others. The publisher feels that all space sold by a competitor is his own loss. If he publishes a weekly, and an advertiser buys a page in every issue of his publication as well as every issue of a competing weekly, each publisher thinks the advertiser should use two-page spreads exclusively in his own publication instead.

Despite this keen rivalry, the Magazine Advertising Bureau is supported by nearly all leading periodicals. The Bureau is a central clearinghouse for much magazine advertising information and promotion. It also sponsors some research to show advertisers the strengths of magazines in general.

More explicit information about individual magazines comes from the individual publishers, from Standard Rate and Data Service (SRDS), from the Publishers Information Bureau (PIB), and from the Lloyd H. Hall Magazine Editorial Reports. SRDS reports circulation and specifications needed for buying advertising space; PIB gives the advertiser a clear picture of how much advertising his competitors and others do on the basis of space and vehicles used; and Lloyd H. Hall reports the space occupied in each magazine by all types of editorial features. This enables the advertiser and the copywriter to judge the interests and attitudes of readers according to what types of fiction and articles are included.

Newspapers

Newspapers are the largest of all advertising media in terms of dollars invested in advertising, although they are somewhat comparable to magazines in the total dollar volume of *nonlocal* advertising. People often buy newspapers primarily to look at the advertisements, and newspapers enjoy the highest advertising approval of any major medium.

Newspapers are timely and flexible, and these characteristics carry over to the advertising to a large degree. Newspapers are also definite entities in the minds of their readers, often championing their causes and occasionally campaigning for the other party.

In many respects the reader identifies himself a great deal with his daily paper and often unconsciously reflects its contents and point of view. After all, there are only about 60 cities in the United States with more than one newspaper owned by a different publisher.

Nearly everything that has been said about the integrity of leading magazines and their editors applies equally to leading newspapers. Some differences are inherent, such as the difficulty of ensuring factual accuracy in the many issues and editions which a newspaper prints almost as soon as events have happened. Balancing this limitation are the physical nearness of the editor to his readers and the frequently personal interchanges to reconcile differences or to correct errors. The newspaper editor is often a community leader, protecting readers from corrupt practices by anybody from an unscrupulous politician to an unscrupulous advertiser.

While the primary function of the daily paper is to report general news, readers are attracted by many other news and nonnews features. Front-page stories and occasionally banner headlines can be overlooked in the search for features of special interest. Society and sports, columnists and comics, editorials and crossword puzzles all have their devoted followers, and editorial changes may cause canceled subscriptions. While the daily life of the daily newspaper is brief, traffic through its pages is heavy, with more than 80% of all readers likely to read certain comics. Despite the search for entertainment along with the news, newspaper readers keep close to a world of reality.

Remember also that *advertising is news* to most readers. Although an advertisement may not be competitive for attention as much as the most exciting news stories and features, advertising is extremely important to readers. Almost any page is likely to carry a familiar local reference or to offer some immediate service. Both the local advertisements and the want ads are filled with familiar landmarks.

National advertisers are a minority group in most newspapers. Like most minorities, they find it desirable to conform. Greater emphasis upon information and upon the immediate need is found in national newspaper copy than in magazines. Again, like other minorities, the national advertiser finds himself somewhat penalized and neglected. He pays an arbitrarily higher space rate than his local neighbor and finds the publisher generally unresponsive to his desires and requests. In return, he enjoys the advantages of timeliness and flexibility in newspapers; he benefits from active advertising interest on the part of readers; and he is protected by the editorial integrity so much a part of the newspaper tradition.

The biggest problem of the national advertiser who wishes to use newspapers is the detail of arranging continuous, comprehensive schedules. Development of "networks" of newspapers has failed to solve the problem.

The fact that newspapers are so predominantly local complicates the process of obtaining comprehensive and general information about the medium. The Bureau of Advertising of the American Newspaper Publishers Association attempts to secure such information for the benefit of advertisers. An outstanding study entitled *The Daily Newspaper and Its Reading Public* obtained information for the Bureau of Advertising on activities and attitudes of a national probability sample of 4,826 people age fifteen and over in the United States population.[17] Attitudes, as they relate to advertising in the four largest national media, were obtained by using a 7-point scale. "It fits very well," counted as 7 points; and "It doesn't fit at all" counted as 1 point. The results reported in Table 25 are based on those rating each point as 5, 6, or 7.

TABLE 25. High Ratings of Media by Adults [18]

Descriptive rating	Newspapers	TV	Magazines	Radio
"Is first to introduce new products."	60	71	57	45
"Has interesting and imaginative ads."	54	66	67	37
"Gives a good description of the products I need."	60	57	59	40
"Shows good taste in the advertising it carries."	63	47	64	44
"Carries advertising that can be trusted."	58	41	57	40
"Tells you all you need to know when buying a new product."	50	40	48	34
"Sticks to the facts."	63	40	56	41
"Gives useful information."	71	58	65	54
"Tells me where I can buy things."	83	53	41	56
"Is meant for people like me."	61	52	50	45

While newspapers were rated high for carrying advertisements which are reliable and informative, it is noteworthy that television and magazines led on new products and imaginative appeals. This tends to confirm the reliance of consumers on newspaper advertising for accuracy and for specific information. Likewise, television and magazines apparently serve the func-

[17] *The Daily Newspaper and Its Reading Public* (New York: Bureau of Advertising, 1961).

[18] Page 54 of citation in footnote 17.

tion intended by those advertisers who must stir new wants for new products through the use of interesting and imaginative copy.

Advertisers in newspapers can obtain detailed information about specific publications from Standard Rate and Data Service, Inc., and from the Publishers Information Bureau. SRDS reports newspaper circulations and gives the specifications needed for buying and using advertising space, and PIB provides a record of media vehicles and space used by competitors and by other advertisers.

Television

Network television, when time and talent costs are added together, is by far the largest national advertising medium. No other medium permits so much internal control by the advertiser, and no other medium offers so many assets for presenting a sales message.

The high costs of network television sponsorship and the limitations of time have encouraged a great deal of sharing and alternating of specific units. As a result, television advertisers have a decreasing opportunity to exploit program content and talent association.

Daytime network television is designed for housewives, late afternoon programs are aimed at children, and the "extravagant" evening shows are for the adult family. Weekends include programs covering a variety of interests and appealing to varied audiences. The strength of evening network program appeal, by type of half-hour program, is reflected in the following Nielsen ratings of homes tuned in during early December, 1961:

Program type	Nielsen rating
General drama	20.7
Suspense-mystery drama	22.8
Situation comedy	21.1
Western drama	22.1
Variety	23.8
Quiz, audience participation	20.8
Informational	12.1

The most striking feature of this list is the relative uniformity of average ratings of several program classifications. These ratings reflect the predominant evening preoccupation of American homes, over 90% of which have TV sets.

Television networks are in a different position from magazines in securing advertising support. All of their revenue must come from advertisers, and all individual programs in prime evening time must gain their own support. There is no subscriber revenue to give stability, and there is not the independence of choosing entertainment features with the freedom of a magazine editor. Each single program failure stands out.

Adding to this pressure is the control exercised by the Federal Communications Commission, since television channels are in the public domain and must be used to serve public interests. Paradoxically, no one accepts the final responsibility for maintaining high ethical standards, a fact brought to light by the first television scandals involving deception in certain quiz shows. The broadcasters, public officials, and advertisers concerned denied either the knowledge of facts or the power to have prevented abuses.

Television programers may even be subjected to pressure from advertisers and their representatives. The Television Vice President of the Columbia Broadcasting System once gave the following examples.

The opening show scheduled for *Playhouse 90* was to be based on the novel by Pat Frank, *Forbidden Area*. This was the story of a supersecret military group whose primary function was to study the behavior patterns of Soviet Russia. This group came to the conclusion that the Soviet planned to attack the United States on a given date. The story then proceeded to show their frustrating efforts to alert the U.S. Military to this danger. Representatives of one of the advertisers were extremely distraught and brought great pressure to modify and tone down what they considered an alarming, sensational, warmongering program, and particularly one which would embarrass and offend our armed forces. They were dissatisfied and unhappy with the show even as it went on the air. Following the broadcast, CBS received a request from the United States Air Force for kinescope prints of *Forbidden Area* to be circulated among key personnel of the Strategic Air Command as soon as possible. These kinescopes became required viewing for S.A.C. thereafter.

On another dramatic series we once scheduled a show with a Jewish hero. We were admonished by the advertiser's representative that this program would be very offensive to Jewish people and would alienate them from the advertiser's products. Somehow or other we managed to get it on the air. It won both the B'nai B'rith and Brotherhood Television awards for that season.

On one of our most successful western series, an advertising agency executive wrote a letter to the producer, urgently requesting and even insisting that he not produce a certain episode, as it was in his opinion the worst western script he had ever read and "full of caricatures, clichés, and bad writing." The program was nevertheless produced, and subsequently won for the author the Screen Writers Guild Award for the best television western script presented during that season.[19]

[19] William Dozier, "Are Effective Television Advertising and Programing Incompatible?" speech before *Advertising Age* Creative Workshop, August 7, 1959.

As has been demonstrated experimentally in an important study of television viewing, watching of television is a different sort of experience for different people.

> It becomes clear that there is no single audience group and that a unitary mode of defining television's audience is overly restrictive. There are at least several audiences, each with a particular point of view toward the medium. These points of view each include a distinctive set of feelings about television, characteristic ways of using it, and a unique manner of selecting, responding to, and evaluating its content.
>
> Three such viewpoints are discussed. The first is referred to as "television embraced"; it signifies a particularly close identification with television, a rather undiscriminating and accepting attitude toward it, and, usually, great use of the medium. In contrast, "television protested" is an audience outlook that signifies the most selective use of the medium and often extremely critical attitudes toward it. "Television accommodated" is a position that rather casually accepts television, one that evidences a "coming to terms" with TV, its meanings, appeals, and shortcomings.[20]

Certainly the advertiser on television occupies an ambiguous position with viewers. As a sponsor, he benefits from a certain amount of good will and sportsmanship on the part of his audience. His commercials place him in a totally different light, since any straight commercial must interrupt the program. Once interrupted, the viewer has no chance to resume the program in the way he can resume a magazine story after passing an advertisement. He must wait out the commercial time, being bored if the commercial lacks interest for him, and growing increasingly resentful if he finds the message objectionable.

It is not surprising that television advertising—over 40,000 TV commercials every year—is considerably less popular than publication advertising. One alternative is to place commercials at the extreme end of a program, but no advertiser feels that he can afford this risk. Another alternative of blending commercials inoffensively into the program format runs too much risk of failing its mission. The only practical solution is to attempt to establish some degree of compatibility of commercials with the program; and this is very difficult to do.

There are many points of view and only a little evidence regarding the

[20] Ira O. Glick, Sidney J. Levy, Edith Arlen, Shirley Greene, and Karol Kane Weinstein, *Living with Television* (Chicago: Aldine Publishing Company, 1962), pp. 43–44.

influence of audience attitudes on commercial impact. The president of General Foods Corporation once said that Jello commercials combined ideally with the program of a comedian, but that breakfast cereal commercials were totally unsatisfactory in the same program. A prominent research company advised an automobile manufacturer to stop the practice of having a clown soberly proclaim the dependability of a certain make of car.

Both audience attitudes and the level of attentiveness of viewers contribute to the impact of commercials. Certainly, emphasis may well be placed on "attentiveness" as an important dimension of an advertiser's use of TV programing.[21] Women, for example, who view long sports broadcasts because of the intense interest of their husbands, may recall very little of the commercials.

Arthur H. Wilkins of Benton & Bowles, Inc., has reported that people who really enjoy a particular television program have significantly higher commercial recall than others who are less pleased.[22] The housewife, especially, may not fully enjoy the program (1) because of competing household activities, (2) because the particular program is not her own first choice, and (3) because no thoroughly enjoyable program is available at the time, and so on. The study by Wilkins showed that these factors led to a decreased recall of commercials broadcast at the time. He was able to confirm this relationship between recall of commercials and enjoyment of programs by using data on program favorites obtained from other sources. Wilkins demonstrated that under certain conditions a program with a lower rating may deliver more measurable commercial recall than a higher-rated program. These functions are, of course, specifically program functions and are only indirectly related to the broadcast channel, the television network, or the general effectiveness of television as a medium.

The relative importance of programs and lack of a clear network or station image may reduce the role of broadcasters in the success of television advertising, but cannot eliminate their influence. While the images of top networks or their local station outlets may not differ greatly in the minds of viewers, the audience distinguishes them from smaller stations. Many viewers recognize station leadership and are aware that major networks can bring them entertainment beyond the budgets of smaller competitors.

[21] "Annual Media Award Winners," *Media/scope*, Vol. 5 (April, 1961), p. 33.
[22] Arthur H. Wilkins, *Finding Program Values That Are Not in Ratings*, paper presented at the Sixth Annual Conference of the Advertising Research Foundation, Inc., October 4, 1960.

This prestige may carry with it some increased confidence in dependability of the advertising, although it is not to be taken for granted. The leadership in television networks is so concentrated that most of the promotion of the medium is carried on independently by each network and by leading stations.

There is also a Television Bureau of Advertising (TBA) for service to the industry and to advertisers. TBA obtains and distributes valuable information about the industry as a whole.

Radio

Radio lacks the nationwide network programing once used like television to serve national advertisers. There are chain broadcasts and a considerable number of taped programs for broadcasts at station convenience. Most national advertising on radio is through saturation of *spot* announcements not involving program sponsorship.

Radio is an important national medium, but it is seldom a primary means for covering total markets. Instead, radio spots can be used to complement magazines and network television in local areas.

The Radio Advertising Bureau has collected a great deal of information on the industry for the benefit of stations and advertisers.

Outdoor

Outdoor advertising reaches a dual audience, since people see posters when going about business and also when traveling for pleasure.

The outdoor plant operators, combining local services into nationwide coverage, take pride in evidences of good citizenship and public service. They combat the outspoken objections and indignation of articulate citizens with organized efforts to inspire and police their industry.

The Outdoor Advertising Association of America serves its industry and is dedicated to promote attractive panels, approved locations, and artistic display. National service to advertisers is available through Outdoor Advertising, Inc., which negotiates contracts for extensive national coverage.

IMPLICATIONS

Since qualitative dimensions of media are automatically aspects which are not subject to measurement, it is not surprising that this chapter reflects few numerical facts about attitudes and motivations. If doubt has been cast on the value of simple, direct attitude questions for rating media, something has been accomplished. The indirect approach to attitude ratings is psychologically superior, although—as in the testing of advertisements in different magazine covers—it may not be sensitive enough to bring out significant differences.

Methods adapted from the psychological clinic have frequently led to only the obvious or the controversial. Growing sophistication of clinical and social scientists in conventional research and in awareness of advertising functions may lead to greater productivity of unstructured and projective methods.

Adaptations of the semantic-differential and other approaches to image studies have produced interesting results in many cases, although the significance of an image in the media function remains to be demonstrated.

Objective evidence of involvement with media, which is abundant with television and which *Better Homes and Gardens* secured for its own reader relationship, is the most convincing of all qualitative information.

The evidence about attitudes is indirect, and its advertising implications are not entirely clear in specific instances. Television programs, for example, can dominate the behavior of individuals and families for long periods. Behavior during broadcast of commercials is less well documented, but at least some of it is negative in its implications. The measured responses to *Better Homes and Gardens* stand out as essentially positive in their advertising implications, but they relate to a publication with a unique function. At this writing, this study is the outstanding example of qualitative media evidence.

Magazines are highly selective. There is no doubt as to the favorable attitudes of readers, and they alone are important to advertisers. Attitudes toward advertisements in magazines are generally favorable, although a sizable minority find them irritating enough to be eliminated.

Newspapers, with their heavy proportion of local advertisements, enjoy reader confidence comparable to magazines, and they enjoy more positive approval of their advertisements. If the national advertiser could achieve the full status of the local retailer with the newspaper and with its readers, the newspaper would offer his greatest qualitative opportunity. However, his superior status with the magazine publisher, the mechanical printing advantages of magazines, and the general content of national advertising copy weigh in favor of magazines.

Television is so dramatic and so compelling that only cost considerations and channel limitations keep it on an equal competitive level with other major national media. The individual and the family loyalty to particular programs must reflect a high regard on the part of viewers. Television, more than any other advertising medium, is a familiar conversation piece.

The contrast with printed media lies in the irritations aroused by televised advertising messages. The general attitude of the public is highly in favor of television, but television probably lacks a majority in general approval of its commercials. This is not an easy situation to remedy, since commercials are necessarily an interruption of programs.

Radio lacks some of the dramatic quality of television, but the reaction to commercials is not generally one of approval. The sales effectiveness of both TV and radio commercials may still make them highly profitable. In other words, a favorable general qualitative rating is not necessary in order for a medium to be profitable for advertising.

The more easily quantified media dimensions, which include the numbers reached by a media vehicle in each desired market classification, and the frequency of advertising contact in a vehicle remain the most important media dimensions. If the right kinds of people make up the audience and if a sufficient number of the right people are reached often enough, there is a reasonable opportunity to advertise profitably. If certain media vehicles can put their audiences in a receptive frame of mind and if they can convey favorable attitudes regarding their advertising messages, the opportunity is that much better.

Research has already produced much useful quantitative data on media audiences and their combinations, showing breakdowns into class groupings. Techniques are well advanced for measuring frequency, and progress has been made in qualitative measurement of attitudes. The future task of research is to provide usefully accurate data on all aspects of media functions so that media may be bought and used with maximum efficiency.

sixteen|

Audience Accumulation and Combinations

Most national advertisers schedule advertisements in more than one medium or media vehicle. The choice of each vehicle and the working out of a schedule requires many kinds of information and much judgment. This final chapter brings together the significance of each dimension discussed previously and shows how all of the available types of information may fit into media planning.

355

A REVIEW

The discussion of *basic media concepts* (Chapter Nine) dealt almost exclusively with the advertising functions of individual media vehicles and their evaluation. It was indicated that consumer media can claim credit for the numbers and kinds of people to whom an advertising message is exposed. Media probably contribute to each succeeding stage of advertisement noting and sales communication, but the part played by media in those stages is hard to isolate. Ultimately, of course, media investments pay off in dollars of sales or profit.

The data on audiences of printed and broadcast media vehicles (Chapters Ten and Eleven) mean a great deal more to advertisers than do such physical media dimensions as printed copies, signal strengths, and numbers of receiving sets. These audiences are people who have been sufficiently motivated to look into a magazine or newspaper issue or to attend to a radio or television broadcast. If the advertiser buys space in the publication or if he sponsors the particular broadcast, he knows that the audience of the vehicle is his maximum audience potential. The size and composition of the audience of a vehicle are helpful guides to its possible purchase.

Actual advertising exposure (Chapter Twelve) has even more specific meaning as a media dimension, since every vehicle has different characteristics of reading, viewing, or listening. The vehicle with the largest total audience may not succeed in getting the greatest number of people exposed to its advertising, may not expose them the longest, and may not expose them the most times. This involves more than one dimension—how many people are exposed and to what extent are they exposed? Both answers may have a bearing on the value of the media buy.

Advertising audiences (Chapter Thirteen), as distinguished from audiences of media vehicles, are highly important as a concept for evaluation. They are composed of the people who not only are exposed, but who actually note or perceive the advertisement. True, the appeal of the advertising copy may greatly affect advertising audience size, and this is not a dimension of media. Nevertheless, the advertiser could not have gotten a single member of this audience if the audience had not first been attracted and then exposed by the medium.

The kinds of people in media audiences (Chapter Fourteen) are almost as important as the total quantity. Advertisers are always choosing their media with the hope of matching their coverage to the particular prospects who make up their best markets. Numbers mean very little unless they can be related to prospective sales. Not only is it important to reach people of the right age, sex, or economic level, it is often more specifically important to reach car owners, home owners, dog owners, or devotees of some particular activity important to the advertiser. The selection of appropriate media will depend upon the size and selectivity of the market.

The attitudes of media audiences (Chapter Fifteen) may also contribute to the effectiveness of an advertising vehicle. This elusive factor is so important that it is the first consideration of many advertisers and buyers of space and time. Just how much of the audience attitudes toward the medium "rubs off" onto the advertising? How much do the general attitudes toward advertisements in that medium affect the reception of the message of a particular advertiser?

All of the above factors enter into media evaluation. If sales and profits resulting from each media investment could be accurately calculated or measured, there would be little need for probing of media-audience size, advertising exposure, advertising-audience size, and the breakdowns of media audiences or for the appraisal of their attitudes.

ACCUMULATION, COMBINATION, AND DUPLICATION

As has been pointed out by George H. Brown (see page 194), the effectiveness of media, like the effectiveness of advertising copy, can be measured through experimental design.[1] Such a design requires that the advertiser allow the investigator full control over the advertising schedule in some major marketing area or areas such as are covered by regional editions of national magazines. The experimenter can employ varied media combinations on the theory that "because one medium supports another medium, the two in combination are more successful than the same amount of money spent on either one of the media separately." Of course, this may take place through psychological reinforcement rather than through patterns of reach or frequency.

The Ford Motor Company has initiated experiments that have implied (1) a relationship between advertising and sales, and (2) no significant superiority, or the reverse, for any one of the limited number of media for which data were adequate, according to research technology and costs.

[1] George H. Brown, "Measuring the Sales Effectiveness of Alternative Media," speech at the 7th Annual Conference of the Advertising Research Foundation, Inc., New York, October 3, 1961.

The stage nearest to final sales effect for which methods and data are currently available is the audiences of media vehicles. Methods are available for measuring not only the total audiences of most national media vehicles, but for measuring the combined and accumulated audiences as reached by varied media schedules.

Audience *accumulation, combination,* and *duplication* are the basic elements in making quantitative estimates of the reach of multimedia schedules. Each term has a meaning which requires careful definition for use in the advertising business. The terms have already been clearly established in usage, even to the extent of having abbreviations which are part of the lingo of those who deal in media.

But very few important national advertisers are willing to suspend or adjust multimillion-dollar media schedules for the purpose of a scientific experiment, nor is it clear that the findings would necessarily be adequate for application in the years following such an experiment.

Two major considerations determine the present course in evaluating media for the national advertiser. One is the need for quantitative information on *all media vehicles* at the nearest possible stage to the final sales effect. The other consideration is the need for such information *across all media,* both in combination and in accumulated reach for continuous advertising. Media purchases are made through individual orders or contracts, but media planning is based on the productivity of combinations and of continuing schedules.

Media-audience Accumulation and Combinations

The chief quantitative basis for planning multimedia schedules is logically the stage of the media function nearest to final sales effect, for which data are available on media combinations. Since the feasible stages are dependent upon survey research for data, the practical limit is *audience accumulation* ("cumes")—a term reserved in this book for the growth in total audience achieved by successive units of the same media vehicle.

Two weekly broadcasts of the same television program will *reach* more total people or households than will a single broadcast. Two issues of *The Post* will reach more people than a single average issue. And this combined audience will continue to build up even after the next and the next issues are published.

The more units of media vehicles that an advertiser uses, the longer is the time for accumulation—until it becomes necessary to plan in terms of some convenient period. The programs of most national advertisers are sufficiently long range to permit planning in periods of a month, or a season, or possibly a full year. The significance of accumulation depends partly upon the characteristics of particular media and partly upon the marketing program of the advertiser.

Combined total audiences ("combos") of media vehicles are defined in this book as the *reach* of two or more units of *different* media vehicles used by an advertiser at or near the same time.

A particular television broadcast, together with one issue of a *Life,* a *Look,* or *The Post,* will *reach* more individuals or households than either of these media units will reach alone. The facts that the broadcast reaches its total audience during air time and that the weekly magazine requires weeks for effective audience buildup must be considered in media planning. These are characteristics of media which help to determine the total advertising opportunity.

Duplication ("dupes") refers to the degree with which different media units, both like and unlike, make repeated impressions on the same people in establishing their total reach. Combinations of consumer magazines and popular TV programs normally make repeated or duplicate impressions on many of the same people, just as successive issues and successive broadcasts reach some of the same people twice and others only once.

The total *reach, or unduplicated audience,* of any media combination is a function of both the size of the audiences of individual units and the extent to which they *duplicate* or overlap. As a specific example, *U.S. News & World Report* stated at the end of 1961 that more than 1 million of its 1¼ million net paid subscribers did not subscribe to *Time*—thus, 83 per cent *nonduplication* of subscribers. Duplication of readers should not be much greater than duplication of subscribers. But a word of caution is necessary concerning the concept of duplication, because what really counts is not *reader duplication* but *prospect duplication.* As Richard Manville has said:

> The entire problem of duplication must be approached from the viewpoint of the individual customer for the individual product. Not all the people forming the total audience of any magazine, newspaper or radio or television program are customers for any given product—unless that product is the magazine's or program's editorial content.[2]

[2] Richard Manville, "What Counts Today Is Prospect (Not Reader) Duplication," *Printers' Ink,* Vol. 236 (July 13, 1951), pp. 27–29, at p. 29.

Duplication, accumulation, and combined reach can be shown very simply for a small number of media units. Two units, such as an issue of *Life* and an issue of *Look* can have their audiences represented by two lines:

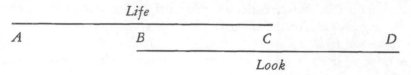

The distance *AC* represents the measured audience of an average issue of *Life*. *BD* is the measured audience of *Look*. The duplicated audience for these two average issues of the two publications is the distance *BC*. The *combined audience or reach* of the two magazines is the distance *AD*.

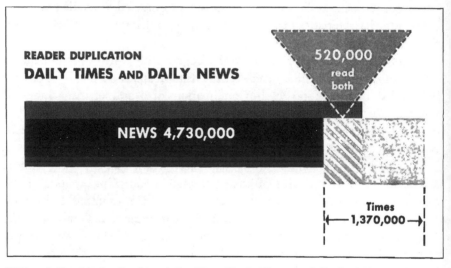

FIG. 16. Reader duplication, daily *New York Times* and *Daily News*. (*Courtesy of The News.*)

If both audiences were for successive issues of the same publication, the distance *AD* would be called the *accumulated audience* of two issues of the publication. Frequently, the total audience represnted by *AD* is called the *total unduplicated audience,* meaning that the same individual or household is counted only once.

Based on work by W. A. Simmons and Associates Research, Inc., Fig. 16 shows how the *Daily News* (New York) represents the combination of its reading audience with that of the daily *New York Times*.[3]

[3] *Profile of the Millions,* 2d edition (New York: *The News,* 1958), p. 48.

When these same dimensions are considered for three media units, the graphical representation becomes more complex. Three units may be represented by three areas, shown in Fig. 17. If the three regular areas M, L, and G represent the average single-issue audience of *McCall's, Ladies' Home Journal,* and *Good Housekeeping,* respectively, it appears that some people read all three magazines, MLG. Others read only one of the three publications—M, L, or G. The *combined audience* is represented by the area within the perimeter of the three overlapping areas.

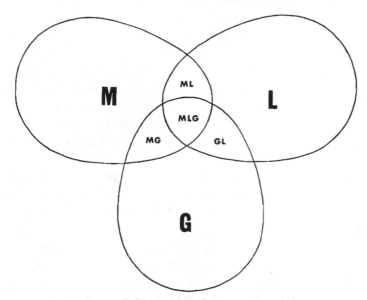

FIG. 17. Relationships of three media units.

While audience duplication and triplication can be shown graphically for three media units (Fig. 17), it is not practical to visualize the combinations obtained by large numbers of media units. Nevertheless, the principles and definitions remain the same, and media planning must consider the interrelationships of all available media vehicles.

MEASUREMENT OF ACCUMULATED AUDIENCES

The measurement of accumulated audiences of successive or added units of the same media vehicle, together with estimates of duplication, differs greatly for television and magazines.

Syndicated rating services, like the scheduling of sponsored broadcasts, are set up to continue through successive broadcast units. The mechanical method (adapted to households) and the diary (adapted to individuals) provide for accumulated measurement and reporting. Sample limitations and losses place a limit on the period for measuring accumulation, but it is not difficult to study several successive weeks of a weekly network program.

Data from the November-December, 1959, Nielsen Television Index reveal that the half-hour evening weekly Ford show reached a total of 23,852,000 homes at least once during a 4-week period when the average total home audience for the individual broadcasts was 13,339,000 homes. This accumulation of more than 10 million additional homes is explained by the fact that only one family out of six viewed all four programs, whereas one-third of the total families viewed only one of the four shows. The pattern of viewing, by number of shows seen, was 33.5 per cent saw only one show; 29.2 per cent saw two of the shows only; 20.4 per cent saw three of the shows only; and 16.9 per cent saw all four shows.

The implication of these data from the Ford show is that advertising campaign strategy must not rely entirely upon a buildup of consecutive messages reaching the same homes.

Data from the July to December, 1960, Nielsen Media Service survey of magazine audiences reveal that four issues of *Life* magazine were read by people eighteen years and older in 28,409,000 homes when the average audience for a single issue was only 20,178,000 homes. With approximately nine out of ten *Life* copies making their original stop at regular subscriber homes, 39 per cent of the total four-week audience of families looked into all four issues. Any family in which at least one adult eighteen years or over looked into a measured issue is counted in the total audience of homes. The pattern of reading (by number of issues looked into) was 20 per cent looked into only one issue; 21 per cent looked into only two issues; 20 per cent looked into only three issues; and 39 per cent of the families looked into all four issues.

Earlier *Life* data on the accumulation of its audience of individuals, issue by issue for six measured issues, shows the following pattern: [4]

Issue accumulation	Total readers
One average issue	26,450,000
Second issue added	38,800,000
Third issue added	46,800,000
Fourth issue added	52,550,000
Fifth issue added	57,000,000
Sixth issue added	60,500,000

[4] *A Study of Four Media* (New York: *Life*, 1953), p. 12.

There is a difference in the rate of audience accumulation for individuals as compared with families. Individual audiences tend to increase at a slightly faster rate. Probably this is largely a result of definition, since a reading home requires that only one person look into the issue. Also, since one issue reaches a greater percentage of total homes than of total individuals, there is a smaller share of homes remaining for additional issues to build upon. This pattern is in general confirmed by independently produced projections on *Look* magazine, as shown in Table 26.[5]

TABLE 26. *Household and Individual Audiences Accumulated by 13 Issues of* Look *

No. of issues	No. of households (Pop. 53 million)	No. of individuals 10 and older (Pop. 139 million)
1	18,460,000	31,830,000
2	24,190,000	42,860,000
3	27,720,000	49,980,000
4	30,230,000	55,420,000
5	32,160,000	59,750,000
6	33,710,000	63,520,000
7	34,970,000	66,730,000
8	36,010,000	69,380,000
9	36,880,000	71,750,000
10	37,640,000	73,850,000
11	38,260,000	75,660,000
12	38,800,000	77,200,000
13	39,200,000	78,590,000

* The figures from 5 through 13 issues are mathematical estimates.

The implication of these data is that advertising campaigns in these national media should not be designed on the assumption that successive messages build up their effect on the same households or individuals. Each message should strengthen the impression made by previous contacts with the same audience, but it is also important that each message have some sales impact on those exposed perhaps only once.

By the same token, media scheduling cannot realistically be based on an assumption that advertising contacts will be mostly continuous if the same vehicle is employed. The potential total audience of many of the leading media vehicles is, ultimately, a great majority of the total population

[5] *Look Audience Study* (New York: *Look,* 1961), pp. 13, 47.

of the United States. The frequency of contacts with the same homes or individuals is extremely varied.

A Technical Problem

In their first efforts to measure audience accumulation, investigators were confronted with a technical survey problem. This was the problem of guarding against "conditioning" of the behavior of the survey sample resulting from repeat interviews regarding the same media vehicles. Going back repeatedly to ask the same person about attending the same broadcast program or reading the same magazine might influence respondents to *attend* to these media. Consumer panels for radio or TV have long been suspect on this point, and this argument has been used to support a policy by one research company of changing TV diary samples every reporting period.

The mechanical Audimeter solved the problem of measuring the accumulation of households tuned to broadcasts. Whatever conditioning may arise from meter installation is unlikely to have a prolonged effect. Similarly, development of the *editorial-interest technique* for magazine-audience measurement (see Chapter Ten), combined with the possibility of measuring several issues in one interview, may have minimized the hazard with magazines. *Life*'s first accumulative audience study called for three complete sample waves eight weeks apart and covered four or five successive issues in each wave with the same individuals.[6] The technique employed diversionary questions to minimize conditioning and included an experimental study of possible conditioning. Index numbers representing audience claims on three successive calls were 100.2, 100.2, and 99.6, respectively. This is not to be interpreted as providing that conditioning is a myth, but rather that the particular survey design overcame conditioning.

The measurement of magazine family or household audiences raises the same question of conditioning, since one member of the family may observe or be aware of interviews with others. The opportunity for conditioning is accentuated when one or more callbacks are required to complete interviews in the same household. This tendency can be measured—and partly discounted, if necessary—by first interviewing a random member of the household, as is customary in measures of total individual magazine audiences. Comparison of the audience measurement of first respondents in

[6] *A Study of the Accumulative Audience of* Life, (New York: *Life,* 1950) pp. 11–12.

each home with the average of all others should expose any conditioning effect.

MEASUREMENT OF AUDIENCE DUPLICATION AND COMBINATIONS

The combined measurement of audiences for a few vehicles of the same medium offers no new problems beyond those of the four-insertion accumulation measurement.

The mechanical method can measure household tuning for the entire broadcasting schedule of all national television networks in one operation. When it is desired to measure audiences of individuals, the diary method meets the need with less precision than metered measurement of set tuning, but the diary is also well adapted to covering the entire broadcast schedule.

On the other hand, magazines require separate interviews with all household members, and early techniques were not designed to encompass all major magazines in a single interview. The accepted standards for magazine-audience measurement require that the respondent be shown a substantial part of the entire editorial contents of each measured issue. Emphasis on diversionary aspects adds to the interview time so that there is a practical limit to the number of issues which can be handled on a single call. National advertisers require information on all major magazines with regard to both average-issue audiences and accumulative audiences for each publication. There are probably more than 30 different publications worth serious consideration, and they are issued weekly, bi-weekly, and monthly. There is no consolidated process of reception comparable to a television set, which can be mechanically metered for continuous information about all magazine reading.

Research talent was applied for many years to the problem of measuring audiences of all major magazines in one interview. The first efforts failed to devise an interviewing technique which would encompass enough magazines without too much sacrifice in basic accuracy. In the middle 1950s, those associated with the Advertising Research Foundation felt so strongly the industry demand for comprehensive audience information on magazines that a special committee was appointed. This committee was assigned the technical task of devising an appropriate interviewing method.

Fortunately the ARF had previously conducted a comprehensive audience survey of the somewhat smaller group of 11 leading Canadian magazines.

The Canadian study had been modeled after studies of smaller magazine groups in the United States and retained the same basic methodology. Controls built into the interviewing procedure made it possible to test whether the adaptations of method had affected the results. The outcome was completely reassuring and provided helpful guidance to the new committee.

The critical problems in a magazine interview are time and possible boredom or fatigue. When interviewers interrupt people in their homes without advance notice, it is unsafe to plan on more than about forty-five minutes of working time. It is not advantageous to schedule calls ahead— even if more time could be secured by appointment, it is likely that boredom or fatigue would set in before the end of an hour. Since it takes ten to fifteen minutes to conduct a respondent through all the pages of a popular magazine—in the editorial-interest interview on specific issues, for example—the practical limit is some four or five publications.

Investigators quickly found that time could be saved by fastening together or removing all issue pages lacking major editorial display features. The Canadian survey reduced each issue copy to the most vivid display page or spread of each of 10 leading features, plus a few cartoons, and rebound the items in the issue cover. Later tabulations showed that 10 major items are more than enough to enable a respondent to identify an issue he has read. Very few additional readers are discovered by showing more than 5 properly chosen items from the issue. Even 10 display items represent an enormous saving of interview time, compared with a whole issue.

A contribution to technique made by Alfred Politz proved a great time saver by eliminating readership questions on individual items.[7] This improvement, based on the principle that respondents should be asked to recognize whole issues and not single items, was readily adopted by the ARF committee. Politz had already measured as many as nine American magazines in a survey, using his revised procedure.[8] (See pages 308–323.)

One of the questions raised in connection with the Canadian magazine study was whether the sequence of showing magazines in an interview might penalize each later measured issue, possibly through increased boredom. Two steps were taken to control this factor. One was to reproduce and actually show the magazine name logotype in the process of initially asking about publications read within the past six months. The second step was to shuffle the logo cards for each interview and then to keep account of the sequence followed.

[7] *McCall's Female Audience* (New York: *McCall's Magazine,* 1960), p. 7.
[8] *The Audiences of Nine Magazines* (New York: *Look,* 1955).

The actual name flags or logotypes added interest to the preliminary question. Tabulation of the influence of sequence showed no evidence of significant deviations related to the order of the interview questions.

The problem of the ARF committee was to combine all of the quickest techniques of interviewing and to arrive at a method which would work mechanically in the field in order to produce valid audience estimates. The basic Politz principle of recognizing whole issues was followed, publication name logotypes were used, and survey issues were stripped down to 10 major items. Since this permitted going through an issue in three to five minutes and since so few people claim even occasional reading of more than 10 or 12 publications, it proved possible to complete interviews on some 35 leading magazines without evidence of undue resistance or boredom.

The contribution of the Advertising Research Foundation was the adaptation and field testing of a technique for interviewing on approximately 35 magazine issues in one call. The expanded interview capacity could be applied to 35 different publications, or to the measurement of accumulated audiences of a smaller number of publications, up to a total of 35 copies.

There remained the need to apply the method to a sample of sufficient size to determine whether the interview combination would produce statistically accurate issue measures. Although the ARF was prepared to execute such a study in 1958, financial support was not forthcoming; as a result the expanded interviewing procedure, which already had the approval of advertising research leaders, was made available for use by others in the advertising industry.

COMBINED TELEVISION AND MAGAZINE AUDIENCES

So far, the description of television and magazine-audience measurement indicates that techniques have been developed for making usefully accurate measures of accumulated and combined audiences for vehicles within each medium. Major national advertisers frequently employ both television shows and magazines in their schedules, and there is need for data covering combinations of vehicles in both major media.

More specifically, the national advertiser needs audience data on his own television properties and on other shows and spots available to him, plus data on the complete magazine list. A concept for measurement to supply such broad audience information requires consideration of advertiser needs, a review of the audience pattern in each medium, and then a search for research methods capable of producing the needed information economically and at a useful level of accuracy.

The viewing of television is often a family or group activity, which may explain the recommendation of the household unit of measurement by an early Advertising Research Foundation committee. Magazine reading, by way of contrast, is basically an individual activity, with more freedom for highly selective individual behavior patterns. Since measurement of individual audiences usually makes possible the combination of family units as well, the only practical approach to measurement of combined television and magazine audiences is on the basis of individuals.

Television research reaches its maximum level of accuracy and acceptance for national projections when the mechanical method is applied to household units (see Chapter Eleven). Data on individuals are not so precise and require a supplemental diary to provide a basis for accumulation and combination of data on individuals. Emphasis on inherent dangers in diary measurement has led to refinements discussed earlier, but the best diary is not generally accepted as a basis for projections of individuals to total national audiences.

Measurement of projected total magazine audiences began with individuals as the unit and reached a level of general acceptance when based on maximum completion of known-probability samples of individuals. Some caution is suggested when magazine interviews are extended to whole families because each individual interview may have some effect on subsequent respondents in the same household. Random selection of the first respondent in each household provides a basis for assessing this influence.

There is a similar hazard in measuring accumulation of audiences of successive issues, although procedures have been tested for minimizing any possible conditioning. The recommended measuring method, both for projecting individual audiences and for minimizing the danger of conditioning, is the *editorial-interest technique* (see pages 227–229).

Combined television and magazine measurement of both individual and household audiences cannot be based on the mechanical method, since meters do not measure individuals. Measurement of household audiences of magazines cannot reach the maximum percentage of sample achieved in measurement of magazine audiences of individuals, nor is such high sample completion possible in measuring total individual audiences of television.

The common core—available for both individual and household measurement for both media—is the sample which can be recruited for diary reporting on television. This sample, somewhat less complete than can be reached for individual-magazine-audience measurement, should be capable of providing adequate data on all audience combinations, provided optimal survey techniques are used on both media.

Nielsen Media Service

The diary refinements employed in the Nielsen Audilog and monitored by the Recordimeter (see pages 251–252) have demonstrated a capacity for making audience measurements approaching those of the electronic Audimeter. The A. C. Nielsen Company, which developed the Audilog operation, decided to initiate combined television and magazine measurement in 1960. The best available method for multiple magazine measurement was the editorial-interest technique, already demonstrated and approved by the Advertising Research Foundation. There appeared to be no obstacles to employing this exact procedure in Audilog homes, to supplement the individual and household television data with corresponding audience information on magazines. The first national survey was conducted from July to December, 1960, and covered all network television broadcasts, along with two to four issues of each of 12 leading magazines.

The Nielsen Media Service 1960 survey measured audiences eighteen years of age and older. Audilog records for viewing of television were obtained by periodical placement of weekly diaries at intervals of one month.

Since a magazine issue requires a month or more to build up its total measured audience, the interval may have made magazine and television data more comparable. Television audiences for widely separated broadcasts of the same program show less overlap than do succeeding audiences of a weekly show. Magazines, whose audiences were measured for two to four successive issues in a single interview, have been shown to have much the same overlap for widely separated issues as for successive issues.

Therefore, it is believed that the accumulative audience data, as well as the data on audience combinations, are obtained on a basis suitable for media planning. While the chief purpose of the survey was not to provide projectable audiences on individual vehicles of either medium, the present authors believe that the data are accurate enough to furnish helpful guides in media planning.

It should be recognized, of course, that many others do not share the view that data on audiences of combinations of different media are useful in planning multimedia schedules. Following is a statement by the Marketing Studies Section of the National Broadcasting Company.

> The Nielsen Media Service makes available information on the undupli-cated number of homes who read a particular magazine and/or see a particular TV program, without taking into account the inherent difference in the two media's definition of audience and the relative impact of each. Whenever a cross-run is made, combining the audience of a magazine with the audience of a television program, there is a basic underlying assumption made: that the advertising "exposure" of one issue reader is equivalent to the advertising "exposure" of one program viewer. . . . The measures are noncomparable.[9]

Additional Considerations

Combination data on households tuned in to broadcasts have been avail-able to the advertising industry ever since nationally projectable Nielsen ratings were introduced in 1948. A half-hour evening network show with a household audience of 15 million homes, for example, might be com-bined with a full-hour Saturday daytime show reaching 7½ million homes, to achieve a combined total of 20 million separate homes.

Such information has been used for years—first in radio and later in television—to guide program choices within the limitations of those avail-able. Less sure guides have been available for combining total individual audiences of the same shows, although the Audilog had improved diary-measuring precision in single markets before substantial television networks were possible.

The data combinations, made possible through magazine-audience meas-urement in a national sample of Audilog homes, opened a new era in media analysis and planning. Most national advertisers, already accus-tomed to data on household combinations for the new network shows and the spots available to them, were enabled to relate these television prop-erties to a dozen leading magazines on both an individual and a household audience basis. Since all magazines are available, generally on any desired schedule, the added data multiplied the available measurable combinations of national audiences enormously.

A growing tendency toward participating television advertising and toward network spot purchases has added to the need for comprehensive television data. As a result, the total number of practical combinations involving television and magazines has become astronomical. Yet audience

⁹ *The Nielsen Media Service: an Analysis,* Marketing Studies Section, National Broadcasting Company, *NBC Research Bulletin,* No. 230 (G-R-TV), May 15, 1961.

data for compiling these combinations are available through a single research operation.

One simple approach to the application of combined data on television
and magazines is to examine both the *reach* and *frequency* of the schedule
of a particular advertiser or to compare competing advertisers. An automobile insurance company which sponsors a half-hour evening network
television show reached 11,866,000 homes, as indicated in Fig. 18. The

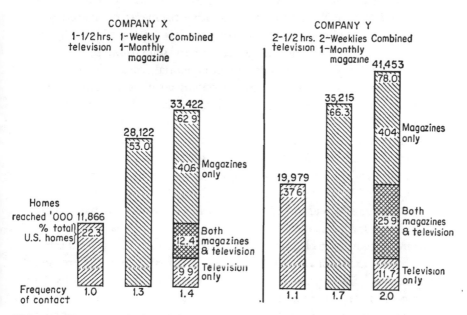

FIG. 18. Homes reached and frequency of contact through different media schedules. (*Adapted from material furnished by A. C. Nielsen Company.*)

company also scheduled one advertisement per month in a weekly magazine
and one in a monthly magazine, having a total combined issue reading in
28,122,000 homes. Because of audience duplication, the total number of
different homes reached by television and magazines was 33,422,000.

The competitor, with two half-hour network television shows and advertisements in two weeklies as well as one monthly magazine, reached
household totals of 19,979,000 homes by television alone, 35,215,000
homes by one or more of the three magazines, and 41,453,000 separate
homes by the whole combination.

A similar, though somewhat reduced pattern can be shown by restricting
the audience analysis to homes with male readers, or to car-owning homes.

These data illustrate how the advertiser with the bigger schedule reaches more households and with greater frequency.

The complementary nature of television and magazines probably extends into message communication as well as audience reach and frequency. *Look* magazine has reported a comparison between interviews with a sample of *Look* subscriber-housewives and with another sample of housewives viewing specific television programs after a uniform interval of twenty-four hours for both print and television exposure.[10] Aided recall of 19 selected four-color full-page food and beverage advertisements compared with 20 comparable sixty-second television commercials produced average scores of 26.3 per cent for print and 24.9 per cent for television.

While this difference may seem inconsequential, comparisons of content showed that the same advertiser might obtain recall of a headline in print well above words on television, yet have high recall of musical effects from television. The assistant to the publisher concludes: "It suggests, for example, that print and TV used in combination (1) reduce the risk of poor communication penetration due to failure of the ad message on one medium or the other; and (2) produce a complementary communication in the consumer's mind." [11]

Look probed the relationship between television and magazines further by obtaining special tabulations from the Nielsen Media Service showing exposure of families to leading units of both media. The top 10 television programs from October, 1960, through February, 1961, were selected along with the nine regular magazines measured for 1960 by NMS. Households in the sample were divided into four equal groups, according to their ranking on the basis of frequency of exposure to one medium, and again on the basis of frequency of exposure to the other medium. The ranking of exposure to television indicated frequency of exposure of at least one adult (eighteen years of age or older) in the household to any of the 10 selected programs. Likewise, the ranking for magazines indicated frequency of exposure of at least one adult in the household to any of the nine prominent magazines.

When the ranked grouping of one medium was superimposed on the other, a number of significant differences in demographic characteristics were evident. The data, representing a universe of some 45 million families exposed to at least 1 of the 19 media units, showed that heavy users of both

[10] Communication from Joel Harnett, Assistant to the Publisher of *Look* magazine, New York, May 15, 1962.

[11] Citation in footnote 10.

media had higher incomes than light users and also were bigger families with better educated household heads. The largest contrasts, however, were between the 25 per cent of all households with heavy print and light television exposure and the 25 per cent with light print and heavy television exposure. Those with heavy print and light television exposure had the following median scores, as compared with the light print and heavy television exposure group: household income, $7,800 versus $5,600; size of family, 3.7 versus 3.5; years of education beyond grammar school of head of household, 4.2 versus 2.1; and age of head of household, 47.6 versus 49.2. Altogether, television and magazines complement each other in the classes of households reached, as well as in the total reach and frequency and in the communication of the advertising message itself.

Advertisers are restricted in their television opportunities by the nature of the medium. There may be little interest in examining data on all networks or on shows other than their own properties, at least for the immediate future. The opportunity for change in magazines is very different. All magazines are available to almost every advertiser and with almost any desired frequency. It is not enough to study the effectiveness of the present schedule or merely to experiment with data on possible substitutions.

THE PATTERN OF GROWTH OF AUDIENCE COMBINATIONS

One of the earliest discoveries through magazine-audience research was the fact that the readers of magazines tend to be a concentrated group. In fact, the reader of Magazine A is more likely to read Magazine B than are the nonreaders of Magazine A. Even within class magazines, such as women's service magazines or weekly news magazines, the person who reads one has a predisposition to read another in the same group.

However, this pattern does not carry over from magazines to television. In connection with this problem, Cornelius DuBois reported, *"In this sample at least the women easiest to reach via TV are different kinds of women from those easiest to reach with magazines."* [12] Again, referring to his own sample, he said, "There is essentially no correlation at all between magazines and evening TV, or between print and broadcast." [13]

In 1960, Nielsen Media Service confirmed the differences between maga-

[12] Cornelius DuBois, "What Is the Difference between a Reader and a Viewer?" *Media/scope,* Vol. 3, Part 1, (September, 1959), pp. 53–58 at p. 55.

[13] Cornelius DuBois, "What Is the Difference between a Reader and a Viewer?" *Media/scope,* Vol. 3, Part 2, (October, 1959), pp. 46–51, at p. 47.

zine and television audiences on a national scale. These differences emphasize the need for audience combination data in order to put together media vehicles for the purpose of obtaining satisfactory audience combinations.

A comprehensive description of what actually happens when the audiences of leading American magazines are combined is not practicable because of the astronomical number of possible combinations. Instead, following a common practice of media analysts, a start may be made with one magazine, adding to it the other publications in the same group, such as weekly magazines. Other magazines or groups may be added, with smaller or greater increments to the total, depending upon audience duplication with previous publications on the list. Obviously, as the list increases, the gain from adding each additional magazine tends to decrease. The following example is an arbitrary selection from Nielsen Media Service, 1960: [14]

Magazines	Total adult readers
Life	28,344,000
Life and Look	41,033,000
Life, Look, and The Post	49,002,000
Life, Look, The Post, and McCall's	53,553,000
Life, Look, The Post, McCall's, and Ladies' Home Journal	56,587,000

Note that the total reach of a magazine combination may increase very little as more publications are added. *Ladies' Home Journal,* with an audience of 13,181,000 adults, adds but 3 million to the total reached by the other four magazines.

True Story has an audience of 6,179,000 readers—about half the number for the *Ladies' Home Journal*—but would add 2.65 millions to the same four magazines. This suggests that the *True Story* audience is a different kind of group, not inclined to read many of the other magazines listed above.

What happens when the above list of five magazines is extended is illustrated in Fig. 19. The letter sequences, such as A, B, and C, are intended to represent magazines in the same class. Isolated letters, such as Z, represent different kinds of magazines. Magazine A, being first on the list, is represented by its full individual audience. Magazine B, in the same class, overlaps considerably, and the addition of Magazine C overlaps both A and B.

However, when a different type of magazine, Magazine J, is added, it benefits from being different from ABC. But Magazines K and L are like

[14] Copyright A. C. Nielsen Company, reprinted with permission.

J, and also overlap ABC, and so contribute little to the total. Magazine Z, which might be a romance magazine or a farm publication, adds substantially since both have different reader appeal than the others.

Further additions are likely to add smaller increments because of duplication with preceding magazines. If they appeal mainly to entirely different groups, they may be disqualified for not fitting the needs of the particular advertiser.

FIG. 19. Incremental pattern of magazine-audience combinations.

Many years ago Seymour Banks suggested the use of *incremental analysis* in the selection of advertising media.[15]

> As we increase an advertising appropriation, we know that we get a larger number of readers; incremental analysis reveals the rate of change of readers at any given level of expenditure. It shows the gain in readers for a given increment of cost—if $50,000 yields X readers and $51,000 yields $X + Y$ readers, then Y is the increment attributed to the last $1,000. The value of this type of analysis is that the advertiser can formulate his decisions in terms of the point beyond which the added increment of readers or rememberers of advertising is no longer worth what it costs to obtain that increment. He can therefore plan a campaign in which the cost of obtaining the last increment of advertising equals, or, in his judgment, is worth the value of that increment.[16]

Banks and Madansky explored the widely recognized tendency of magazine-audience accumulation and combinations to follow largely predictable mathematical patterns.[17] They made a unique contribution by noting that

[15] Seymour Banks, "The Use of Incremental Analysis in the Selection of Advertising Media," *The Journal of Business,* Vol. 19 (October, 1946), pp. 232–243.

[16] Page 232 of citation in footnote 15.

[17] Seymour Banks and Albert Madansky, "Estimation of Multimagazine Readership," *The Journal of Business,* Vol. 31 (July, 1958), pp. 235–242.

patterns of duplication deviate from random in a way which can be largely predicted for mass publications by accounting for editorial differences. Special equations which they developed made it possible to *predict* from single-issue audiences the duplication and accumulation of audiences of combinations of two, three, and four magazines within one percentage point of available survey measures. They were also able to estimate the patterns of combinations of up to six issues of two and three different publications. For magazines, it was indicated that audience combination patterns (derived from simple functions of audience size and the basic editorial content and format of the publications) such as income levels of audience members or pass-along ratios made no significant improvements over duplication estimates provided from the two primary factors.

More recently, a mathematical procedure has been developed for the purpose of eliminating the nearly infinite tabulations and bulky reports required to present combinations of audiences of more than two large groups of magazines.[18] The procedure does not ignore the differing audience composition of differing magazines, since it requires survey measurement of all audience pair combinations. The inventor of the procedure worked with the findings of a survey of 30 French magazines, which had been reported in all combinations of 15 magazines. His empirical formula was developed from a random selection of 98 of the 32,767 possible combinations of two magazines.

When applied to the original data and to one American magazine survey, the formula produced usefully accurate estimates of total unduplicated audience combinations in almost every instance. While this would indicate that all possible combinations of audience totals and breakdowns could be computed from data on individual totals and pair combinations, with breakdowns, the author noted that applications beyond the observed data remained to be proved.

The pattern shown in Fig. 19 is relatively simple, since it assumes that there is a fixed sequence of adding publications and that total unduplicated individual audiences are the only goal. But there are many other possibilities, all apart from the considerations of cost. Each magazine, depending on its frequency of issue, may be scheduled more than once in a particular period of evaluation. The number of publications and insertions in the total schedule will vary according to how many publications and issues are

[18] J. M. Agostini, "How to Estimate Unduplicated Audiences," *Journal of Advertising Research,* Vol. 1 (March, 1961), pp. 11–14.

required to reach a predetermined goal. And the publications can seldom be safely selected in a fixed order.

Such an order might easily forfeit the most important advantage of planning on the basis of combination audience data. If there is no starting point or fixed number of publications, the number of possible combinations becomes so nearly infinite as to make manual trials impracticable.

OPTIMIZING MEDIA REACH BY MATHEMATICAL PROCEDURES

The problem of selecting from a nearly infinite number of possible combinations was solved to a considerable extent when John Mauchly and J. Presper Eckert submitted a plan to the U.S. Army Ordnance Department in 1943 for an electronic computer.[19] This marked the beginning of the evolution of the modern high-speed computer. The first UNIVAC was delivered by the Remington Rand Company nine years after the original plan was conceived by Mauchly and Eckert. "Mathematicians, physicists, and chemists were able to make calculations long desired but which defied solution because of the sheer volume of work."[20] The high-speed computer also has a place in helping to discover the best media combination; it can deal with the numerous variables which enter into such an advertising decision.

The ideal media plan is one which makes most efficient use of a particular advertising expenditure. No plan can safely be established in a "vacuum" which lacks any of the vast number of important variables contributing to advertising effect. Mere calculation of the optimal total unduplicated audience, on the basis of minimum cost, is not sufficient. This concept overlooks many important factors, not the least of which is the value of all the duplication occurring when vehicles overlap.

Nor would this simple concept arrive readily at solutions by the cut-and-try method because of the multitude of possible combinations. Even if the national advertiser chooses to stand by his existing television properties and to consider only four-color full pages in magazines to complement his broadcasts, the task of optimizing expenditures is too tedious to be done by hand.

[19] J. Presper Eckert, "Executives 100 Feet Tall: The Invention of the Computer, Computers Today, Computers Tomorrow," speech for the Executives' Club of Chicago, April 6, 1962.

[20] Page 6 of citation in footnote 19.

The media scheduling problem is well adapted to systematic solution through *mathematical programing* methods employed in *operations research*. Mathematical programing, sometimes restricted to linear programing, may be used for calculation of the one most economical or efficient combination of media for a particular purpose.

Mathematical programing is a systematic approach to problems and represents one of the primary tools or techniques which are grouped loosely under the name of "operations research." The essential steps are as follows:

1. A clear statement of definitions and philosophy related to the problem

2. Careful formulation of the problem, indicating relationships and weights of the various factors involved and the kinds of data required

3. Assembly of appropriate data of sufficient accuracy for solving the problem

4. Choosing or developing a mathematical model or formula which is capable of being solved, with all of the variables indicated in the problem formulation

5. Turning over the materials to a technician to program and solve the problem, usually by means of a high-speed computer

6. Applying human judgment to examine the outcome to make substitutions or alterations and to arrive at a solution which meets with human judgment and experience

Examination of the above steps will show that there is provision for applying "weights" to factors in media selection according to their estimated importance. There is no alternative to the specification of weights in numerical terms. This is done automatically when "no" weights are assigned, as each weight then becomes unity. Reluctance to convert subjective weights to numbers is understandable, but illogical. After all, every purchase that is ever made of a medium or of media requires the matching of subjective judgments with numbers—dollars of media costs.

The steps in mathematical programing also allow for decisions to be made after the computer has put out its findings. Mathematical programing and computers do not make decisions. Decisions are made before the computer goes to work, and decisions are made after the output is obtained. The procedure is primarily a means of aiding the decision process. The competent media man may arrive at a somewhat similar solution on the basis of experience and intuitive judgment. In that case, the mathematical confirmation ensures his judgment and indicates whether the solution is a clear-cut choice or one of several reasonably similar solutions.

Subjective Considerations

There are many considerations, both objective and subjective, in choosing and combining media. Some of the many ways in which media differ are as follows:

1. The number of persons exposed to the advertising messages in each medium
2. The number of persons who have their attitudes toward the advertiser changed by each medium
3. The number of persons who are conditioned so that they will buy the advertised product when something necessitates a brand switch
4. The number of persons who immediately go out and buy the product because of the advertising in each medium
5. The extent to which each medium encourages present users to retain their brand loyalty
6. The extent to which each medium encourages present users to use the product more frequently [21]

The above generalized differences must be extended to include many detailed dimensions and assumed qualities of individual media vehicles before the problem formulation can be completed. It is also essential to assign values to every acceptable advertising unit in each medium. Then it is important to consider the values or weights to be assigned to possible impressions to be made one or more times through every possible kind of contact, duplication, and repetition.

All these elements are implicitly weighed in every media decision made on a subjective basis. Mathematical solutions only require that these factors be individually specified and accorded weights in proportion to their importance to the media buyer.

Significance of Media Audiences

The measurement of media audiences is the closest stage to final sales effect for which research methods and surveys have made comprehensive media data available. It was for this reason that the first publicly announced business application of mathematical programing to the optimizing of media schedules was based on media-audience data.

[21] Howard D. Hadley, "Newspapers vs. Television—Which Is the Better Buy?" *Media/scope,* Vol. 2 (November, 1958), pp. 31–33, at p. 31.

[22] A presentation by Batten, Barton, Durstine, and Osborn, Inc., before the Eastern Annual Conference of the American Association of Advertising Agencies, November 16, 1961.

The fact that audiences have such different meanings for different media vehicles and for different types of media accounts for the elaborate process of weighting required to reach a meaningful media pattern.

The television audience includes all persons who have viewed some part of a program. The magazine audience includes all who have looked inside an issue, on an average, and have seen one or more editorial features. The newspaper audience includes persons reporting the reading of any part of a newspaper on the previous day. Both the media and the definitions differ and have a different significance to the advertiser.

Weighting of the value of an advertising cost unit in any media vehicle must allow for likelihood of delivering the message to each of those persons who qualify on the media-audience definition. It must also take into account the kinds of copy which the medium can carry, the physical form of the message, the intensity and frequency of impression, and the atmosphere or attitude pattern in which the advertising operates. In order to establish a value, these factors must be combined with an understanding of the kinds of people in the audience of the media vehicle.

Other Stages in the Media Function

It is in this part of the problem formulation that all of the stages in the concept of the media function are given consideration. The analyst estimates on the basis of available data the likelihood of one or more advertising exposures to the people in the audience of each media vehicle. He also tries to estimate likely perception of his advertisement and the likely degree of communication of its sales message. These factors and the attitudes stimulated in the minds of advertisement-noters contribute to the weight which is assigned to each unit in the audience of the vehicle.

Variable Market Values

It is hardly necessary to point out that national advertisers place a considerably different value upon various segments of their markets, actual and potential. The primary advertising function of media is, of course, to seek out the particular markets of interest to an advertiser.

The manufacturer of breakfast cereal may place some unit value on adult women, another value on men, and still another on children. Regional markets may differ according to climate, wealth, or eating and shopping patterns. Formulation of the media problem must take into account the weights of different audience segments. It should also take some account of the possibility of effective communication of advertising to each market segment, as related to characteristics discussed in Chapter Fourteen.

Some Basic Decisions

The problem of each advertiser is different—not only different for each product, but different for each season and market. Some of the basic decisions essential to problem formulation are as follows:

1. Which is more important in determining product purchases, the individual or the family unit?
2. What are the basic units acceptable in each medium, by size and cost? If television, there is not only the question of commercial time, but also of the relationship to a particular program.
3. What is to be the basic unit of media planning—a week, a month, a season, or a year?

Such decisions or restrictions are judgmental, and additional factors may be the advance decision to put one-third of the budget in spot TV, the decision to buy women's monthly magazines only in units of 12, the decision to use center spreads because that has been a company custom, etc.[23] The most fundamental judgmental decision—usually made by the advertiser himself—is the size of the total advertising expenditure. Whatever these judgmental decisions may be, they become a part of the problem formulation. If these restrictions must be a part of the final solution, then there is no point in allowing flexibility on these points in the mathematical plan.

Consider also the environmental restrictions, such as the availability of only 12 issues of a monthly magazine annually.[24] There are also the specifications by which each medium sells its time or space, and the availability of such features as color only under certain conditions. Technically, the size of the advertising expenditure is also considered environmental. These factors are in a sense the "facts of life," and media solutions would be meaningless if they did not conform with the advertising units and schedules available in media and the money made available by the advertiser.

How Weights Are Assigned and By Whom

Insofar as reliable data are available on any point, they may determine or aid in estimating the appropriate weight. Lacking full data, it is neces-

[23] David Learner, "The Translation from Theory to Practice," speech on mathematical media programing presented at the Eastern Annual Conference of the American Association of Advertising Agencies, November 16, 1961.

[24] Citation in footnote 23.

sary to make actual numerical estimates of each particular value. Fortunately, assigned weights are not permanent commitments, and they can
come from a number of sources. They can also be varied to suit products or
other considerations related to any particular advertiser. The advertiser may
assign weights, or weights may come from media buyers, creative people,
account men, or any combination of these. In fact, if the final decision is
made by one who differs greatly from a consensus, he should have sound
reasons for such differences.

Some of the more important considerations entering into the estimate
of weights for each unit in a media audience are as follows:

1. If the value of each opportunity for impression by a magazine advertisement is unity, then what is the relative weight of an opportunity in
television? Or, if the value of an opportunity in Magazine A is unity, then
what is the value of a similar opportunity in Magazine B? This weight may
take into account the expectancy of rereading of the same magazine copy
or the expectancy for multiple exposure to the same person in the same
issue (see Chapter Twelve).

2. If the first insertion in Magazine A has an opportunity worth unity,
then what is the value of successive impressions in Magazine A, provided
it can be scheduled more than once in the basic time period studied? Are
two opportunities worth double the value of one, or how much more or
less than double?

3. What is the value of one advertising opportunity or impression for
each person or family unit in a total combined audience, compared with
opportunities for two, three, or more contacts reaching varying percentages
of a smaller combined total? For example, if Magazine A has already made
an advertising contact on an individual or household, how much is a second
contact worth through Magazine B, as compared with the value of reaching
an entirely new person or household with Magazine B?

4. If different individuals (men or women, for example) or households
(rich or poor, for example) have different prospective values, what is each
worth numerically in comparison with the other?

The above factors are not exhaustive, but merely identify some of the
elements which cannot safely be assumed to have equal weights for most
advertising situations. Some of these factors and others involved in media
evaluation are nonlinear, which means that strictly linear solutions are not
adequate.

Altogether, the problem formulation for mathematical programing of media on the basis of media audiences calls for assignment of weights regarding the following:

1. The likelihood of the individuals (or households) in each media audience carrying on through the remaining stages of the media function

2. The influence of such factors associated with each medium as the kinds of advertising units and the mechanics of communication

3. The influence of audience attitudes

4. Audience breakdowns in relation to potential advertising communication and market potential

5. All of the relationships involved in multi-media combinations, duplication, and accumulation, and their contributions to the values of each added advertising opportunity or impression

All these considerations and many more enter—consciously or unconsciously—into every media purchase. This complex is involved in the choice of media combinations, as well as in choosing the particular vehicles which make up a combination. Bringing mathematical or numerical concepts to a media man's thinking does not add any single new element for his consideration, but it may bring some elements to the forefront of his consciousness.

Final Mathematical Solutions

The process of putting factors and weights into suitable form for mathematical programing is beyond the scope of the present book. Nor is it necessary to consider which mathematical model suits which problem.

Progress in the development of high-speed computers continuously adds to the scope of problems which can be solved and to the speed of solution. Both the mathematicians and the designers of electronic computers have proved their ability to handle the problems of mathematical programing of media. What research will do to supply adequate data, and what procedures will be followed in applying mathematical programing to media planning, remain for future development. Computers are certainly helpful to the media planner in reducing the amount of guesswork.

When mathematical programing of media is carried on by means of high-speed computers, the output is an actual schedule of advertising media vehicles. The process arrives at the one most efficient combination to fit the advertiser's designated purposes according to the formulation of the problem. It does not stop there.

The optimized schedule in the solution may not suit the planner in every respect. He may find some favorite vehicle left out entirely, whereas he had expected at least some minimum use of it. Part of the output of the machine is a series of assigned values for every advertising unit in each available vehicle. It is then easily possible to substitute any desired media vehicle and quickly to determine the numerical impact of its use.

If a small loss is indicated and if the media planner feels that he wants to add enough more weight to that particular vehicle to justify its inclusion, that is a matter for him to decide. On the other hand, if a substitution causes a numerical loss out of proportion to its estimated value, the media man can immediately see what the consequences would be. Actually, he must always increase the weights he has originally assigned if he is to "convince the computer" that any substitute vehicle or advertising unit should be included.

"Machines can make mathematical computations and relate one set of factors to another set of factors. But only a human being, exercising judgment, can determine the relative importance which ought to be assigned to each of the factors." [25] The machine works only with what is fed into it, but it rigidly adheres to its solutions until someone changes the rules under which it operates.

A highly significant outcome of the process just described is that it reflects on the *accuracy* required of input data. If the tolerances of survey data are so great as to indicate possible variability in the mathematical solutions, then it may be necessary to secure better data. On the other hand, if the tolerances could be greatly increased without indicating changes in the optimal media program, then perhaps the available research has been unduly costly.

The mathematical approach does not tell the operator whether or not his input data are accurate. It only tells him how accurate they need to be!

Another method of using computers as an aid in media selection involves what is called the *simulation* approach. The Simulmatics Corporation is the main proponent of this method.

> The computer storage includes descriptions of hundreds of hypothetical consumers according to their demographic characteristics (age, sex, education, income, etc.). Each of these mythical people is also described according to his habits of reading various magazines, watching various television shows, listening to various radio stations at certain times of the day and days of the week, and so on. These people are sometimes also described in terms of their owner-

[25] S. R. Bernstein, "Judgment Is More Important Than Ever," *Industrial Marketing,* Vol. 47 (July, 1962), p. 127.

ship, purchase, or usage habits for the advertised product. This hypothetical consumer horde that is "trapped" in the computer is supposedly a representative sample of all U. S. consumers.

With this information in the computer, a tentative media plan, developed in the conventional way, is fed into the computer. This input describes the tentative plan according to so many units of a given cost and type in one media vehicle and so many units in another. The computer output is an estimate of the reach and frequency of advertising exposures which will result from the media plan, broken down according to various consumer types.[26]

Of approximately two hundred books, articles, and program proceedings that are listed in Robert D. Buzzell's bibliography of mathematical methods that might be useful in work in marketing, 32 of the items relate to the use of computer methods for setting advertising budgets or allocating promotional efforts.[27]

IMPLICATIONS

Beginning with 1960, there were great gains in industry acceptance of new advertising media concepts; in the production of data for the purpose of evaluating media and media combinations; and in the procedures employed for scientifically planning media schedules.

While the accepted concepts show the desirability of measuring media more and more closely, problems of research methodology and interpretation make the measurement of media audiences currently the most satisfactory basis for comparing and combining media. Survey estimates of combined audiences of television programs and leading magazines are also available to national advertisers. Methodology also exists to extend comprehensive measurement to the other chief national media, namely, newspapers and radio. Outdoor and car-card displays are actually advertisements, more than media, and any measure of their media exposure is actually advertising exposure.

The problem of using media data scientifically is almost as complicated as is their measurement. The reason is that media are bought in combined schedules with a relatively fixed budget. Typically the possibility of variation of media combinaitons is so nearly "infinite" as to make it imprac-

[26] John C. Maloney, "The Use of Computers in Marketing and Advertising Today," speech presented at the Advertising Club of New York, April 2, 1962.
[27] Robert D. Buzzell, *A Basic Bibliography on Mathematical Methods in Marketing* (Chicago: American Marketing Association, 1962).

ticable to select the best combinations by hand methods. To meet this problem, media planners have brought the skills of the mathematician and the speed of electronic computers into the process of media scheduling. The mathematical method is capable of taking relevant media data along with the value judgments of media buyers and converting these elements into the one most efficient schedule. The significance of these procedures has been described as follows:

1. To force us all to put down in figures those judgments which we always have matched against figures, namely, media dollars

2. To enable us—for the first time—to make real sense out of and maximum use of our media research facts

3. To produce for us specific, optimized media schedules from the facts and judgments on hand when media decisions have to be made.

4. Finally, and most important, to provide us with a scaled framework on which we can superimpose our considered alternatives and intelligently remold the media plan—knowing what we pay for and what sacrifices we make regarding each change in the schedule.[28]

The spectacular gains in evaluating and programing media have come very rapidly, following many, many years in which media planning was practically on a plateau.

There is still lots of room for future improvement, of course. The necessity for making subjective judgments can be decreased to the extent that comprehensive data are obtained nearer to the completion of the media function. In a lesser way, every new measure of a meaningful dimension of any advertising vehicle will reduce or eliminate the necessity for judgment in establishing weights for the performance of that vehicle.

[28] Darrell B. Lucas, "A Summary Perspective—Some Implications, Questions and Comments," speech on mathematical media programing at the Eastern Annual Conference of the American Association of Advertising Agencies, November 16, 1961.

Index

CPSIA information can be obtained
at www.ICGtesting.com
Printed in the USA
LVHW03s1536250818
588127LV00011B/861/P